Puppeteers on Puppetry

Puppeteers on Puppetry

Interviews with Influential Puppeteers
conducted and edited by

Jeff Bragg

This book is dedicated to the memories of

Doris M. Baldwin,
Jean Reges Burn,
and Caroly Wilcox.

Their work and love of puppetry
changed the world for the better.

Puppeteers on Puppetry - Interviews with Influential Puppeteers

Conducted and edited by Jeff Bragg

First published in 2022 by
The Imaginary Ranger Station

Library of Congress Control Number: 2022922727

Bragg, Jeffrey Phillip, 1954 -

ISBN-13: 979-8-218-12045-0

First edition: December 2022

TABLE of CONTENTS with brief biographies

FOREWORD

Jim Henson started making and performing puppets on television in 1954 with virtually no previous exposure to the art form and brought a unique style and sensibility to his craft. He thought this was a phase, and that he would move on to other areas of the TV and film medium as his career progressed. Jim pivoted in 1958 when he traveled to Europe and encountered a wide range of puppet theater artists who were telling diverse stories in captivating ways. He recognized puppetry's immense possibilities for visual communication and returned to Washington inspired to pursue puppetry as his primary means of expression.

Jim had seen Bil Baird, Shari Lewis, and Burr Tillstrom on television and cited them as influences along with the Russian great Sergey Obraztsov, whose book he had read, but he was eager to learn from and share ideas with the greater community of artists. With his wife Jane, he joined Puppeteers of America and began attending festivals and local guild events. Over time they explored international puppetry, joining UNIMA and meeting puppeteers around the world. Jim treasured the relationships he developed with his fellow artists and valued the creative collaboration that enhanced his work and provided long-lasting friendships. As his success grew, he used his visibility to encourage and promote the art form, producing a series of documentaries about puppet artists, establishing The Jim Henson Foundation to support new puppet works, and remaining active in puppetry organizations.

One such group is the National Capital Puppetry Guild. Established in 1964, the NCPG runs workshops, performances, and special events, creating a community for puppeteers both experienced and new to the field. When Jeff Bragg joined the organization while researching a personal project, he saw the NCPG as a valuable organization that could benefit from fresh energy to maximize its impact and have a broader reach. He joined from outside the field but was immediately swept up by the extraordinary artists working with puppets and sought to celebrate and amplify their craft.

Jeff's interviews conducted for the NCPG's Puppetimes newsletter serve as vital documentation of remarkable people working in every aspect of the art form. As designers, builders, performers, directors, company managers or guild leaders (often all at the same time), the featured puppeteers demonstrate the intense creativity and dedication to their craft found across the field. Their detailed stories provide inspiration to peers and novices alike, and through this collection, they will be available for future generations.

As a historian, I value these primary records for storytelling, not just on the page, but in the classroom, in museums, and beyond. I also came to puppetry from another field, eager to learn about it. I appreciate the window Jeff has provided to explore and connect with this vibrant and welcoming community of puppeteers.

Karen Falk
Archives Director, The Jim Henson Company
2022

Introduction

Puppeteers are a unique artistic sub-species of the human animal. They often work long hours, in isolation for months or even years before they get to see the fruits of their labor. Puppeteers are artists of synthesis and must be masters of multiple artistic disciplines: design, puppet building, set creation, writing, costuming, music. They are often their own advertising, promotion and marketing, too. Their visions are singular and the worlds they create can be compelling, unique and engrossing.

And sadly, they are often not taken seriously as artists by much of humanity or even by artists from other disciplines.

I believe puppetry to be one of our highest art forms, combining theater, music, art, writing, and craft. I believe puppeteers, boldly and against all odds, continue to occupy the highest levels of art, creating works that embody the human experience in the deepest way, allowing the observer to participate at a level that is truly visceral. There is a reason that children respond well to puppets; they invite participation and allow full expression that is not threatening.

This is a book of interviews with puppeteers who I believe are important. They are also snapshots in time and are just some the puppeteers that I had to good fortune to interview during my tenure as President of the National Capital Puppetry Guild, and publisher and editor of its newsletter, Puppetimes. I am grateful for that opportunity, for without it, these interviews would not exist. I continue to interview people involved in puppetry. Perhaps there will be additional volumes. We'll see.

I am very grateful to all those who participated in these interviews. Their wisdom and insight into the world of puppetry is invaluable to future puppeteers.

They are an eclectic group. Some are exclusively live performers. Others embrace video and film work. Several have worked for Jim Henson. One has founded a theater dedicated to puppetry in the Washington, D.C. area. All are noted for the excellence that they have brought to the field through their work and I want to thank them all.

I want to thank Elise Handelman whose contribution as a proofreader of most of these interviews was invaluable.

I also am especially grateful to Heidi Rugg for all her help. With her dedication to puppetry and the puppet community, her fine work and attitude, Heidi continues to exemplify all that is good in the art and its practitioners.

Jeff Bragg
11/14/2022

DON BECKER

Jeff Bragg: How did you get started in puppetry?

Don Becker: It started with God. (he bursts out laughing) The reason I say that is that I'm getting ready to go see "Hand to God" and that's how I got started because a friend of mine in high school was a church goin' fellow and he was a ventriloquist and I had made a puppet and we got together and we started doing started doing puppet shows together. So we would perform for church groups. And in the town I grew up in, in Manassas, there was a Christian television station there and they used to do a children's television show there in the afternoon. We were flipping through channels and found this thing and they had these puppets lip-syncing horribly to Christian music. That kind of stuff. So we grabbed all our puppets and we went together down to the station and said, "Hey we can lip-sync a lot better than that." And they said, "Okay, you're hired." So that's how I got started, was lip-syncing to Christian stuff for this television show. That's what I did during high school, so that's how I got started.

JB: So this was in the late '70's and early '80's

DB: So this would be, yeah, I graduated in '81. So '79, '80, '81.

JB: That must have been an interesting experience.

DB: They would just hand us cassette tapes of music and say, "We want to film these songs." So, then we would pick out which puppet we wanted to do and then we'd just lip-sync. It was very...no production values whatsoever or anything like that, but you know, it was kind of fun. But it was a good way to get into puppetry, finding that you could do it, kind of thing.

JB: How long did this go on?

DB: It went on for about two years. Yeah, sophomore, senior year and then the show ended up closing, they stopped filming episodes and sort of faded out just as I probably getting ready to get out of high school and that's when I met Bob Brown. I met Bob doing a show and I gave him a card, I wrote down my name and said, "Hey, if you're ever looking for a puppeteer, give me a call."

JB: Now Bob primarily does marionettes and TV work, that was all mouth puppets, not even rod puppets.

DB: Right, because my influence was The Muppet Show. I'd never seen a marionette show before in my life! So even the mouth puppets that I built looked like the Muppets. So that was my influence. So the patterns that I had were from Christian puppetry how-to-build books. So I'd take those patterns and alter them from there.

JB: So working with Bob must have been a bit of culture shock.

DB: What happened was I was seventeen and getting ready to go to school down south and when I met Bob he was like, "Oh, yeah, we can always use puppeteers." So at that point I decided, I'm not gonna' go to school down south. I'm going to go to school locally, so I went to George Mason and about three years later, I finally heard from Bob (laughing). I'd dropped out of college and I was working in retail, I was working in a job that was getting ready to move me to Atlanta and I really didn't like the job at all. I didn't know what to do and I was twenty and I'm never late for work and this day I was late for work.

It was on a Friday afternoon and all of a sudden I got this phone call and it was Donna Wiedeman from Bob's and she said, "Is this the Don Becker that does puppets?" And I'm like, "Yes." And I hadn't done puppets in a couple of years, since high school. And she says, ah, "Can you start Monday for a two week gig with the National Symphony Orchestra?" And I said, "Sure!" So… (laughing), so, I arranged it all and showed up for work for Bob there and then ended up doing the show with him and then once I did that two week run with him, they found a way to work me in.

They had a show that needed a total of five puppeteers and they needed three more. And what had happened was they had tried everyone they could think of to fill it out and for some reason people had another gig and blah, blah, blah. And going through the rolodex and stuffed in the back of the rolodex was that piece of paper I'd given Bob three years prior. And Donna just pulled it out there on a whim to see what (laughs), what would happen, if the number was still puppetry there, 'cause at that point I started working for Bob, but I good.

wasn't working for Bob fulltime. There was a guy in the area, Jimmy Rowland and Jimmy did all the puppet shows at all the King's Dominions, King's Islands and Carowinds down in North Carolina and he did the little twenty-minute puppet shows they would do throughout in the park, so he was always looking for puppeteers, so he hired me for King's Dominion and I had no marionette experience whatsoever and that's how I learned to work marionettes, because you do the same show five times a day, you know, five days a week and just repetition and learning, you know, how to do it. And it was a one man show, just me.

So I went down there, like, two or three days to rehearse kind of thing and Paul (Malerba), Jimmy's partner, showed me, kind of, basically how to do it. That's how I learned to work marionettes and once I did that run, then Bob was hiring for the Jack and the Beanstalk production and I started working for him there

JB: How long a time did you spend working with Bob? I know it was off and on, but how long did the gig with him last?

DB: So when we did the National Symphony it was '84. So I consider I've been working with him since '84.

JB: Because you're still doing work with him now.

DB: Yeah, when he broke down the large company and it just became him, I was still doing all the symphony shows.

JB: Tell us some more about the Jack and the Beanstalk shows.

DB: Jack and the Beanstalk was a two person show and I've got Jack and that first day of rehearsal…Judy (Barry Brown, Bob's late wife and partner) directed all the shows… and I would sit there and I'd start working the puppet and she would go, "NO, NO, NO, NO, NO!!" And she'd grab the puppet she goes, "I WANT THE PUPPET HERE! (motions to the left) I WANT IT OVER HERE!" (motions to the right). And she'd just GRAB the puppet from below! Just grab the whole puppet.

And I left that first day and was like, "Oh my god, this is just horrible. I'm not going to…I can't handle this. I can't do it. I'm terrible.

I can't do it!" And I just went home that day and I just thought about it and then the next day when I came back in (to work at Bob's), I don't know, something clicked.

JB: Let's talk about puppet building. When you started out, how did that go?

DB: So, I was building in high school and that was all foam rubber stuff, off of a pattern. It was fun and I was building big costumes, too. I built like a big, kind-of-a long-necked, monster kind of thing that I would walk around in parades and things like that and I just enjoyed doing it. I really enjoyed the craft of building puppets a lot, and performing…I'd go back and forth, but I really like the building aspect of it, the designing and building of 'em.

JB: Did you work from sketches or did you do it organically and just start putting things together?

DB: Yeah, just putting things together, yeah. And that's the way I've always worked for the most part. I'll just pick it up and start doing it. Although, within the last three or four years, last three years in particular, I have worked more from sketches. I've sorta' found that working from a sketch is a good thing. When I built the little guys (his art miniatures pictured), I'd just pick up clay and just start going at it. I think that because now that I'm carving more in wood, I'm "taking-away" rather than sort of being able to "add-to," you know, like with clay and stuff like that. That's the thing, I don't want to be wasting the wood.

JB: The subtractive process is very different than the additive process.

DB: Yeah, so I don't know if that's changed me to using more sketches or not. Also I'll use the sketches for proportions and things like that. Also, too, when I started building automata, because I started building automata a couple of years ago. That in particular, I thought, "Okay, you just take a puppet and throw some rods on it and some gears and away you go!" And, ah…no (laughs). This is much more precise than, you know, sorta' what you think. So at that point it's like, ah, I need to be drawing these things out. I need to sketch these things out and get this kinda' going first, before I actually build it, before I prototype it out.

JB: What was the transition from soft puppets to building marionettes like? Was there a point when you decided to stop making foam puppets and just concentrate on marionettes?

DB: No, no, it was more that I was working with Bob and I was doing shows and building puppets for Bob and Bob does everything, you know, carved out of Styrofoam. We didn't do a lot of mouth puppets. Even the mouth puppets were carved Styrofoam covered in felt. There weren't a lot of soft "Muppety" type figures when I was there. Most of it was always carved Styrofoam and we'd cut a mouth into it and make it hinge and do it like that. There were never any soft sculpts. Except when I built "Carnival of the Animals." That's all foam rubber and fabric. For the most part.

JB: Commercially available foam rubber...

DB: Yeah, yeah!

JB: Or things like Scott Foam?

DB: No, no! It was just carpet foam padding. That kind of stuff, yeah. Yeah, I didn't learn about Scott Foam until Barry Gordemer, I think, or Ingrid (Crepeau of DinoRock Productions) may have told me about it. And that was probably the early '90's, I guess. And I was like, "Oh! You can actually get that kind of stuff? But working with Bob, we were always building Styrofoam and felt, Styrofoam and felt, Styrofoam and felt. Everything, all the rod puppets and everything was like that, was all that. That's all I did.

Because I didn't build for myself, you know, I was always building for Bob and then I didn't build for myself until after I left Bob and started my own company

JB: Let's talk about Don Becker Puppets. You've been devoting your work to art miniatures, lately set in these beautiful backgrounds. Do you get commissions for larger works?

DB: I used to. But no, not anymore, because I just don't have myself "out there," either (promoting his work). People don't know that I'm around and I haven't made a real effort to let people know that I do that. You know, I've built some stuff for different theaters around town for different productions and things like that, that's been bigger stuff. I did a production at Woolly Mammoth a couple of years ago. I built this bird puppet in a show called Velvet Sky and then I built these puppets for Constellation Theater, you know, a Greek tragedy kind of story and we had to build these doll rod puppets out of soft… out of fabric, because they were supposed to be built by one of the characters. I built some puppets for Folger Shakespeare, some hand puppets of Henry the Eighth, for the play "Henry the Eighth." They're not in the play, but the director put them into the show. There were these three puppets, hand puppets, that were the characters of the actors. Taffety Punk, in town, I built this big owl figure for one of their shows.

But you know, theaters around here really don't have a lot of money to spend and right now, it's kinda' like do I want to do this for almost nothing or do I want to do it? I don't know, now I'm kinda' like, I just want to do it. So I've reached out to a few people and we'll see what happens.

JB: Let's talk about your miniatures. Some of them look very human, some of them look like they came out of a horror movie, those more eccentric figures, the "grotesques," where do they come from? Childhood influences?

DB: You know, it's funny, because I'm not a science fiction guy, so I know it doesn't come from there. It's funny when people say to me…ask me where the monsters come from or that they're scary, because I never see 'em like that. I never see 'em as scary and I see them more out of…I think your term of "grotesques," actually, I like better, because I tend to see it as more that it starts off as a face and then I "grotesque" it, I exaggerate and however that comes out, then that's how it comes out. Almost everything is a human face, to me, I guess, in a way and then let's jut out the jaw, let's pull out the ears, let's pull this around, let's squint the eyes, let's take the nose and squish it up, let's give him a piggy nose, that kind of thing and "Oh!" there you go, that I like.

JB: What other influences would you say were important?

DB: Well, you know part of the thing, I worked for Bob for so many years and when I started my own company, my puppets looked like Bob's! Everything that I built looked like Bob's. It looked like I was just doing a Bob Brown ripoff in a lot of ways! My hand puppet show, my tabletop show, they just looked like Bob Brown Puppets. And also at that time Jimmy Rowland, who was dying.

I came in to help him sculpt figures for his shows and I overheard Jimmy say to his partner when I happened to be in the other room and he was looking at a one of my puppets and he didn't know I was there and he goes, "God, this thing reeks of Bob Brown!" So, I started off ripping off the Muppets and now I was kinda' ripping off Bob! I found it very hard to break that and to find a style of my own.. and Michael Cotter (Blue Sky Puppet Theatre). About that time I started a friendship with Michael Cotter, this was in the late'80s, early '90s. He was hiring me to build puppets for him, rebuilding his shows, fixing puppets, stuff like that and Michael's style is completely different than Bob's. Michael is really, really just one of a kind, a really wonderful person. And he's been so wonderful in my life and one of the first things he said was you DO have to find your own style and vision and don't be afraid to do that. You have to. It's nice to be able to imitate everybody, but you've really got to make yourself stand out. I want people to be able to look at the puppet and say, oh yeah, that's a Don Becker Puppet. As compared to, oh, that's someone copying Bob Brown.

JB: So many people do copy the work of others and I'm as guilty as anyone.

DB: Well, you see television and you see the movies and everything is a Muppet ripoff, it's just the strong Muppet television influence. And even the way that they're performed. Even the way the lip-sync is done and the movements. You can tell, oh yeah, there are Muppet performers underneath those things.

JB: One of the things I talk to my students about are archetypes. And I see many of the puppets of different puppeteers as being archetypes of a certain style and I wonder if the Muppet archetype is especially resonant. I wonder if there are only so many styles that will resonate.

DB: No I don't think so. I think people will accept anything. And I think if the story's interesting people will watch two peanut butter cans talking to each other. I don't think there are archetypes. I mean, there are definitely styles.

JB: You knew Terry Snyder. How did he influence you?

DB: I wouldn't be building miniature marionettes if it wasn't for Terry Snyder. Terry, I think almost from the first time I met him, he was so open. Most puppeteers, in general, are willing to talk about what they do and their secrets. It tends to be a very open group. I would not be building little miniature marionettes if it wasn't for him. He was the one who showed me that. He built a little marionette out of polymer clay and I'd never hear of polymer clay. I'd never thought about building small marionettes and he had built this little figure. He had this elf head and it was so inspiring to me. Then, I built this figure and I showed it to him, it must have been a couple of weeks later and he bought it. Then a little bit later on, I built this other figure and he bought it. He was a big influence. From him buying those marionettes from me, he then introduced me to this guy named Bill Nelson, who's a famous illustrator in the Richmond (VA) area. And I didn't know who Bill Nelson was. And Terry said, "I think we need to show Bill Nelson your work." And so we hopped in his car and we went over to Bill Nelson's house and had me pull out the work and show Bill. Terry would send me work building puppets. Not for him, but for other clients that he couldn't do, he would send me work that way. He was just a fantastic fellow.

JB: Well, I think I've taken up enough of your time today. Thank you for talking with me.

DB: Likewise. Thanks for coming over.

BOB BROWN

JB: Bob, this started in New York City, right?

Bob Brown: Actually it's not. I actually started in New Jersey.

JB: That's New York City, isn't it? (we both burst out laughing)

BB: Yes!! I mean, you know, I was born and raised in New Jersey and I met Christopher Piper's father and mother, Leonard and Pat Piper who lived in who lived in Morris-town, New Jersey. And I lived in a place called Hillside and I sort started my career there. Now, a few years later I moved to New York and that's when I was really getting into puppetry on my own, because before that, I'd worked for Len Piper we did Cole Marionettes (a Chicago touring marionette troupe founded by George and Lucille Cole) shows. There was a puppeteer named Evans Web and we did shows for him. So I actually worked for three or four companies before I went out on my own, but when I went out on my own was New York City.

JB: The first time I ever saw you perform was in Bil Baird's company at the 1964 New York World's Fair. You were doing the Chrysler pavilion's show.

BB: Right, we did an automobile that assembles itself onstage and Ollie Oil Can and there were the dancing motor blocks, I don't know if you remember them.

JB: Yeah, that experience was one of things that inspired my love of puppets. I saw so much good puppetry at the World's Fair.

BB: I have to tell you a really quick, funny story about that, I actually got out of the Army a little bit early to work the New York World's fair. So Bil Baird introduced me to some of his puppeteers at his studio, going "Oh, Bob Brown's the greatest puppeteer and he went to India with me and he went to Russia. He's absolutely terrific!" So I get this whole big buildup and I get up on the bridge, and they hand me this tandem set of dancing motor blocks, and you know, you kick them, which was easy to do, and I'm workin' 'em, and all of a sudden, in the middle of the number, the girl swiveled her hips from side-to-side, and I'm looking at the control, and I'm looking at the control and I can't figure it out! And they'd go, "Okay, Bob can you get in step with the rest of them?" and we would do it again. We kept doing it and doing it and I couldn't figure it out! And finally, I said, "I'm sorry." And I was mortified because of the big buildup about what a great puppeteer I was. It turns out, the main bar looked like a heavy dowel and when you twisted it forward and back it swiveled the hips! But I didn't know that! I'm just holding on to this thing and I'm working the leg bar and the girls going back and forth with their hips and I'm not and the funny thing is my team leader was Jerry Nelson from the Muppets.

JB: When you were in Russia and India, those must have been amazing experiences.

BB: It was absolutely amazing, because I went back later on because I kept thinking, 'I'm making this up" or not remembering it correctly… We had seven tons of equipment that we carried with us! Because there were actually three shows that we took overseas with us. One that Bil called the big theater show, were the shows he did on Broadway and in his theater and all. Then there was something called the village show. Where we performed out in the middle of nowhere, like in remote loca-tions and jungles, and we had to take generators to operate the show. Then, he just had a collection of puppets and things that we took around to hospitals and orphanages. So it was an informal, kind of little, you know, show.

But yeah, there were three different shows that we did. And I remember at one point, we were in the middle of this jungle setting up the show and we always set up late in the after-noon and we waited until it got dark, of course, and then we'd turn on the generators and turn on the lights and I'm going, "There is nobody around anywhere! WHERE is the audience going to come from?!?" And they said, "Don't worry about it. Before the show starts we'll start blasting some music."

People were literally crawling out of the woodwork! I mean it was unbelievable! There were hundreds and hundreds of people that showed up for the show! And they had these enormous speakers that were up on great big parallel stands and the puppet stage we had was kind of a hand puppet rod puppet stage, so we were hidden from the audience.

At one point the speakers started to topple toward us and I realized the crowd was pushing from the back (of the audience), forward, right up against the stage and I don't know how they got control of it, but I was scared to death! I mean I literally thought we were going to be crushed to death doing this show, you know.

You know, what was funny was a lot of the posters said "Bill Baird All Electric Puppet Show," which I never quite understood! (breaking down in convulsive laughter). Another interesting thing was that all the shows were done in English, of course, so what would happen is during a key part of the show, everything would freeze and just stop, and the lights would come on, on a side stage, because we had three stages. There was the main marionette stage in the middle, and there was a hand puppet stage on one side, rod puppet stage on the other side. The lights would come up on the side stage and there was a little figure of an Indian interpreter who would speak in Tamil or Hindi or whichever the local language was. And there are dozens and dozens of different Indian languages, which I didn't know. So they had to hire an interpreter who spoke half a dozen different dialects and languages, and then at some point they had to switch and get another interpreter because we were going to another part of India. So one of my jobs was to work this little figure, which was very much like a miniature ventriloquist's dummy, because you put your hand in the back to operate the head and the mouth, and because, of course, I didn't speak the language, the interpreter would sit right next to me backstage on a stool and I would watch his lips and just absolutely follow his lips and they kept saying, "You know, your manipulation of the mouth is terrific because it's right in sync." And I said, "It wouldn't be if I couldn't sit and watch him!" So I literally sat and watched and he would pause at different times and different places and I never knew quite what he was going to do and so the only way to follow was to sit there and hang on his every word. I remember at one point we did a show at some ambassador's home or something and they set up this enormous tent in the yard to do the show. And I remember just sweating to death and Bil had his theater curtains for the marionette stage were regular heavy theatrical velour and there were two towers in the front of the stage and there were pulleys inside the towers and you would hang these curtains on a batten and then pull it up with these ropes. And it took four people, that's how heavy this curtain was, to raise the curtain in place. It weighed a ton! An absolute ton! But I remember just sweating through every pore in my body. I want to say this was in the spring or the fall because it seemed to me that when we were leaving, it was getting REALLY hot. And the interesting thing was that they wanted to extend the tour, be-cause we were there three and a half months. But after three and a half months, we were like, “this is great, we all want to go home,” you know. And Cora actually has a couple of little kids she wanted to get home to that she’d left behind, Peter and Laura.

JB: Tell me about the Russia tour.

BB: When Bil first hired me I had done a couple of Broadway shows and I had done a couple of concerts with him and a few other projects and at one point he said to me, “Now I need you to get your passport in order.” And because Bil had this, what I consider, sort of a warped sense of humor, I thought he was kidding, and so I just kind of ignored him and at some point he said, “You know, we’re running out of time. Have you gotten your passport?” and I went, “Oh yeah.” And he went, “No seriously, have you gotten your passport?” and I said “why?” and he said, “We’re going to India.”

And I was absolutely bowled over. Because I still thought he was kidding. I absolutely thought this can’t be true and so I went, “I’ve got to be the luckiest person on the face of the Earth,” because after we got done with India, he went, “Well next year, we’re going to Russia.” So we did three and a half months in Russia. And as much as I enjoyed India, I thought Russia was going to be more interesting and it turned out to be all the cloak and dagger that you heard turned out to be true. You know, the whole thing! Our interpreter was spying on us and there were just all kinds of weird, weird incidents.

JB: After this it was back to New York City and then you met Judy.

BB: It was actually during the New York World’s Fair, by the way. Or just before I did the fair. Judy and I met at a puppetry convention, oddly enough, in Florida. Got married a couple of months later on and then because Bill couldn’t keep me on salary all year round, you know, I was kind of a swing puppeteer that he brought in when he needed. I decided that the only way I was going to make a living was to go out on my own. So Judy and I actually did a whole bunch of television commercials and at one point we were doing this commercial and this company called me up and said, “Now we have the puppet al-ready made and all you have to do is manipulate it,” and I went, “Okay.” So they had this potato chip that stood up on end on a box and all it did is tip forward and back and we spent two or three days try-ing to film this commercial with a technician, trying to work this puppet and you can’t work it! So I bring it in and I’m going,

"The thing tips forward and it tips back and it tips side to side, because it's on a spring and that's all it does. What do you want me to do?" And they had Henny Youngman, if anybody's old enough to remember Henny (Take my wife…please) Youngman had record-ed these jokes, because it was a potato chip made with corn and it was called the Joey Chips Show, the corny potato chip and Joey Chips would tell these stupid jokes.

Now this looked just like a real potato chip standing up on end, no face, no arms, no legs, just this potato chip. So I worked this for a couple of days shooting a whole series of commercials and they went, "You know, it's absolutely fantastic, the work that you've done. Bottom line is, while we were filming the commercial they had sent out samples all over the country and the word came back everyone hated them! So the commercials were never shown! But as a result of that, one of the women who was work-ing in the production said we'd like to hire you and your wife, not as puppeteers, because that has a certain connotation to it, but we're going to call you "product animators." And I'm going, "So, another word for a puppeteer?" And they went, "Yeah!" And they said, "We have all kinds of technicians who can build this mechanical stuff, if you can manipulate it. And my reaction was, you know, if you can build it I can probably manipulate it!

So we did a couple of commercials, one of them was for Griffin Shoe Polish, where they took these real shoes and they put mechanisms inside them so that they can bend and twist and do stuff, you know. And at that point my youngest son was born and he was like two years old and we lived in the Village, in New York City and we decided it was just too hard to try and raise a family, because we were planning on having more kids, so the Smithsonian wanted somebody to come down and do shows on the Mall for the summer, and we did that. And speaking of hot as blazes, we were in a circus tent that just held the heat. And this was July and August and I thought we were going to die, it was so hot in that tent! We got through the summer and the Smithsonian kept saying, "You know, if we get enough positive feedback, we'll consider opening up a marionette theater. We'd like you guys to do it."

Well, people aren't going to give them positive feedback, because they're on a tent on the Mall. Who're they going to talk to? They could come up to us and say it was a wonderful show. Well, I can turn around and pass on the word, but they may believe it or not! So what happened was, we made up these postcards that said if you enjoyed the show, please fill out your response and it was pre-addressed to the Arts and Entertainment division and people sent them in saying what a fantastic show! So basically we were hired at the Smithsonian and worked there for a couple of years. Until we had a falling out with them.

JB: Any situation you're involved with can have difficulty and as I read that part of your book, I tended to think that the biggest problem was staying strong enough to use the puppets, but it seems that the politics of any given situation can be worse.

BB: Well the problem was, I had just never worked for a government agency before and I just wasn't political. And I wasn't used to dealing with the crazy stuff we had to go through. We literally had to put in a requisition to get a pencil for the box office. And we would give the entertainment office a write up about the show. By the time they okayed it, the show had opened and closed! And they'd go, "we're releasing the thing about Hansel and Gretel. " And I said, "It closed two weeks ago!" Because they just couldn't get their act together. It was almost like they were doing everything they could to circum-vent the theater from operating properly. It's like they were going against it and at one point they were trying to claim that the puppet theater was not making money and I said, "There's no way, no way that this is losing money, because we built a production of Wizard of OZ. It was so popular, we used to do two shows on the weekend, it was so popular that we would add shows. Because we almost literally had riots at the Smithsonian from people that were showing up. I remember there was some father who couldn't get in to see the show with his three or four year old or two year old, because he had driven around the mall, circling around the Mall for an hour trying to find a place to park. By the time he got in the theater was sold out and he was mad as hell and he literally attacked the box office person. Physically kicked her. She had blood running down her leg! She called a security guard and I don't know if they arrested him or what they did, but that's just what we went through, you know! And people would show up and they'd be angry, because they couldn't park, they couldn't get into the theater on time, then they would find out it was sold out and we weren't taking advance reservations, so we would add shows. We'd say, "Okay, we have enough people to do another show." We would sometimes do five shows, back to back, on a Saturday or Sunday. We were absolutely wiped out. But because Wizard of OZ was so popular, they wanted to continue it. I was so sick of it!

By the time we had run it for a couple of months, I couldn't stand it anymore! 'Cause the show was prerecorded, so you couldn't alter the show or, you know, do anything different, you had to do it exactly the same way. It was a great, great show and I can't take credit for it, because we had hired a guy who had figured out how to do all of the scene changes during the entire show right in full view of the audience, where towers turned around and they turned into something else. We had, you know, wagons and things that went across the stage with scenery on it and stuff. And at one point, when they go walking into the forest, the forest comes rolling across the stage and as they're walking, they're walking in place and everything's rolling across into the wings. We had to extend the floor of the puppet stage, by like twenty feet or more on the either side, in order to accommodate all these things that had to roll across on the stage.

JB: It sounds like quite an elaborate production.

BB: It was fun. It was a good, good show. I think it was one of the best shows we ever did.

JB: And wasn't there this one fellow at the Smithsonian who really became your nemesis? And he just tried to undermine you at every step.

BB: And I could never figure out what the problem was and at some point we tried to talk to Dylan Ripley, because they didn't want to renew our contract and I said, "This is just a personal thing. It really is a personal thing." Because when I was saying they were claiming that the theater was losing money, what they were doing was they were putting all of the money together from all the other projects, which were losing money. Ours was like one of the few things that was literally making money. And I kept saying, "Call in the accountants. Have them figure this out, because there's no way that this theater can be losing money. Because I knew approximately how much we were pull-ing in and how much they were paying us and the interesting thing is when they left, they were going to hire Fred Thompson to take over and they kept announcing, you know, that this was the world's greatest puppeteer. Well I had never hear of him. And Fred had worked for Rufus and Margo Rose. So what they did is, they brought Fred in when I was not in the theater and said, “All of this is going to be yours, as soon as you take it over.” Well, it turned out that was not true, because all of the puppets, we made.

At some point the Smithsonian was like, “well, we’ll give you a budget to build the puppets,” and I said, “Uh, uh! We’ll pay for it out of our own pockets. Because then they belong to us. If you pay for it, they’re going to belong to you.” So there was a knockdown, drag out fight, because they’d literally promised Fred he could have the hundreds of puppets that were all hang-ing backstage, it’s like, “This is all yours.” And so when I left, I took every puppet, stripped all the lights, all the curtains, be-cause we provided all that stuff and he (Fred) was left with a framework of a stage and that was it! So it was quite a shock! And he was ill prepared because the day before the theater was supposed to open, they were staying late rehearsing and they were so nervous, because everybody kept saying, “Oh, the Browns were so good and their shows were so nice and they were such nice people!” And then you’ve got this thing you’ve got to live up to. And Fred and Russell Metheny, who worked with him, were a nervous wreck! Because they had this whole buildup about, oh, you know the Browns did great shows or whatever. So they were staying late to rehearse and it turned out the Smithsonian literally caught fire. And the theater burned down!

Now, Fred grabbed the puppets, because they were all on loan from Rufus Rose and Fred was in a panic and he got the stuff and they’re (the Smithsonian folks) like, "You can’t take any-thing out of the Smithsonian," and he’s like, “Oh, yeah?!?" So, he got the stuff out. So then what happened is, they had Fred on salary and they had a contract, so they had to pay him! So they were getting annoyed because there was no theater that they could put him into, couldn’t do shows, so then they decided to send him out on tour. So he did one of the shopping malls in Maryland, I can’t remember which one, and it was at Christmas time. They stuck him out in the middle of the mall, completely out in the open, to do his version of Pinocchio, because at this point he had borrowed, I think, Rufus Rose’s touring stage. So what would happen is, everything backstage was exposed, because the audience could walk completely around the setup, so they started to do the show, the kids got restless and the kids got up, went around the back of the stage and saw all these marionettes hanging from the bridge and started to hit them and swing them back and forth! And Judy and I had gone to see the show and I went, “You know, I know they’re taking over our job, but I can’t see any puppeteer going through this. I’m going backstage and see what I can do to help.” So I went backstage and scooted the kids out of there, because what was happening is Fred Thompson would hand his marionette to Russell, because it was the two people doing the show, so that Russell could go down and chase the kids. Well, by the time Russell got halfway down the steps of the bridge, the kids would just run around, disappear into the crowd, Russell would go back up, continue manipulating, the kids would come back and start swinging the puppets back and forth! And I went back stage and stood guard through the whole show and that’s how I met Fred Thompson!

And I said, "I feel so sorry for you guys!" and Fred had told us how he'd heard all these horror stories about us and , I said, "Yeah, of course! You know, but that none of them are true" And the Smithsonian had said what awful people we were to work with and how difficult we were and how we were making all kinds of demands and all kinds of things... turned out none of it was true! And Fred found it out the hard way!

So what happened is that after he did this shopping mall show he said to the Smithsonian that in December, he and Russel had tickets to go see the Saltzburg Marionnettes doing The Nutcracker, so don't book that date! They (Smithsonian) booked it and they said you have to do it! And Fred said, "I'm not doing it!" And they said you're either doing it or you're out of here.

So Fred said, "Goodbye!" (laughs) Which I admire him for doing. (more laughter)

When we started out on the Mall, at some point my wife (Judy) was walking across the Mall with thousands of dollars in a little tin cash box and she kept saying, "I need security or somebody. I can't keep walking from one Smithsonian building to another to deposit this cash." And they wouldn't do it.

JB: Perhaps it had to do with the fact that puppetry is often not taken seriously as an art form.

BB: We told them from the very beginning what kind of shows we were going to do. And I told you that this happened both at the Smithsonian and the Rock Creek nature Center. They would go, "Well, we need you to do shows related to the Smithsonian." And I said, "Okay, can you give me an example?" And they said, "Yes, we'd like you to do a show about the first ladies gowns." I looked at them and I said, "Could you run that by me again? Do you realize that the average child that comes to our theater is in a 2-5 year old range? The last thing they care about is what Dolly Madison wore back in 18-something or other and it's not going to make for a very interesting puppet show! And they just wanted to do things related (to their exhibits) and I can understand that, but I went, "Okay, fine. If you want to do that, then I think you should not charge, it should be part of the Smithsonian exhibit budget."...and not expect it to be a profit making enterprise. And the same thing happened at Rock Creek Park! At one point the Park Service called us in and said, "You know, (we) think the stuff you're doing is fantastic. You're pulling in crowds all the time. (We're) busing in all these school kids and they come to see this puppet show about the Rock Creek Park Nature Center and when it's all over, they get on the bus and leave." And I went, "And what's your point?" They said, "Well, they're not staying here." And i said, "They're not staying here because there's nothing interesting for them to see. We pull 'em in, your job is to keep 'em here. That's not our responsibility, we're doing what we're paid to do. We're pulling in the audience. If you want them to stay you need to have something that appeals to these little kids." It was almost like they didn't understand what I was talking about!

JB: And this was in the mid-1970's, right? And this was the time that Bob Payne brought you in to do some work for Jim Henson when he was on Ed Sullivan, correct?

BB: Yep, yep. Bob Payne was one of the puppeteers who started with Jim and Jane (Henson). I had met Bob at the New York Worlds Fair (1964/65) and I hired him when we were at the Smithsonian and he painted scenery for me and puppeteered for me and he did hysterical puppet voices. He was a funny, funny, funny guy. He had me come work for Jim, just, you know, on a part time basis and one of the first project's I had was working on these puppets. They were two squirrels that get into a fight and basically the fight escalates and they take out cannons and do all kinds of stuff. They're blowing up stuff and it was typical of the era when Jim was blowing up things and they brought in the producer for the Ed Sullivan Show and we did this whole routine and they hated it. No, let me backtrack. It's not that they hated it. They thought it was much, much too violent. The squirrels were little hand puppets and they're (the puppeteers) working behind a masking. Standing on these tiny platforms were puppeteers, of which I was one of them, inside these life-sized trees, these foam rubber trees. And you had to stand there and hold a pose and the squirrels would run up and down the trees and tear off branches and whack each other and do all kinds of violent things and eventually the trees come to life and they start going toward each other and attacking one another. Well, what happened was because there was no floor other than the little platform we were standing on, some puppeteers would slide a section of floor in next to you, you know, on your left or your right and you'd step on that and as you were doing that, they would take the one you'd just got off of and move it over. But the problem was, you'd couldn't see in this tree and I was only maybe six feet off the floor, off the ground. But I kept thinking, one step and I'm going to fall! And you're inside this thing which had chicken wire and foam rubber! And I was terrified. (laughing). And I kept going, "I'm a puppeteer, how have I ended up doing this?!" But it was absolutely fascinating, but they decided not to do it! And then at some point the Muppets did a Christmas show with Ed Sullivan and Arthur Godfrey, you have to be a certain age to know who he was, played Santa Claus. Other than the squirrel project, Jim and Jane had these frames that were suspended on monofilament and they had these Muppety monsters that were supposed to be paintings in a gallery or something and I remember Jane coming in and giving me some really good advice on what I was manipulating.

JB: Let's talk about your time with Bil Baird.

BB: For years and years and years Bil would sent me letters, going back to the 1950's and some of them were so funny, so funny! And I go back and read them every once in a blue moon. And I'm going, I have no idea what he was talking about, because it'd just be these absurd things. Speaking of which, when I was in the Army, somebody said, "You know, you could get out if you have a job that's seasonal." and I said, "Well, I don't. I'm a puppeteer." Because I kept talking about how, gee, I was going to miss the World's Fair and I had just finished working for Bil. Actually, I got my draft notice in Russia, by the way! And I went immediately from Russia into the Army. At that point they were drafting people, so Bil actually got a letter saying that they would defer drafting me until after the tour, so I could have possibly gone in right after India, but they waited until Russia, because Bill kept saying, "Puppeteers are not a dime a dozen, they're hard to find. We need this guy to work in the show. Can you give him a deferment until the tour is over?" So the minute the tour was over, before the tour was over, as I said, I got my draft notice and got pulled into the Army. So what happened is somebody said, "Get Bil Baird to write a letter to the commanding officer saying that he really needs you, maybe you can get out of the Army early." And I thought, that's the most ridiculous thing I've ever heard of. First of all, backtracking again, when I went into the, I wouldn't put down that I was a puppeteer. I wouldn't admit it, because I had been teased mercilessly, of course, as a kid, you know, oh, you're playing with dolls again, so I went, I'm not telling anybody I was a puppeteer, well what happened is somebody got a'hold of a press release from the Bairds saying they just returned from Russia and listing the puppeteers and my name was on it and somebody connected it and told them at Fort Dix, where I was stationed, that I was a puppeteer and they were like, you need to go get some puppets, we want you to put on some shows at the hospitals, while I was still in basic training. And (I said), "No, no, no, I can't do that, because all my stuff was in storage in New York and they literally had a Sargeant drive me to New York to pick up my puppets and I would do shows on the weekends and stuff. And then they were trying to figure out what to do with me, in the meantime, I was learning how to be a teletype operator, which I hated or learning to be a file clerk or whatever they call it in the army. They couldn't figure out what to do with me and they couldn't just say I was going to be a puppeteer, and they wanted me to do shows, so they put me in special services and they wanted me to teach photography, which I knew nothing about and they literally said, "Here are the chemicals, here's the developing stuff. Here's how you do prints." And people would come into this arts and crafts center and they'd want to do pictures and I'd go, "Well, if you know what you're doing, here's all the stuff, go ahead and do it. If you want to know the very basics, really basics, I can show you. Beyond that you're on your own. So I taught photography for a while and then they wanted me to do lapidary work, polishing stones, making jewelry, which I also know nothing about. Well, okay, show me how to do it. Because what would happen is that then they could pull me whenever they needed me to do shows. So I was always going to the officers clubs. Now if you heard my wife tell it, you'd swear I did nothing but puppetry in the Army, which wasn't true, but I did do a lot of it.

So, going back to the Bil Baird letter, he writes this to the commanding officer and typical of Bil, wrote it in his phonetic way, putting little cartoons on the bottom, some of them probably 'dirty' and I get pulled in and the commanding officer says, "What the hell is this?" holding up Bil's letter and I said, "I don't know." And he said, "Read it!" And I started laughing and he goes, "Who is this gentleman?" "Oh, this is Bil Baird." And he said, "Well, if he wants to be serious about this, tell him he needs to write a serious letter." So I wrote back and I said, "Bill, you can't do this to me, I'm already having trouble, so do it seriously." The next thing I know they're releasing me a couple of months early to work at the New York World's Fair. I still have a collection of letter's I've saved from him that are just funny as anything. But I have to go back at some point and explain the story behind them. Because in reading these things, you don't know what's he's talking about.

JB: I have to say that that sounds like a wonderful project, to collect those letters.

BB: It's one of those in my spare time. I did start months and months ago, speaking of which, we have hundreds and hundreds of publicity pictures, we're talking about sixty years here and I suddenly went, you know, when I drop dead nobody's going to know what these things are. So I started making notes, putting on the back or these were puppets that were made for the commercials for the shopping mall and whatever. And here's the Fred Rogers photographs. I haven't even gotten through a tenth of it!

JB: Let's talk about your visits to Fred Rogers' neighborhood.

BB: Sure! So what happened is that while we were at the Smithsonian, the Smithsonian Magazine featured an article on our theater at the Smithsonian and at the time we were doing Peter and the Wolf. Fred Rogers got the magazine and saw it and said, "Check out these puppeteers and see what you can find out about them." So he sent David Newell, who played Speedy Delivery on the show. I had never heard of David Newell. I sort of knew about Fred Rogers, but not really, I hadn't seen the show. So they came down and they decided that they wanted to do Peter and the Wolf and we were like great and we were all enthusiastic, except Judy had recorded a sound track using several different recordings, which you could not do and they couldn't get clearance for it and they could not do it with an orchestra and it can't be done on the piano, because all of his music was accompanied on the piano.

So that decided that we couldn't do it. But from what I gathered he liked our work, he liked what he saw, so we ended up doing jack and the Beanstalk, which was the first show we did. What I didn't know was that we were written into the script as neighbors who'd moved into the neighborhood. What I did know is that we were going to do some acting on it because we were appearing as ourselves. So the first script I get, I'm interacting with Fred's hand puppets and they did a playback at some point and I said that's the worst acting I've ever seen in my life. Because what was happening is I was used to doing children's theater and doing voices for puppets where you overact, because none of our puppets, for the most part, had movable eyes or mouths or whatever. So you tend to overact a little bit to compensate for the lack of expression in the puppets faces. So everything is a little more melodramatic, vocally.

So, I'm on TV going (yelling) "WHY MISTER ROGERS!!" And they played back the tape...I look like I'm on drugs of some sort! Like take it down about ten notches! Because Fred's like (whispering), "Well, Bob.." and I said (to myself), this isn't working at all. So I had to learn to calm myself down a lot when working with Fred. At one point, I'm talking to Daniel Tiger, which was one of his little hands puppets and I had this little toy horse and I'm going, "Daniel, this is a very fine horse. This is a very, very, very fine horse. This is a fine horse." And the director goes, "Stop! Stop!...Do it again!" So I do it again and I do it three or four times, and I go, "I'm sorry, but I don't really consider myself an actor. If you tell me what you want, maybe I can do it. Am I doing it too fast or too slow, too whatever. And he goes, "No, we want you to sing it." And I said, "Excuse me?" They said, "We want you to sing it." And I said, "Why in the hell would I sing it?" And they said, Because it's a song." And I said, "No, it isn't." They had sent me a script with the lyrics, (with) no indication it's a song and had forgotten to send me the sheet of music. Which it wouldn't have done me any good, because I can't read sheet music anyway! So they went, "Okay, we need to stop and take a break for a minute and go sit down with Johnny, who is the piano player, and he'll teach you the thing." Well, it was a typical Fred Rogers song, which I couldn't get the melody to at all! I kept trying to sing it and I'm going, oh, this is awful! And they said, "Okay, just say it." So I'm on the show going, "You're a very fine horse. You're a very, very, you're a fine horse." Which makes absolutely no sense. I'm not sure if it would have made any more sense as a song, but it was just one of those weird incidents.

They did not have an audience in the studio, at all and usually, most TV people, most technicians, most theater people are sort of broad-minded. So we would have to report to the studio at eight o'clock in the morning. We usually wouldn't start filming until ten or eleven and they'd be getting microphones, checking feed back. So these twenty minute segments that we would do on the show would go from literally go from eight o'clock in the morning and sometimes not get out until seven or eight o'clock at night. I remember one of the first days I did something. I never, ever swear in front of kids.

And I dropped a puppet or tangled something badly and I went, "Oh SHIT!" Everything just stopped dead, I mean the silence was deafening! And I looked up and everybody was staring me down and I suddenly realized, oh, I guess this is a no-no. So I apologized and I said I'm terribly sorry, I never do that in front of children, but since there were no kids here I thought it would be okay. Fred came over and lectured me for the next ten minutes, going, "Oh, that's okay Bob we all express ourselves in different ways, and you need to be you, and you need to tell us the way you really feel." By the time it got done, I'm like, I'll never do that again, because I can't stand listening to the rest of his lecture. As sweet as the man was, it's like, this is just a little too much for me. So I had to be very careful what I said around Fred, 'cause Fred of course was a minister and I had to watch my mouth, I learned that very quickly.

JB: Bob, thank for your time. I think we'll need to have another conversation sometime, because I don't think we've heard everything yet. In the meantime, do you have any advice for young puppeteers?

BB: People sometimes ask me how I learned and where they can study to be a puppeteer. I just got out there and did it. And I worked for quite a few puppeteers. I did some work with Paul Ashley, who did a lot of stuff with Chuck McCann. So I learned by doing and I think that's the best way. You have to get out. Get out there and do it. And you learn to hard way, you make mistakes.

JEAN REGES BURN

JB: Tell us about your early life and when you became interested in puppetry.

Jean Reges Burn: When I was a child I did a lot of make believe. My mother died when I was six and a half, almost seven, very unexpect-edly and eventually my father's two aunts came and took care of us. I was the youngest of four. My sister was away at college so we moved from Douglas-ton, Long Island to Great Neck and we lived in a house that was owned by Oscar Hammerstein. We lived in this beautiful house with a back staircase where you could go and do make-believe. I even had an imaginary play-mate named Millicent!

Many sad things sort of happened that shaped my childhood. My brother unfortunately got polio at fifteen after we moved to house in Great Neck. My brother fell down, they took him to a hospital, and then we realized he's got some kind of paralysis, we don't know what it's called. But he had been playing football with three other men and they all went swimming in Long Island Sound, which they were not allowed to do, it was polluted, and it was posted, but they went swim-ming there anyway and so they all came down with polio. The other men died and my brother survived and so they brought him home and he was bedridden for three years on the sunporch in that house and so I did a great deal of make believe, paper puppets, paper things. My father was a lawyer on Wall Street so every day he walked to the Great Neck railroad station, took the train to New York and then came home.

And then my father, six years later married an extraordinary woman who was like an angel that came to our family. She helped my broth-er. She made suggestions, you know, "I think if this young man had a brace on his leg he might be able to walk again," and he did, so, you know, she was instrumental in emancipating the family from a great deal of pain and sorrow. And also she had a tremendous sense of hu-mor, and she was a musician, she had lived in Berlin during World War I and she was famous. She was an opera singer or intended to be an opera singer. Her father was a famous military man who was Per-shing's aide-de-camp. She was in Boston when she met my father, then she moved to New York to be with us, so she did many, many things, but one of the best things she did, I did a puppet show every Saturday night, you know, in the door-way with a blanket. There was something in Child Life, Bertram the Puppet, she bought things for me and no matter what I did she enjoyed it, she was one of these wonderful, extraordinary people and encouraged me and so, I had that background. But I didn't know anything about puppets. I didn't see a show, they had some players come to our town, you know, to do programs. The Clare Tree Majors did the fairytales, they were adult actors, so really, I mean, let's say I had just a passing, I had played with puppets as a child.

And then my father, six years later married an extraordinary woman who was like an angel that came to our family. She helped my brother. She made suggestions, you know, "I think if this young man had a brace on his leg he might be able to walk again" and he did, so, you know, she was instrumental in emancipating the family from a great deal of pain and sorrow. And also she had a tremendous sense of humor, and she was a musician, she had lived in Berlin during World War I and she was famous. She was an opera singer or intended to be an opera singer. Her father was a famous military man who was Pershing's aide-de-camp. She was in Boston when she met my father, then she moved to New York to be with us, so she did many, many things, but one of the best things she did, I did a puppet show every Saturday night, you know, in the door-way with a blanket. There was something in Child Life, Bertram the Puppet, she bought things for me and no matter what I did she enjoyed it, she was one of these wonderful, extraordinary people and encouraged me and so, I had that background. But I didn't know anything about puppets. I didn't see a show, they had some players come to our town, you know, to do programs. The Clare Tree Majors did the fairytales, they were adult actors, so really, I mean, let's say I had just a passing, I had played with puppets as a child.

I graduated from Barnard College and immediately got married, we lived in Forest Hills a year, then we moved to Boston for three years and then after that I went to Philadelphia for three years. I started learning how to make puppets because I thought that if I made puppets my children would stop watching television. Puppets were too expensive for me to buy so I decided to try to make some for my children.

I had a friend who made some puppets for her little boy, and I saw him playing with them, I drove them around, I could see this little boy playing with these puppets in the back of the car and I thought "I need some puppets for MY children. I can make some puppets and they can play with them, maybe they won't watch as much television.

JB: Were you successful in keeping them away from the television?

JRB: No! But I read about a puppet meeting in my neighborhood and that is where I met Marion and Bill Duvall (a couple who were active puppeteers in the '50s and '60s). They were from New Jersey and they were lovely, very friendly people and they encouraged me and suggested I go to the local library and borrow Mabel Beaton's book, Marionettes, A Hobby for Everyone. That is when I started making puppets.

Then we moved from Haddonfield to Michigan. The Grand Rapids Press published an article about me "She literally is on her knees to her art". That was because I made a 3 sided puppet stage I had to kneel in to per-form. After that was published, I met Burr Tillstrom's brother, and he didn't love puppetry the way his brother did. he turned his business over to me, so people were calling me and I said "Well, I can make puppets, but I don't perform, I simply can't perform, I don't know how," and finally a mother said "You WILL; I'm going to play a RECORD and you will do SOMETHING to that record," and so it sort of launched me out into reality. We lived eleven years in Grand Rapids, Michigan. That's where my puppet business flourished.

Eventually George Creegan called me from Steubenville, Pennsylvania and said, and asked me if I would do Pip the Mouse, do you know about that? Yeah, and so I agreed to do it, and I had to go to Steubenville and be trained for a weekend and so I did that one year and it was quite an experience but my children were young and I felt that I it's such a special time, so I told him I couldn't do it the next year, and he hired somebody who started doing the six shows a day, six days a week, and the young man just decided to stay in his hotel room across the street from Herpolsheimer's and WAIT to see if anybody stood in front of the store win-dow, so George called me like November, I mean, yeah, it was November, December 9th, and he said, "Tomorrow is the biggest day, it's a Saturday, December 10th, will you take over?" and I said, "Well I have a few conditions, I want twice my salary." I was getting peanuts, I could have made a lot more money just independently booking my show, my OWN show. So I did, I finished his contract, and I knew the ropes, and then the design, the display design man at Herpolsheimer's, asked me if I would build an Easter show, and this was really a puppeteer's dream come true. I wrote a special show, Mrs. O.C. Rabbit, and she had two sons, Oglethorpe and Hugo. I had learned some things from watching George Latshaw. Once he did a puppet show where there was a little bathtub, you know, where you could pull the curtain and you could put a puppet in there, so I had Herpolsheimer's, they had their carpenter build me a set to my design, so I wanted all these little things, I wanted a window box where flowers would grow. Well he did that, all I had to do was push up a stick, you know, and the flowers grew. He built me the bath-tub with a half-circle so that Hugo could give his little brother a bath, and I made all the puppets, and so I was booked to do probably two weeks. They brought that set to my home in East Grand Rapids and set it up in our basement, which was quite nice, you know, it was comfortable and it was carpeted. So we lived near, I think it was Collins School, anyway, it might have been Woodcliff. Every grade came to my house and came downstairs¬ and I rehearsed with this captive audience. So first through sixth grade came and saw my puppet show and then I went down to Herpolsheimer's, they took the set down and set it up in Herpolsheimer's, in the children's clothing department, someplace where the mothers would be.

I was commissioned to do a British fortnight of Punch and Judy at Steketee's Department Store. I had an entire summer to prepare so I made all of the puppets, I memorized the script. I still had not met any more puppeteers. After, I became a member of Puppeteers of America. The Detroit Guild was very active. There was a festival in

Detroit and I began going to Detroit to meet people who were puppeteers and I was taken into the puppet community, especially the Detroit people, and I saw a lot of marvelous performances there.

In 1959, I took my two oldest children and drove to my first Puppeteers of America Festival in Ohio. It was there that I heard of Martin Stevens. He was publishing a correspondence course for puppetry. I subscribed to this and started studying the art of puppetry seriously.

I wrote to Steve that I was not satisfied with my stage, what should I do? Steve lived in Middlebury, Indiana – only 3 hours from our home in Michigan! He offered to sell me a hand puppet stage for $75 payable "when you can". This meeting became a special friendship with him and his beloved wife, Margi. They were my mentors. They helped me build my first marionette variety act. Steve built me a marionette stage that was portable and I had the hand puppet stage. I can never express my gratitude and affection for these two people who were the driving force of my puppet life.

And then I had to leave Michigan, I had to get my family out of Michigan due to some unfortunate circumstances. I took my children, my puppet show, my sewing machine, and my typewriter.

So we wandered, first to Albuquerque. I thought I wanted to get my family to an Indian reservation, away from society as much as possible. So I went to the Bureau of Indian Affairs, and they said "Oh no, you have to apply through Washington, DC." So I sent away for the application, we were living in a ten-man tent for the entire summer. And then I took the family and we went up to Colorado Springs in ONE day. The boys said "You know Mom, school's gonna start, what are we gonna do about school?" and I said "Well, I see there's a job in the paper for a bus driver at a school. I'm gonna go down there and apply." So I did, I drove down Ute Pass and went into the school, this woman said, "There's something about you, I don't know what it is, I think you'd make a better teacher, I think we need a teacher." It was the end of August, I mean like that, bin-go, I was hired, so I thought OK, now we need a place to live, this is all happening in one day. I said I don't have a telephone number because I'm living in a tent, but I'm gonna find a place to live. So I'm driving down the road in Nevada, and I looked over, and I saw this beautiful big Victorian house for sale on a corner. It was 504 Nevada, the address. I see a realtor's name, it was for sale, so I went to the payphone, and called and I said "Would you consider renting that house?" and he said "I'll be over in five minutes." Well he took a shine to me, and he said "Name the price you would pay" and I thought, well, I might be able to pay $200 a month. "Yeah, that's done, deal," so I rented a house. And he said, well this was formerly a tourist home, it had seven or eight bed-rooms and three or four baths, and it was beautiful, and it faced the mountains, and across the street was the Methodist Church. He said "I'll get everything turned on and you can move in tomorrow." And he said "You can do anything you want with this, if you want to rent out rooms you can" and on the second floor there were maybe five beautiful bedrooms and there was still furniture left in the house and like seven fireplaces with these beautiful tiles, a huge kitchen and a back stairway, you know, like we had in Great Neck, the old-fashioned house where you had two stairways. So I went up to Ute Pass and told the boys "So we've got a place to live, do you want to come and see it? We can move down here tomorrow." So the boys came down, they ran through the house, and Wendy came down. And [KNOCK-KNOCK] knock on the door, I opened the door and a young man stood there, and he said "Do you have any rooms for rent?" This is ALL the same day. "I need four rooms for four Vietnam vets." I said "Let me show you what I have, what we have" and I showed them, I said "You can have four bedrooms upstairs" and he said "what will you charge?" and I, "well how about ten dollars a week apiece?" forty dollars a week, maybe I can make two hundred dollars, I could pay my rent. So he said fine, done deal, they moved in, we moved in, and it was quite an adventure, I mean just living in that house was an adventure. We lived there for a year. I had a beautiful German Shepherd dog I had to take care of my stepmother's estate when she died, this beautiful German Shepherd, King, and he went with us to Colorado. Bruce had just gotten a driver's license so he drove.

One of the extraordinary things, this has nothing to do with puppetry, but about what sort of emancipated me from worrying about material things. They came home from school one day and there were boxes on the back. It had a Victorian porch around three sides of the house. A minister was there from the Unitarian Church and he said "Do you have a big dog and a lot of children?" and I said "Well I have a big dog and six children" and he said "Then you are the person. A young woman died in childbirth. She said that you were kind to her and she, when she died, and her husband agreed, he's in Canyon City Jail for writing bad checks, but as she died she said 'I want everything I own to go to the woman that lives on the corner of 504 Nevada, that has a big dog and several children" and I thought "No, no, no, no, this can't, this isn't happening" and all of the clothes fit my daughter Wendy and we got her china, we got her wedding rings, everything else, we felt guilty, I mean, we couldn't look at the stuff, we felt so badly, but I mean, that this young woman had died. Rex had been her favorite boy so she knew, she liked Rex, and she came to the house one day, and this young woman was sitting on the porch, and I think we had some kittens running around there, I don't know, feral kittens or something, and she was sitting there with a book, and I came out of the house, and I said, I said "Hello, isn't it a beautiful day?"

JB: And this was mid-60s, I take it, roughly?

JRB: 1968, yeah, and I said, she said, "Is it alright, is it alright if I stay here?" and I said "Oh yeah, I want you to stay here, I want you to enjoy it," and I said, "You have a lovely book to read and I have to get going, I have to pop off to school." That was the only time I ever saw her and he said, as she was dying she said, "There was a woman who was kind to me." So you never know how you're going to affect people in life, you know, you just don't know.

JB: Well eventually you get to Virginia and our guild. You're on the papers of incorporation, you, Don Becker, John McAnistan, and some of the other names escape me right now. JRB: It was Donna Wiedemann.

JB: I know about Donna Wiedemann.

JRB: It was Allan Stevens who rescued us; we didn't have a place to meet, we didn't have order, we didn't have officers, and so we pulled, we started pulling things together, ALL of us. So I sat down one day, and I thought, I don't know, I mean, we weren't on the computer, you know, at that point. I sat down, I looked to Bob and Judy, but they were busy. They had small children, so I sat down and I wrote every puppeteer whose name I could find within a fifty or seventy-five mile radius of Washington, DC and invited them to a guild meeting. And "out of the woods" came this young officiant, whatever you call them, someone that was going to be a priest, who called me and he said "You're welcome to meet here," so we met at the, first we met at the Paulist House of Studies, which is in, near Howard University. That's where I met Bill Hopkins, Doris Baldwin, and Jimmy Rowland. The guild was gathering all this energy together. John McAnistan was an integral part and con-tributed his humor and help in our reorganization. Bill Hopkins wrote a constitution for us and we became an authorized Puppeteers of America Guild.

We still didn't have a permanent place, some people didn't want to drive into Washington, and that's when I picked Don Becker up, when he was seventeen, in Reston and drove him in with me to the Paulist House of Studies and so he could become acquainted with everybody. Then there was Allan Stevens, who had his theater in Alexandria, and then the next thing you know he had a yurt out at Glen Echo. He was very kind to me. He let us have a Day of Puppetry there. I remember I put on some secondhand, long dress from some thrift shop. I remember my son Rex came and he had two of his children. I just stood there with Allan and then we greeted people. They came and rode the carousel, they saw a pup-pet show and they saw the yurt. After that Allan moved to the Spanish Ballroom and then Christopher Piper came to join him from Hawaii and they became partners. Allan and Christopher invited the guild to have our meetings there and we had a home. Thank you Puppet Co! My vision for the guild was to support younger puppeteers, or emerging puppeteers, or people that were interested in puppetry, librarians, wherever we could to promote puppetry. We had a mission statement and it was to primarily to promote puppetry, to encourage young people, we had a young man that came, we had junior members, we were nurturing these people and trying to nurture their love of puppetry for educational purposes.

JB: I know that our guild has gone through some lean years over our history. When you put out our calendar was one of those times. Tell me about that.

JRB: Judy Brown had this incredible idea. She said, "I want to do a calendar!" And we launched on that project and it was a good thing we did, because we caught Marjorie McPharlin the year before she passed away. I interviewed her. But you know about the calendar. We were in the position of having to raise money to get it printed and get the artwork done, but we got it all done and we went to the printer and we went to the festival that George Neff put on up there in New Jersey. And we went and sold raffle tickets because Bob (Brown) had donated a couple of puppets. Everybody wanted a Bob Brown Puppet. And we raised another $500.

I think when we really got together was when I said, alright I'll be president of the guild and we did some money making things and Bob was very generous, as always. And this was 1976, 1977, 1978, we're putting the guild back together. We've got Bob Brown on board and then I met John McAnistan. I would come and visit John and John was the one with the ideas.

JB: How did you get to Seattle?

JRB: The Seattle thing. Well, our house here in Reston, we were away, and I got a call from Joy, and she said "Mom, your ceiling, I'm in your house and your ceiling's falling down." Both Jim and I had gone off on separate vacations and some little odd piece of plumbing broke, and the house flooded. So, that was a turning point. That was 2005, and so eventually Jim and I ended up having the house renovated and we sold it. We went to live up in Princeton for a while and Joy drove up and took care of things. Joy's been my savior. Any-way, eventually Jim passed on and so I went to live not far from here in a house that my youngest son owns, and I was there for a couple years, well I had, I've had a couple of scares with my health, and so now it's down to Joy and my son Stuart who I live with. So I finally said, "Joy, I don't know what to do," and so Stuart said, "Do you want to come live in Seattle? I'll take care of you," so I decided to go to

Seattle to be near my son Stuart. He's very brilliant, he's a mathematician.

JB: So, let's talk about modern puppetry. How do you feel about a lot of the trends going on now?

JRB: I mean, if you're gonna do it, do it right, but I think that my personal feeling, and I'm sure the world would disagree with me, but that puppetry has changed because of Jim Henson and the Muppets and now everybody is making foam puppets. I don't know how much you're on Facebook but I'm on this puppetmakers thing. And I just scroll through it. I mean, I could make any foam puppet, I made tons of them, when I was teaching in high school I made sets of puppets, just the armature part, just the basic parts and the students put on the noses and stuff, and so it isn't that I can't make them, it isn't that I'm against them, but they don't last forever, you put them in the back of your car and they're melted! So it's not as much an art form anymore, where you have, like when Luman came and stayed with me, he photographed Alan Cook's collection. It's all been sent to Seattle.

JB: I'd love to know what you think about the new digital puppetry, where you have an armature on your hand, that reads all your motions and then turns that into a digital image. How do you feel about that? I'm sure you've seen stuff like that.

JRB: Well, I'll tell you, I have an open mind. I am interested in seeing how these things evolve, but you have to have high standards. If that is digital, whatever they're doing, I don't care as long as the standard is high, I mean, who knows what's gonna happen, who knew what the cloud was ten years ago? We didn't know we could store unlimited information in some "where" somewhere out there.

I'm very interested in modern puppetry and what they're doing. We are all explorers and exploring new ideas and new frontiers. I am looking forward to the next chapter in the history of puppetry!

DOCTOR SCHROEDER CHERRY

JB: You grew up in DC. Talk about going to school in the nation's capital.

Schroeder Cherry: I grew up in Northwest Washington, DC. Years later, I understand now I'm what they call an uptown guy. I played with puppets in elementary school. I had a pretty playful childhood. I grew up in DC. I spent my summers in the country in Virginia. When I was very young, we lived close to Rock Creek Park, so I spent a lot of my time in the woods in Rock Creek Park. In high school I was an art major. I went to the closest thing, at that time, to an arts school in DC. It was called Workshops for Careers in the Arts and that was the predecessor to the Duke Ellington School for the Arts. So, I went to McKinley High School to study art and then I hung out with these kids who were part of the city-wide Workshops for Careers in the Arts. That's when I was exposed to other kids from across town and studied visual and performing arts. At the time, I thought visual art kids were just kind of…dry, so I hung out with the theater kids and the dance kids. But I knew I wasn't one of them. I just liked to be with them. My talent was really in making visual stuff. I liked dancing and I enjoyed the effusiveness of those kids. They were just so, so expressive. I really enjoyed that. But I knew I wasn't one of them. I was a painter. I liked to draw, to paint.

In my senior year of high school, I went to Switzerland. And there, the learning environment is very different. It's highly structured. Even the art course that I took was regimented and highly structured. You learn this, then you learn this, then you learn this, then you learn this. And I stuck through that. I don't think I appreciated it as much at the time, but when I look back at it now, I think, oh, foundation is really important. What I lacked was the effusiveness. I didn't speak fluent German.

JB: Yes, that could put a damper on things.

SC: I had to learn German on the spot. Well everybody in that program had to. So, I am the non-language speaking person taking classes. Recently, within the last couple of years, thanks to Facebook, I have reconnected with three people who were very instrumental in my Switzerland year, just kind of helping me get through things and it's interesting seeing us now as all adults. But they were also creatives and they've gone on to other things in their adult lives. One is still a theater-slash-musician type and he plays with a band and he travels around Switzerland and Italy with an Italian wife. His English was not that strong, but it was good enough for him to communicate with me and was certainly much better than my German. After I came back from Switzerland, I studied German as a minor, just to keep the language up. So, when we're communicating now, when I wrote letters back to these guys, (they asked) how is it that you went back to America and your German is much better? And really it gave me a pause; yeah, I was the foreign kid. I was the one who didn't speak their language. Which makes me very sympathetic to kids in the U.S. whose first language is not English. I'm really sympathetic to that. I get it. Someone can have a conversation with you and I can tell where you're at the point where you're nodding your head, yes, as if you understand, but your eyes are glazing over. You didn't really get those last three sentences. But coming back after college, I'm still on the museum track. I'm working in museums and I keep the puppetry interest on the side. And I'm a visual artist and I keep the visual art and the puppetry going simultaneously. The thing with puppetry is, for me, I wasn't so excited about the making of the puppet as I was about performing with them, so I would go through periods of making them and then I wouldn't make them anymore because I'm performing with them and the materials I'm using last for years, so it's not like I had to make another puppet every month. My first puppets were hand puppets and by third grade I had marionettes. I still have a marionette from that period, today. He's a Jed Clampett marionette, a string puppet. Let me get him. He needs surgery, but his strings were attached.

JB: Is this a Pelham?

SC: I think so. He's missing his hands. This is what I was playing with in third and fourth grade. As a kid I became masterful at untying knots, because that's the thing that happens with string puppets. I was pretty adept at untying knots. I stopped playing with puppets just before going to junior high school because I thought, you know, junior high school, puppets for a guy is just not cool. But I was still fascinated with puppets. I was always watching puppeteers. As a kid in DC early on I remember watching coffee commercials with Jim Henson and those fascinated me. Even before I could tell time, I sensed when they were about to come on, on Saturday afternoons and I would be right on front of the television to see the characters who were selling coffee. Later I came across puppeteers like Jiří Trnka. I found an old book with some of his stuff in it. I kick myself that I didn't buy the book. I liked what he was doing with the figures, they fascinated me as well. I went back to puppetry in college in my freshman year. I had an instructor, Martin Puryear, a well-known sculptor, and he was doing these amazing kites. So, I said, "Why are you doing these kites?" "Well, I did kites as a kid and I wanted to know how I would respond to something from my childhood." And I thought, wow, that's a fascinating idea. For me, my childhood thing was puppets. So, I went back to puppets and I realized I still loved puppetry. And the imagination, and the construction, and the playing around with characters. So, in my next year I was at the University of Michigan and I devised a way to have puppetry as a minor. Someone introduced me to a puppet master in Chicago and I said, "If I go study with this guy in the summertime, can I get credit? Because I wanted to do puppetry. And they said, "Well, you have to have a structure and do a proposal." And so, I put all that together and they allowed me to do it! So, while I was working at the Art Institute of Chicago in the daytime, I hung around with this guy in the evening in his warehouse and studied his puppetry. Later on after graduating, I just kind of did puppetry on my own, but I combined it with my museum work. I was always doing something with puppets in museums. I was a museum educator by training and at one point, I wanted to produce play spaces for adults. I wanted to create "safe spaces" for adults to play in a very serious artistic environment.

JB: And it's during this time after Chicago that you began to really use puppets in your museum work, right? And Ms. Lily was introduced.

SC: At that time, I was working at the Baltimore Museum of Art. So that became the incentive for a character whose name is Ms. Lily. She is a bonified docent. We came up with this woman whose got bouffant hair, (with a) sliver streak, pearls, white knit sweater, red skirt, black patent leather pumps and she only deals with adults in galleries. She does not do children. That was the character. And she was wildly popular! We had great fun with her. It got to the point where people were calling in and asking for Ms. Lily's tours and I had to pull her off because we had live docents. So, we took her off of the floor and gave her a special spot. She started doing television. She did a short clip on Monet when the Baltimore Museum of Art had the Monet exhibition, which was a blockbuster exhibit. Ms. Lily did a tour for adults with Monet. Later on, some of the other curators thought, well, this actually does work, it's not as quirky as we thought it was going to be, so can you do our collection? So, she ended up doing modern art. She did African art. She couldn't do etchings because it just wasn't feasible in the gallery space. The etchings were just too small to have a crowd around the puppet and look at the etchings. So, we weren't able to do that, and I found that I was having to discern what was most appropriate for a puppet in the gallery. We asked for reservations and people would reserve spots. And one day, we had fifteen reservations, but by the time Lily got into ten minutes of her tour, we had forty-five people following her around from gallery to gallery, so it was a huge crowd. I remember one day this woman, tall, elegant, white female, very coiffed, after the tour she pulled me aside and says, "I just want you to know, I've been divorced for twelve years…" And I thought, where's this going? She said, "Today is the first time I've laughed in twelve years. Thank you for this tour." I thought, that's a great validation! There were some challenges. Ms. Lily starts off the tour by announcing that there are no children allowed on the tour. "I don't care how much of a genius your child is, they are not allowed on the tour. The tour is for adults." One woman just insisted that her five-year-old could understand everything. And the child became disruptive, so Ms. Lily didn't address the child, she addressed the mother and said, "Dear, I don't know if you were here at the beginning of the tour, but this is not a tour for children. There is a wonderful family workshop, down the stairs to your left. Would you please go there?" And people said, "Yeah, take the child to the workshop!" There was another instance where this guy would not talk to Lily, he would address me.

Also, at the beginning of the tour, Ms lily introduces me as her technician. I'm her "handler," and if there are any questions to be addressed during the tour, they are to be address to Ms Lily, not "the handler. He does not speak to you." And he was there for that introduction, I saw him. He would not talk to Lily. And he had multiple questions, so he kept coming to me. And Lily just got to the point she says, "Excuse me dear, I know that you were with us at the beginning of the tour. If you have any questions you are to address me. He is my handler. He is not speaking to you." And the crowd went, "Yeah! Talk to Lily!" [we both burst out laughing] I think he kind of annoyed the crowd, because he was kind of obnoxious.

JB: Did he address Lily after that?

SC: I don't remember the man having any questions after that. So, she became known as the puppet docent. And now, even today, she does little spots, because I'm the member of an art gallery in Baltimore. I thought, wouldn't it be great to have Lily introduce the artists? So, we did these very short clips, just a minute or a minute and fifteen seconds. One of the more hilarious points was with an artist who didn't know Lily was a puppet. I said, "Matt! You got these great ceramics on the wall. Can Ms Lily interview you? It's just a short interview. Can she interview you?" And he said, "Yeah, yeah, yeah. Good!" Matt is a big guy and I'm setting her up and he's standing in front of his work and Lily taps him on the shoulder and says, "Well dear, are you ready for your interview?" And Matt turns around and looks and he almost loses it. But he holds it together and Lily interviews him, and he talks to her about his ceramics and the technique and his medium. And it lasts for a full minute and then we cut the camera off and he says, "I'm going to go home and tell my wife that I was interviewed by a puppet." So, we were having fun with that.

JB: It seems that your friend almost instantly accepted the puppet as just as real and valid as he would a person.

SC: Puppets are very seductive and I think that because of that seduction, people can get sucked into doing something. It's called the suspension of disbelief that makes it really work for a lot of folks. In my style of puppetry, I'm in full view. I'm just in all black. I'm not a ventriloquist. I truly do turn everything over to the puppet.

JB: Do you have some folks who just reject the puppet?

SC: Actors. I've had some interesting interactions with actors. Some of them say, "I will never be on a stage with a puppet. Just don't ask me to do it." It freaks them out. Or if you put a puppet in an actor's hand, you have to get them to switch gears, so that they're not the focus.

JB: What material are you using these days to make your puppets?

SC: Mend-All. One of these things I like about it is that it's reusable, so if you do something and you want to change it, you can melt it down and re-sculpt. Unlike Plastic Wood which has its own character. I'm not in love with a material. I like when it works. Since I've found this new material, I'm in a phase now of making puppets during the Covid period and I'm having a ball.

JB: You got your BA in painting and puppetry from the University of Michigan. This was the period of the "independent major." Was your Puppetry major one of these do-it-yourself majors?

SC: They allowed me to do it.

JB: Was it difficult convincing them to let you do it?

SC: I approached one of my professors, he was a painting professor and said "This is what I'd like to propose. How do I go about doing it?" I had to go to the dean and he told me what I needed to pull together so it could be viable, so it could be tracked as a study course. We're only talking about one summer actually, because after that year I went back to Chicago. So we're talking about a summer course that was intensive and once I laid out what the expectations were, when I came back, I had constructed four puppets, I had constructed a collapsible stage with drawable curtains, and I had put together a scenario, which mostly, at that point, wasn't a story, it was really puppets performing to songs. That whole package became part of my graduate performance. That's what got accepted. On my resume I say painting and puppets just to let people know I was doing more than painting.

JB: And your master's and doctoral degrees are from George

Washington and Columbia Universities, respectively. Your graduate work is in Museum Education. What drew you to specialize in this field?

SC: After undergrad, I was living and working in Chicago. I had landed a summer job at the Art Institute of Chicago and realized that's the environment that fit me. I liked being surrounded by people who were dressed in all black and speaking in very articulate terms about art. They'd also given me the opportunity to put together two summer programs. They gave me money for a yellow school bus, lunches, and my job was to introduce high school kids to public art and art in the museum's collection. A dream job for me! Because of that, I was working out of the education department, so I got to see what the education department does in a museum setting, and I thought, this is what I want to do. I was an art major, but I knew I didn't want to teach art. I thought I would just be miserable and also abysmal at teaching art on a day-to-day basis. But I could certainly talk about art and on the side, continue to make my own art. That was a fit for me, so I realized that if I wanted to advance, I had to get a graduate degree and then I started looking around at museum education programs. At the time, there were only two. One was in DC, the other one was in Bank Street [College, Manhattan]. They were offering master's degrees in museum education specifically. And I thought, well, George Washington looks like what I want to do, so I interviewed for that. And that set me on the course for working in museums. I did think, at one point, that I wanted to leave museums and go into television, because of the work that was going on with educational television and puppetry. I got into a graduate program in Columbia, again another program where they allowed you to design your course of study. The focus was education, but they allowed you to choose the discipline, so I chose education and my discipline was museum work, but I wanted to explore television. I got an internship at a television station in New York and in my second week I realized this is not my herd. I like what they're doing, but I'm not the one to do that. I really do want to do museum work. I didn't want to leave museums, it was just the museum I was in, I needed to get out of, so that was my epiphany. My experience with television served me well later on, because in my museum profession

I ended up working in situations where I wanted to have museum people collaborate with television people and so since I understood a little bit of both sides I could help them communicate. Literally help them communicate because the vocabularies are very different! And the learning styles are very different for those folks, so I was able to bring that together and bridge the gap. I've been in museums thirty-five-plus years. Later on, I became more of an administrator. I became a Grantmaker. I'm still connected with museums. In New York I was with the Lila Wallace Fund. I was a Grantmaker there. Later, I was Deputy Director for Museums for the United States with the Institute of Museum and Library Services. In that situation I got to see museums across the country and how they actually serve the public. It allowed me to focus on my passion, which is programming and serving public audiences. I stayed with IMLS for eight years and then left. It's a Presidential appointment. I was only supposed to stay there for four years. I stayed for eight. It was time to go. All along I've been making art and playing with puppets, so now that I'm freelancing and have more time, I can devote more time to puppetry and making art. I still teach museum studies at a university. I teach graduate students at Morgan State University. These are students who primarily already have some museum experience, but they need a graduate degree in order to advance. I feel pretty good about working with that population.

JB: What brought you to Baltimore?

SC: At the time I was working at the Getty Museum in California. I got a call from the director of the Baltimore Museum of Art asking if I'd be interested in applying for a job and I said, "Well, I've only been here for about a year. It's too early for me to leave." He called me six months later and said, "So now what do you think?" And I said, "It's worth a conversation." At that time, I realized I had hit a ceiling and I wasn't going to get any further at the Getty. Also, I had gone through two earthquakes and was not happy about that experience, so I thought it was worth a conversation. So, he sent me a plane ticket and I came and interviewed for the job and they offered me a position as Director of Education. I thought, yeah, it's time for me to be a director. It's time to make the jump. If you had sat me down at a table with a map and said, "Choose your next spot anywhere in the world," Baltimore would never have been on my radar. I just had no experience with Baltimore, but it turned out to work really well for me. I enjoyed the latitude that I was given to do the programs and work with the public. And then it was time to go and I landed a job in New York with the Lila Wallace Fund as a Grantmaker.

JB: Let's talk more about your puppet work. Does your painting influence your puppet work or puppet work influence you painting? Or neither?

SC: I see myself going into "split-brain" when I'm producing. When I'm working on puppets I'm generally not painting. I'm in puppet mode. And when I'm painting, just the reverse. I'm not really making puppets. I usually have to carve out a space mentally to do one or the other. In terms of putting objects together and a narrative, my paintings tend to be narrative, they always have a story behind them. That's a connection with puppets. I have to say for me, they're still disparate. What I do think melds together…there's a triumvirate, the puppets, the painting, and the museum work. I think for me that all comes together, because they are all about narrative, they are about objects, they're about presentation and when I'm working puppets, I think of myself as manipulating objects. In museum work, you're interpreting objects. With the artwork, I'm making objects. It's object-centric, it keeps coming back to the object center and the storyline. Even in museum work, there's a narrative connected to the object.

I also have an interest in African puppetry, so I've been traveling to Africa starting in the '80s and I started collecting African puppets.

[first photograph Brazilian puppet]

He was inspired by a cowboy at a real black rodeo.

Preacher is actually from my undergrad days. He was one of the puppets I made in college.

JB: Tell me, why is puppetry so central to your work and viewpoint?

SC: Puppets are very seductive and because of that, you can get across large pieces of information in a way that wouldn't go across the same way if it were delivered by a talking head. Because of that fascination, something is loosened mentally that frees you up to absorb the information. You're fascinated by this creature who's being animated, but you're also paying attention to what's being delivered. After the fact you realize, oh, the puppet said this. Oh, I was talking to a puppet. All of these things are really effective in terms of getting across information. I've been experimenting with these short clips about Covid related items: how to wear a mask; when you should wear a mask; how not to take cleaning fluid to cure Covid. I'm watching the news and thinking, okay, there's another example for a snippet. We can do this. I'm experimenting with that. I realize that on the spectrum of recording, I'm at the very beginning. I have a large learning curve in terms of dealing with "green screen" and doing puppets on camera. My first couple of takes, I was literally holding a cell phone in one hand and the puppet in the other and doing the dialog. So, since then I've gotten a tripod and I'm experimenting with the phone and then I'm going to go to the next piece of equipment and a stronger tripod. When I started doing those little snippets about Covid, I didn't realize the impact it would have. I just posted on my Instagram and Facebook. Maybe it's because people are starving for some type of entertainment right now because we're all stuck at home, but they really responded to the puppets. A few people said, thanks for reminding us about the importance of wearing masks, thanks for doing this. I love Khordell! Khordell happens to be the first puppet I created during Covid, so his storyline is connected with Covid. When I created him, I sculpted him, his face, body parts. I had a shirt on hand, but I didn't have pants for him and I didn't have a rod. I had to go to Home Depot, but at the time, the stores weren't open. So, Cordell would appear and say, "Hi, I'm a rod puppet and I'm in progress. I'm waiting for my rods. HEY MAN, WHEN YOU GO GET MY RODS, MAKE SURE YOU HAVE YOUR MASK ON BECAUSE YOU CAN'T GET INTO HOME DEPOT WITHOUT A MASK!" It was that kind of delivery. And then finally, he got his rods. Then the next snippet that he did said, "I want to thank everybody who wished me well when I was in quarantine with Covid, but I have my rods now! I GOT MY RODS!! I'M GOOD TO GO!!!" Smooth Earl is developing into a sidekick for Khordell, that was not my intention for Smooth Earl initially. Smooth Earl calls from off-camera, "Hey Khordell!" And Khordell's response is, "Hey man, I'm doin' a film here. What's goin' on?" "Well, I'm gonna go meet with Dark Anne Lovely and we're gonna be six feet apart." The next shot is six puppet shoes. "We're gonna be six feet apart!" And Khordell says, "Well, that's good man. Make sure that Dark Anne Lovely's got her mask on too, cause you need to have that social distancing." That's how that snippet ends. People are having fun with it. I got a call from Smithsonian's Anacostia Museum, "Do you think you'd have enough material with Khordell for a thirty-minute show in October?" I said, "Yeah, by that time I'm sure we'll have something. Let's do it." Because museums now are trying to figure out how to accommodate the public during Covid and a lot of them are going to virtual. Some of them are doing spaced visitations, but many are going virtual. Anacostia Museum is going to be doing a series of programs for kids and family. They started off being Saturday, but now it's Thursday afternoon, so Cordell is going to have a spot and he gets to be promoted in their materials. We're going to call it Khordell and Friends. Between now and then, I have to come up with a couple of scenarios.

JB: The first time I saw you perform you did, If I can't Sell It, I Will Sit On It.

SC: That's Ms. Lily! That was for a puppet slam. We've done it a few times, in different spaces, but it was developed for a puppet slam. It was initially done at Black Cherry Puppet Theater. When they put out a call for puppet slam pieces, I thought I'd like to do a song, so it's basically lip-syncing or acting out a song. I heard the Blues song and when I heard it on the radio I thought, that's a puppet song, that's a narrative. And I ran around and found a chair, and then sculpted the chair and let Lily do it. I had two puppets songs for that slam. That's how that came about. That's Ruth Brown talking about having a second-hand shop. There's a guy coming in and he likes what he sees, but he's too cheap to pay for it. That's all Ruth Brown. That's actually a signature song for Ruth Brown.

JB: What was your first show, when you came back to puppetry?

SC: We'd have to go back to my museum work. Because I was working as a museum educator. I got an invitation from Smithsonian to interpret an exhibition of three-hundred and sixty sheet music covers.

The curators were a little concerned that, on its own, the show was dry and it needed something to perk it up and attract an audience, so I thought, how about a puppet whose name is Ragtime Roucheaux? He's an old guy, an old musician and he knows all of these guys who are on the sheet music covers and he can go through the exhibit and point out old stories connected with the covers and he would move the audience through the galleries. That was a traveling exhibition, which is why it was tricky, because it's what I call a library exhibition. They're sheet music covers, they're all flat and they had to be designed in such a way to make them interesting in an exhibition, so Ragtime Roucheaux shows up. He was a hand/rod puppet and he talked about the sheet music covers. That was an early show. This would have been around '78, '79. Later on, when I was Director of Education at Studio Museum of Harlem, I had a small staff and they allowed me to teach them to work puppets. Then they got into it. We did shows that were based around exhibitions to help kids understand those shows. One of the early shows was about Rosa Parks and there was a chant. Those early shows all had chants. "Rosa Parks was a heroine. H-E-R-O-I-N-E." Those were shows that were developed around an exhibition. We did a number of those. The big show that I developed that I thought would last for a couple of months that I'm still doing today, thirty years later, is Underground Railroad, Not A Subway. I was in New York talking to some junior high and high school kids and I said, "Well, you guys know about the Underground Railroad, right?" One kid looked at me with disdain and said, "Yeah man, everybody knows about the underground railroad. That was a subway to help black people get to freedom." And I thought, okay, for him, the Underground Railroad was more than a hundred years ago. He knows that the subway is more than a hundred years old, so that makes sense to him. But I thought, we've got work to do. So, I came up with this show called Underground Railroad, Not A Subway. And it has a chant to it. I'm running into people, now, years later who are saying, "My child saw your puppet show and my child now is in college and she still knows that Underground Railroad chant." I've had parents say to me, "I saw your puppet show and I can't get that chant out of my head." It's Underground Railroad, not a subway. People travel farther north-way. Walk, run, swim, travel far. Follow the drinking gourd.

Throughout the show you hear pieces of that chant. By the end of the show, it's really familiar to you and also, the audience has a copy of the chant in hand. After the show, I come out and I say, "Thank you for coming to the show, but we're not done yet. The puppets would really like to hear you say the chant. So, can you do it for the puppets?" That's when I conduct the orchestra of the audience and they do the chant. That's the way they participate and end it. Again, I thought it would last for a couple of months. The technology has changed. It started out on reel-to-reel, moved to cassette, moved to CD, and now I have it on USB, but it's the same story. Interestingly enough, someone would like me to change the script, because of the word "slave." The narrator, Mister Zeke, talks about slaves, so I got pulled up after an audience, this has happened a couple of times, someone would say, "Could you just please not say slave? Can you just say enslaved people?" And I thank them for their comment and I say, "You know, that's a really good point and it's a conversation you should have after the show, but Mister Zeke is speaking in time period and in time period, they did not say enslaved people. They said slaves.

JB: Let's talk about your Tuskegee Airmen show.

SC: Oh, that was fun. Again, a museum-oriented show. The challenge was: do something about the Tuskegee Airmen, we don't know who the audience is. [laughs] Which is typical of museum work. You don't know who the audience is until you show up. So, I had to ask them, "Well, typically who shows up?" "Well typically, it's young kids. Like preschool and early elementary." Well, that gives me a handle, "And I would imagine these are family groups" "Yes well, they are family groups." So, for Tuskegee Airmen I came up with a puppet whose name is Tevin. Tevin can spell his name and his name begins with the letter "T." And that whole show opens up with him trying to write the letter "T." So, he says, "My name is Tevin and I can write my name and it starts with a 'T.' Do you want to see me write a letter 'T?'" So, he does this [makes writing motions] and he shows the letter "T," but the "T" is sideways, and he says, "T!!!!" And the audience goes, "NO!!!" He says, "No, I can do it. I can do it." He does this several times, it's upside-down. Finally, he gets the "T" right. It's right-side-up. He says, "'T' stands for Tevin and it's also for Tuskegee.

Tuskegee Airmen." He talks about the Airmen. He talks about flying. Tevin also has a large sack that is supposedly filled with things that fly. And it's sitting right there. He says, " I have some things in my sack that can fly. You wanna see 'em?" "YAY!!!! We wanna see the things that fly." So, he digs into his sack and he pulls out a gorilla. And he says, "A gorilla can fly!! YAY!!!" "NO!!! A GORILLA CAN'T FLY!!!" "Oh, a gorilla can't fly. I think gorilla just wanted to come here to see you guys today. Okay, I got something in my bag that can fly!" So, he pulls out a boat. "A BOAT CAN FLY!" "NO, A BOAT CAN'T FLY!!" He pulls out a gorilla, a boat, a book, and finally there's a bird. "YAY! A bird can fly!" So, we're in the Air and Space Museum and we're surrounded by airplanes. That's when we turn it over to the gallery and the puppet says, "Well, look around to see if you can find things that have wings. " And they are literally under these planes. The planes are dropping down from the ceiling. The kids actually get, in-hand, these toy planes and they start making motor sounds and going into flight. That segues into a gallery tour. Tevin says, "We're going to take a gallery tour. You're going to go with me and I want you to find some things in the gallery." They go in the gallery, but they're making their motor sounds with their planes and they're flying through the gallery. They stop at a point and Tevin has them look for different things. "I see something that an airplane pilot would carry with them and it was a good luck charm and it's a monkey. Where's the monkey?" And it's actually a little stuffed animal. The pilots carried these good-luck-monkeys with them when they were in flight, so we talked about the good-luck-monkeys. "I see a photograph of a woman who was an airplane pilot and she flew over the ocean. Where's the woman?" And they look around and they find the woman. And we come back to the gallery space where they sit on the floor and we ended it with another chant about the Tuskegee Airmen. That particular chant engaged the kids about not being forgotten. You are not forgotten. You are not forgotten. You are not forgotten. We know your name. It starts with… And it starts with a letter, so we'll go around to each of the kids, "What's your name?" "Oh, my name's Mary" You are not forgotten. You are not forgotten. You are not forgotten. We know your name. Your name starts with "M." And everyone would sing the song and several kids would get their chance to do it. We ended it with Tuskegee, but by that time, Tevin can't get the letter right. "Tuskegee is your name it starts with "S." "NOO!!!! TUSKEGEE DOESN'T START WITH "S!!!" He finally gets it. It starts with "T." And that's how the show ends. For that presentation, since I knew I'd be working with younger kids, I had to make it very basic, but repetitive, so they had some take-aways and they would remember this. And Tevin's great with kids. He's this tall loopy guy with bright red tennis shoes. He's gangly and he digs into his bag.

JB: How about the show Can You Spell Harlem?

SC: Again, my style keeps coming back to repetition and chanting. That was inspired by my childhood watching cartoons. I learned how to spell Mississippi by watching television. It was the "bouncing ball." (In) Can You Spell Harlem? I wanted to get across the idea that there were a number of people who were "creatives," so the storyline is: there's a boy who likes to rap, he rapping in school and he's a little disruptive, and so his teacher says, you know, the classic line, "Is there something you'd like to share with us?" The boy says, "Yeah. There were a lot of black people who were making things a long time ago, in the Harlem Renaissance." And the teacher says, "That's very good. Who are they?" And he doesn't know who they are, so he's embarrassed. It turns out that his dad is a radio talk-show person and he has a call-in show where people are talking about someone who did something in the Harlem Renaissance. "Hi, this is Puppet Radio, the smooooth radio. Today we're going to be talking about the Harlem Renaissance. Do you have anything about the Harlem Renaissance?" So, people are calling in and giving information about different people: James Van Der Zee the photographer, painter Aaron Douglas, and some other people. By the end of the show you have this information on these people. The boy is listening to the show and he puts it together. He has an older sister and she's asking him what he's doing. He says, "I'm doing research." "Research on what?" He says, "Harlem." And she says, "Can you even spell Harlem?" So, they had this back and forth thing. By the end of the show he has the chant. He says, "I'm going to take my rap song, 'cause you know I'm bad and I got this information about the Harlem Renaissance. Harlem is a place in New York City. Artists there make things real pretty. They use pictures, and words, and colors, and sounds. Harlem is a place, the best thing around!" He gets his sister to say the chant with him, by the end of the show. Typical of my style, we end the show with the audience doing the chant for the puppets. It's locked in their brain. That's a show that had to change, because initially the storyline was the father was a writer and he was writing a story about the Harlem Renaissance. Well in this day and age, that was not suitable for the attention span of young kids. That's when I rewrote it to the dad being a radio talk show host, because then we could do back-and-forth quick sort of things. Also, different members of the family came in and introduced different characters. The mother came across some photographs from James Zan Der Zee. Aunt Marguerite, who is very prim and proper talks about Langston Hughes. The boy is getting information not only from the radio, but from family members.

JB: Are you still doing this show?

SC: I'm not actually doing it that much. The show that I'm doing a lot is Underground Railroad, Not A Subway. As I look at it now…you know how you look at work that's older? It's a little tedious.

JB: How about The Land of Primary Colors?

SC: Another museum show. We were dealing with abstraction. Really abstract works. And I thought, one of the best ways to break this down for younger audiences is to focus on colors, so we talked about primary and secondary colors. It takes place in a land where everything is a primary color: red, yellow, and blue. One day, the young boy who is responsible for delivering the color pots is juggling the color pots and he drops them, and he mixes them to each other. He's freaking out because he's got to deliver the colors before the sun comes up. Because the color painters paint everything red, yellow, and blue. The only person who can get him out of this mess is Color Wizard. She lives on Blue Mountain, she's an African puppet. In this show I'm using African puppets, as well as my puppets. Color Wizard is this quirky character. He [the young boy] has to go to Blue Mountain, so there's this bird who has to fly him to Blue Mountain to meet Color Wizard. Color Wizard is waiting for him to tell him why he's there, but she knows why he's there. "I know what you're here for. You've done an awful mess of things in the Land of Primary Color. And now you're trying to figure out what to do." And the boy says, "Well, yeah! What do I do, what do I do?!?" And she says, "Well honey, what you got is some new colors." And he says, "What am I going to do!?" "Well, you just got some new colors. They're secondary colors!" And she breaks down the secondary colors and he can't conceptualize it. And he just says, "Well what am I gonna do now?" "You're gonna have to go back and tell people that they got these new colors: orange, purple, and green." And he says, "Well, what about the chant?!? What about the chant?!?" Because every day there's a chant: "Separate red, yellow and blue. These are primary colors, true." That is the chant. And she says, "Oh yeah, I guess we're going to have to change that chant. Well, it's about time. Let's see… secondary colors…see orange, purple, green. That's the new chant, honey." So, he has to deliver the chant to the north, south, east, and west before the sun comes up, so everybody knows these new colors are coming along. Bird handles it. Bird is an African inspired puppet that I made. Gazelle who has legs that are so fast you can't see her legs, she's a puppet from Mali and she's got a drummer on top of her head because the people in that part of the Land of Color understand drums. Bird is a raffia puppet that flies over the audience. By the end, they've got this new chant. Well, it turns out that not everybody likes these new colors, so there's this big confusion, you know, "Who ever heard of green grass!? Grass is supposed to be BLUE!! BLUE!!!" I insert a song by Randy Crawford, Everything Must Change. Africa Brown comes out in the crowd and sings Everything Must Change. And after that the people think, "Well, maybe if we're gonna to get better, things will have to change. Okay, we'll go with these new colors." So, they sing the new chant. The color painters come out, they wave these new colors just in time for the sun to come up and that's how it ends. It is a workout, because those African puppets are heavy.

JB: You were also a finalist for the 2019 Sondheim Award. Tell us about that.

SC: The Sondheim is an annual award given to regional artists in the Maryland, Virginia, Delaware region. It's a wide-open art competition. You submit your work and they select six finalists and they each get a chunk of money. Out of those six, there is one who gets twenty-five thousand dollars. I was one of the six. Each of the six gets an exhibition at the Walters Museum of Art. That was fun.

JB: I'd like to talk about your artwork. Your Barbershop Series is especially beautiful. The black barbershop is such a central place in the culture of black men.

SC: It's got an interesting history, too. Black barbers in American started in the colonial period when white men of means wanted to emulate European aristocracy and that means they have what they call a man-in-waiting, who would shave them and cut their hair. That's when they allowed black men to have a knife at their throat! And then later on, black barbers just became professionals.

JB: Your series on Barbershops and the Pullman porters are remarkable. You've portrayed these important aspects of black culture through these series. I find the insight about the porters being so instrumental and important in black culture fascinating. These men, traveled across the country and became a communications network, connecting black communities, so people would know what was going on and they wouldn't have to rely on an all-white owned media to accurately tell their story. Let's talk about that.

SC: That's the type of information I wanted to share, the fact that these men were doing very hard labor on those trains and they took that opportunity and manifested something beyond what anybody ever anticipated. They were largely responsible for establishing a black middle-class. Everyone I've talked to at least knows somebody or had a relative who was connected with the railroad, at some point in their lives. I think initially it was an opportunity to work. That was steady paying work. It was also pretty harsh, because Pullman porters were essentially seen as servants. George Pullman primarily hired only black men from the south, because he figured they knew how to interact with white people. That's why they got the job. Inside the enterprise, you had intra-racial issues going on. Porters tended to be dark-skinned. They were the ones handling the luggage. Men working in the dining car however, tended to be light-skinned, because white passengers didn't want to have darker skin handling their plates.

It was fine for the kitchen, but they didn't want to be served by them, so you had all these racial limitations going on. And there was a tension between dining car guys, who were light-skinned, and the Pullman porters, who were dark-skinned, because although the dining car guys had a lighter workload in terms of manual labor, they weren't paid as well, because the porters were the ones who made tips. The porters were the ones who fine-tuned that whole "aura" of serving the patron in order to get, in addition to the salary, a higher tip, so they were making money.

JB: When did you begin developing the series?

SC: Around 2010 and it came about because of some research I had done about porters. There was a short story, I think it's James Alan McPherson [from the book Hues and Cry." It was a short story about a railroad porter, an older guy, who's in the last week of his employment. He's all set to get to retirement, and on their train the inspector shows up, and everybody knows that something's up. This inspector's a white guy. He's the one who's very picayune about everything being in order. The dining car guys, they also share information with each other. Every two weeks or so, there's a pamphlet about regulations on how to handle customers in the dining car. This guy is illiterate. He doesn't read, so he depends on a younger guy, who's a college kid to tell him what the latest changes are. The inspector comes in and he specifically asks this older guy to serve him, so they all know that something's up and they're highly alert to make sure everything's tight, everything's tidy, everything's done exactly the way it's supposed to go. And the guy who's serving him knows he's got it down; he's been doing it all the time. The inspector keeps trying to goad him into doing something. He says, "Well, why don't you come sit with me?" "No, sir. I can't sit with you." Because that's a violation, that's a transgression, so he wouldn't do that. But the guy keeps engaging him in conversation and the waiter is very anxious, because there's something wrong about this. The guy says, "Well, you're up for retirement. Congratulations." And he says, "Yes sir, thank you very much." He's still not going to sit down with him. And (the inspector) says, "Will you serve me some tea? And I'll take a wedge of lemon." He brings him the tea with a wedge of lemon and he places the wedge of lemon on the saucer, and a spoon, to the right. Well, that week they changed the regulations; the wedge of lemon is supposed to be on the other side of the teacup. The young guy that was supposed to give him the information didn't get to that part, so he missed catching it and telling him the new thing. And that's when the inspector caught him. "The wedge is on the wrong side of the cup. I'm sorry, but you can't get your retirement pay, because you've broken one of the rules." And at that point, the guy just sits down on the chair [laughs]! It was such a riveting story for me, I thought I need to find more about that whole culture, the railroad culture. That inspired the series.

JB: You were also involved in the recent African American puppetry exhibit at UCONN.

SC: That came about through a conversation with John Bell who wanted to know, is there such a thing as African American puppetry, so talking to some people in the field we thought that rather than trying to define it, let's raise it as a question and produce some examples of African American puppetry and let the audience come to their own conclusion. Paulette Richards became the curator for that. She did the yeoman's work on the research. We scoured the country. We had to come up with some parameters. What is an African American puppeteer? So, we had to define that, and in that discussion, we had to shave off what we described as people who happened to be African American and they made a puppet. Or an artist who's known for his sculpture and painting and they did a puppet. That's not a puppeteer. That's an artist who made a puppet, so we were trying to figure out who we could identify, and we came up with a number of people who are actually working with puppetry in various forms. In live theater and also on television. The earliest puppeteer we could find, we got an example of his work. We put up what I thought was a pretty striking exhibition of puppeteers at the Ballard Institute. You can get that information online, too. And Ms. Lily got a chance to be the docent for the show. She actually gave a tour of the exhibition. I wish we had recorded it. The audience turned out to be largely the puppeteers who were in the show, so she talked to them about them! Their work. They weren't quite sure what to expect in the beginning, but that's where my museum education background kicked in. We gave honor to every segment of that show and we put it into context, so it was fun to do.

JB: If you had a basic creative process theorem, what would that be?

SC: The creative process starts with everything out and then you winnow down.

JB: You also live in an area with a lot of fine puppeteers. Baltimore has been a hot spot for a while.

SC: Baltimore happens to have a pretty lively puppetry community and that's partly because of these "arts kids" who have connections with other people who are doing puppetry. And Black Cherry Puppet Theater (no relation). It goes back to connections.

JB: Thank you Doctor Cherry. This has been a delight.

SC: You're welcome. I had a great time.

INGRID CREPEAU AND MICHELE VALERI

JB: How did you get started together? When, where and how did you meet?

Ingrid Crepeau: It's her fault, she started it!

Michele Valeri: I made a record with my friend, Mike Stein, called Dinosaur Rock. This is back in 1983. I had a friend from graduate school who was the artistic director at The Discovery Theater at the Smithsonian and she wanted it to be a show, and she kept bugging me about it, and finally I said okay, fine, we'll make it into a show… somehow. I asked around and I said does anybody know anyone who makes big things, because what I wanted was the foot of a T Rex, and the leg, that would come out from the set, and the head and body of a parasaurolophus…

IC: You just asked for the head…

MV: I asked for the head, right. I didn't know what I was going to do with it, but I thought we could somehow make one of the characters, the parasaurolophus, using just the head. And then an egg and a baby diplodocus, to come out of the egg. That was it.

Everybody said if you want big things, call Ingrid. I didn't know who Ingrid was, I just got the phone number from (children's author) David Wisniewski, who was working with Ingrid at the time, and I called her and introduced myself, and I said I was looking for these things (head, egg, etc.). I didn't have a whole lot of money. And she said, "Well, why don't I take you to dinner?" So she took me to a place called…Horsefeathers?

IC: Beefeaters.

MV: Beefeaters! That was it! Up on Capitol Hill!

IC: I'd just made them a mascot and part of my fee was a bunch of free food at the restaurant. That didn't cost them much of anything! And it's lots of fun to take friends to a restaurant!

MV: So, in the middle of dinner she said, "I could make a puppet that small children would believe is a real dinosaur and when they left the theater, they would have thought they met a real dinosaur." And I thought, terrific, I can't afford that! Anyway, I said, gee, well, that's lovely

IC: I had just made some dinosaur parts for (Thornton Wilder's) Skin of Our Teeth and I was anxious to do some more. I thought, what fun! Here's my perfect opportunity. I had just made a lot of money and I didn't care if I got paid at all!

MV: So I invited her to my house, I lived down at 21st and S, just up from Dupont Circle, to talk money, and I thought, this is not going to work. So Ingrid and I were sitting in the living room haggling about the fee. And what I said was, I could probably pay you about $2000.

IC: I said, how about $500?

MV: And I said no! $500! That's not enough for what you're thinking of doing!

IC: So she said, how about $1500? And I said, how about $300? (now we're all laughing)

MV: So I said no! $300! Are you crazy?!? So she didn't charge me anything for the puppets, but by the time she was done, we had a giant stegosaurus…

IC: It was a four-legged body puppet…

MV: ….and a long neck and head, that came up from the back of the set, that was a diplodocus head and neck, very, very, very tall.

IC: Sixteen feet.

MV: And an entire parasaurolophus, including the tail and a leather jacket. So, I split the fee with her, my fee, because I had already hired (musician) Pete Kennedy to be Professor Jones and I wasn't going to pay him less than I had quoted. So we performed five days a week, for four weeks.

IC: Two shows a day.

MV: And they were sold out.

IC: Oversold! We set a record.

MV: Part of the thing was that the (Dinosaur Rock) record had come out. And it was popular and the kids really liked it. And it was the first wave of "dinosaur fever." It was October of '84 and what threw me was that these kids came to the show knowing the lyrics. So there I was singing and the audience would sing along. It was the most amazing feeling. It was a real thrill.

IC: So after that experience I had to take Michele out again. This could be a career. We could do this. And so we did.

MV: Well, what happened was somebody from the Science Museum of Boston called the Smithsonian and said they were doing a whole weekend about Dinosaurs - did they know of a show? So our very first out-of-town gig was the following January ('85) and we went up to Boston and performed at the Museum of Science for a weekend.

IC: It was six shows, Friday, Saturday, and Sunday. It was a huge hit.

JB: When you write a show, do you write it together?

MV: Now we do. The show had been written before Ingrid came aboard for Dinosaur Rock. But then we did The Great Dinosaur Mystery, which was the next show that we did, and we hired Joe Pipik to work with us and Joe set down some rules.

IC: He said I'll join the company if I can do a puppet and if Ingrid plays a musical instrument.

MV: And we wrote the show together.

JB: (to Ingrid) What did you play?

IC: Accordion. I play accordion.

JB: Michele let's back up a little and talk about your musical background a bit, because you didn't get into this because you were a puppeteer, it was because you needed a puppet.

IC: Michele will deny this, (but) she is a puppeteer and she has done a lot of puppets, long before I ever met her. She did the puppets and sang the songs with the puppets and had a musical accompanist.

MV: I played guitar from the time I was about nine and went to graduate school at Penn State and one of my teachers did children's musicals and she had a little children's theater traveling company, which I became a part of and she needed music for one of her musicals and she turned to me and said, "You play the guitar. You write the songs." I had never written songs for a show before, at all. Maybe a couple of tunes just for myself. So it was frightening. But I did, I wrote songs for this musical, which was called The Beeple, it was about bee people, and the hero of the play was played by a young undergraduate named Jonathan Frakes and went to Hollywood and became Number One on Star Trek (Next Generation). He was a really good looking kid and he could sing!

So I wrote that show and I wrote another show in graduate school and then I came home and after I got my Masters, I decided what I really wanted was to run a children's theater company, have my own. And I was, at one point, in three different children's theater companies at the same time. Which was a little more exciting than (what) I'd had asked for! Just to see what they were like. You know, how would I do it? Then I did a record called Me Casa Es Su Casa and decided to showcase for Montgomery County Schools and made some puppets… sort-of. Hand puppets. And started getting work. So, I was already in the performing arts in the schools in Montgomery County, Fairfax County, in D.C., a little bit in PG (Prince George's County, Maryland), not a lot. But they had showcases and you would come and showcase. And I had already done that when I met Ingrid. And I was also working for the Wolf Trap Institute. It started in '81, so I had been working there even before I put out Dinosaur Rock record. We went up to New England for the New England Kindergarten Conference, which was at Lesley College (now Lesley University)

IC: It's one of the premier teacher's colleges, an educationally groundbreaking teacher's college. MV:

So my boss said, "Come up and bring Ingrid and a puppet or two. And when we talk about the program, you and Ingrid could do a number and that would gather an audience." So, we did a couple of songs, we brought the Hadrosaur from Hackensack and pretty soon, we were performing in schools around 128 (Boston Beltway).

IC: We were better known in Massachusetts than we were here in Washington.

MV: It was like a treasure trove! So we did a lot of performing in Massachusetts and around the East Coast. And then we got a call from our friend Susan Swarthout, who was the artistic director for Discovery (Theater) at the time, and she said somebody had called her from Albuquerque and wanted a dinosaur show and could we do it. And we said, "Okay! Sure! We can drive to Albuquerque!"

IC: We'll just have to buy a truck! We made a pretty decent living, touring at least six months out of the year. Michele and I know a lot about early childhood. We've studied it, we've taken classes in it…

MV: And we've worked for the Institute since…

IC: …the Wolftrap Institute for Early Learning Through The Arts. Their area is early childhood and they have trained us, taught us.

MV: The idea of the Institute is to take performing artists, people who are working in the arts, put them into early childhood classrooms, show teachers, demonstrate how you can use the performing arts from day to day in your classroom. Especially with 3 to 5 year olds, because they have to move and you have to move with them and learning by doing is actually serious business.

IC: A lot of puppeteers don't like that age group. They don't understand a lot of the things about that age group. If you get into a dinosaur that's huge and they watch you do it, then they're not afraid of the dinosaur, you've taken their fear factor right out and once you're in it, they don't remember that you got in it. That's not how their brains work. We were trying to do a little video work, and there was this 3½ year old. And I was in Stella Stegosaurus, which is me on four legs. I got in Stella, did my scene, got out of Stella, got in Stella, did my scene, got out of Stella, so this 3½ year old, who's also in the video, saw this happen, over and over and over again. Finally she went up to Stella, when I was in Stella, and she said, "Stella, did you know there's a lady inside of you?" And Stella said, "That's alright sweetheart, she's a good friend of mine!" And she was fine with it then, by "kid logic." There is a definite kid logic and that's something that Michele and I are proud of that we understand it. We strive to honor it.

MV: The most important thing to performing for young children is to realize the focus of the performance is the children. You're dead in the water if you think you're the star. We came to develop that show, where the kids watch as Ingrid gets into a puppet.

IC: These things are scary to little kids!

JB: To little kids these things are very real.

MV, IC: Yeah!

MV: Exactly!

IC: "How come Mickey Mouse isn't the same size I see him on television?"

MV: So the reason we developed this show, that was presentational, was because we were hired at Wolf trap for the Institute to do Head Start, to do dinosaur shows for Head Start in the Barns. They have these field trips and they invite the classes that have been doing the residencies with performing artists, to come to come to the barns and see a show that is just for 3-5 (year-olds).

IC: Their very first theater experience. These were underprivileged kids, by in large.

MV: Most of them were in Head Start. So we were very close to them, they sat practically three feet from us.

IC: Nose-to-nose with a dinosaur that is 12 feet long and 9½ feet tall. The very first week we were at the Smithsonian, when this all started, the house manager did not know that you could not sit late-comers in the front, because of the dinosaurs. So there were some kids were VERY late! I mean the show was almost over and she sat them down at the front of the stage. So Stella Stegosaurus comes out and she's two feet from these preschoolers and as she's coming out towards them, they jumped up, screamed and ran! There were wet spots on the rug.

MV: And it wasn't just that, the very first show, it was Ingrid's idea, it was supposed to be a display in a museum and the long necked dinosaur, which was…

IC: Sixteen feet tall…her head came through the curtains, so you only saw about ten foot of neck.

MV: Yeah and she was still for the first ten minutes of the show and then she spoke.

IC: Then she comes to life.

MV: Yes….well, that was a bad idea! That was the first time we had spots on the rug! So the second show…

IC: …she (the dinosaur) talked to the house manager and the house manager says, (to the audience) "This is my friend Dina." Then everybody says, "Hi, Dina." Then the kids feel safe.

MV: We learned our lesson!

JB: Ingrid how did you get started?

IC: When I was six I went to the local community center and made a puppet and did a puppet show and my older brother went to it. He made Davy Crockett and my mother made the costume. It was the most gorgeous thing in the world. My father carved him a powder horn and a musket and this puppet was spectacular, and I made a clown. So when it came time to do puppet shows, I did a show of Davy Crockett with my clown playing Davy Crockett and my brother did some show where he was…not Davy Crockett. I mean it was totally ridiculous, but that was my first experience. And I really quite liked that, so I kept making puppets. Then my dad was in the service and we got to live in Germany. I was eleven and there was this wonderful German treasure. They have these designated artists that are considered treasures in Germany and he was a treasure in the art of Kasperle, which is the German version of Punch and Judy. The military base had asked him to take some of the Kasperle shows, translate them to English and perform them at military bases around Germany. So he was gonna' do four performances on a Saturday. It was a big Army base. I bought tickets to all four performances and I was the oldest kid probably in the audience and a head taller than everybody my age, so I stuck out in the back of the audience. And he saw me. So he saw me in line to see the next performance and he gives me the come-here sign with your finger and I go up to him. "So you like ze puppets, ya?" Oh yes! I loooove puppets! "So, okay! In zhis show you vill be ze chicken!" And I'd seen the show and the chicken was wonderful, so I said, okay, whatever! This is thrilling! So I went backstage and he started showing me…I'd never seen a metal thunder clap! You know, that you shake the metal and make thunder! And he had gizmos! Oh my, this guy, he had gizmos that were amazing!

And he said, "Okay. Zhis is number one hand," and he raises his right hand. And he says "Zhis is number two hand," and he raises his left hand. And he points at a knee, "Zhis is number three hand." And he points at a foot, "Zhis is number four hand." And he points at the other foot, "And zhis is number five hand. Zo, I'm the perfect puppeteer; I have five hands!" He had things that his feet did, things his knee did, it was just clever beyond imagination. So, when it came time to do the chicken, he says, "Time for chicken, I go like zhis and you be ze chicken!" Okay, fine. So, I'm watching the show backstage, watching him do all these gizmos and stuff and then he (signals), and I take the chicken and stick it up and I go "BWAAWK! BWAAWK, BWAAWK! BWAAWK, BWAAWK, BWAAWK!" And I got this HUGE laugh, which hadn't happened in the first show. So after the show he says, "Vas is zhis bwawk, bwawk, bwawk? Is zas vhat chicken say in America?" Because like so many performers, who do international shows, they don't translate the animal sounds. People forget. In Germany it was cluck, cluck, cluck! So before shows and after that, I translated the animals for him. And I would watch one performance, out front and then the next three backstage and he would assign me something in every show. One show there was a lot of thunder, so I did all the thunder. The chicken was wonderful! It was made out of a feather duster. So, I announced to my family, after a couple days of (puppeteering), this is it, I'm going to be a puppeteer and I never deviated, everything from then on was puppets, puppets, puppets. I had a company in high school and in college, then I graduated from college and went to work for Allan Stevens. Decided with a friend to start our own company (Patchwork Puppet Productions,

Inc.). Allan was so wonderful, when Sarah and Julien (Yochum) and I decided to start our own company, he gave us three puppet stools, an air compressor and an airbrush to start our company with. Allan launched us, it was just great. And we went on and did some live stuff. Our big claim to fame was that we had a show on channel 9 called Sneakers, which won a couple of regional Emmys. After three of us did a half hour show a week, wrote it, built everything, practiced it, went to the studio, did it…we pretty much hated each other after two years and that was the end of that company. But that's okay. I'm still really good friends with Sarah, but we had to take about three years off. The friendship, which was very strong to begin with, came back. After Sneakers, I decided I wished I knew a lot of things I didn't know and I went to work in every single theater in Washington, in costuming or props. And then I briefly had a business working for ad agencies. I made lots of money, but when I started with Michele, I said, you've saved me from ad agencies.

JB: This was when?

IC, MV: '84.

IC: And we had eleven friends in common. I counted then up one day.

MV: We both knew Joe Pipik, we both knew Michael Cotter, and David Wisniewski, David and Donna.

IC: John Spellman

MV: Liz Lerman.

JB: Lets' talk about your work in the mascot world.

IC: We can't remember when, but it's been within the last ten years.

MV: Here's what happened.

IC: It's all Michele's fault again.

MV: It's very serendipitous. The Congresswoman from D.C., Eleanor Holmes Norton, has a holiday show…

IC: For ALL the Boys and Girls Clubs in the city.

MV: In D.C. And she has it at the Congressional Office Building.

she called us and asked us to do some dinosaurs. One of the guys in her office called.

IC: Who had seen us perform.

MV: So we were going to go down and do the show and it took us forever to get through security. "What's in the truck?" Dinosaurs.

IC: We had to be inspected three times!

MV: So we brought the Hadrosaur from Hackensack and Momma Myosaurus, and a couple of baby dinosaurs, I think and we did our thing.

IC: Eleanor Holmes Norton was so sweet. She actually danced with one of the dinosaurs.

MV: And the Nationals sent "Teddy," with a handler. And of course, once again, all these little kids, it's one look at Teddy and it's "ARGGGHHH!"

IC: And the mascot from the DC United (soccer team) was there.

MV: And we all got dressed in the same little anteroom, so when it was over, Teddy was upside-down and we were putting away the hadrosaur and Ingrid said, "Gee, I'd love to look inside and see how Teddy works." So, I just walked right up to this guy and I said, "You know, the woman who made all our dinosaurs? She'd like to look inside Teddy, if that's okay."

IC: And (he) said, "She MADE that?"

MV: And I said, yeah. And he said, sure, sure, if she wants to look inside.

IC: I look up Teddy and I say, oh my goodness, they didn't re-temper the aluminum! It was all busted!!

MV: The frame was cracked!

IC: It was just in pieces! Wired and duct-taped together!

MV: So the reason Teddy was never winning the race was because that poor guy couldn't see anything…

IC: The insides were so broken!

MV: …he was like, leaning over. So he would come out and fall down!

IC: Because that's all he could do! He could see out about the size of a quarter!

MV: So Cory, their handler, says, "So you know about this stuff?" and Ingrid said, "Well, yeah I do, obviously, see what I did!" And he took Ingrid's card.

IC: And then it was an uphill battle to break into the "boy's club". First they had to test me – "can you make a baseball cap?" Okay, I made a baseball cap. "Oh, this is really nice! I like this! The brim on the one we have is all floppy and it just always looks a mess!" And I put the magnets in so he could take it off for the national Anthem, because mascots originally had their hats sewn on and the audience would boo them, "Hey MASCOT!! Take your hat off!!!"

The mascots are there for families. And the people who do mascots, understand mascots. I watched this group children sitting at the front rail of the ball game and all they did was watch Screech the Eagle and the Racing Presidents. THAT'S WHAT THEY WERE THERE FOR! And when the mascots are good…and the mascots in D.C. are EXCELLENT…that makes it easy to work for them, because they're creative, they understand business, they all have big hearts and good souls, they love kids, they know why they're there, and they are some of the hardest working people! You have no idea!

There are mascot rules. Which I love! This is my favorite rule. Because there's often more than one set of mascots. For practical reasons you have to do that. So, if Teddy is appearing in Fairfax County at one o'clock, he can't appear in Baltimore, until he's finished in Fairfax County. If they finish in Fairfax at 1:30 then he can appear in Baltimore at 1:30, but he can't appear at one o'clock if he's appearing somewhere else at one o'clock. Those sound like silly rules…

MV: No, they're great rules.

IC: When you impress upon these people who are mascot performers the carefulness and beloved-ness of what you're doing and that's what the rules do and that's why you can't photograph them when they're not "alive."

MV: The other ones, I think, seem more obvious. They're not allowed to talk.

IC: Yeah, that's the difference between puppets and mascots.

MV: They're not allowed to show skin.

IC: And that comes right out of Ringling Brothers Clown College. That's one of their rules.

MV: They're not allowed to pick kids up. They're not allowed to "handle" people.

IC: I really respect how they come up with these things. My favorite project this year, the Wizards played the Chicago Bulls, and the mascot performer (for the Wizards) said, can you make me a matador costume to fit the mascot! So I did! G-Wiz is the name of the mascot. He's from that era, probably Harrison Erickson made the original (editor's note: that's correct). So, G-Wiz comes out with a red cape as the players, the Chicago players came out. And one of the Chicago Bulls really liked jonesing with mascots, so he really played it, and he did the horns. The mascot performers told me really funny stories about this guy, and G-Wiz went down in one of those poses on the floor and the Chicago Bull player went, grabbed the mascot by the leg and dragged it off and the audience went bananas, they loved it! So if you can get any players to play with you like that, the mascots are just thrilled out of their minds.

JB: Let's talk about some of the interesting experiences you've had doing shows. What stands out?

MV: The show was Dinosaur Rock and we were doing it in a little town in New Mexico called Secorro, which is just below Albuquerque. So, we did it there and then two years later. And there's this part in the show where we have a baby dinosaur, who hatches out of an egg hungry. "Feed me! Mom, I'm Hungry!" And then we have a little number that we do called, Tiny Little Babies and a Great Big Momma, because according to scientists, the smallest babies who were ever hatched out of eggs compared to the size of their mothers were the long-necked dinosaurs.

IC: So it's a combination of that and the fact that dinosaur parents take care of their babies. This is a conundrum. If your foot is bigger than your egg that the baby's coming out of, motherhood gets difficult.

MV: How do you see them for one thing? So that was what the song was about. Well this is one of those theaters where they have a side platform that goes out to the audience.

IC: There's no stairs or anything. It's really easy to get onstage.

MV: It's like a ramp that goes from the stage, right into the audience. So, I'm in the beginning of this little routine that we do with Danny Diplodocus about being hungry and these two little girls come up the ramp, and they're holding flowers and grass. And I looked at them and I thought, okay, what's happening and I said, "Danny, I think somebody's here to feed you!" And the little girls reached up with their grass and Danny "ate" it. And they giggled, and then they went back and sat down and we went on with the show. The show's over and they came up with their mother. She said, "For two years, these children have been worrying about Danny because he didn't get fed." TWO YEARS! I was like, oh my god! It's my favorite story. I floated for days after that.

IC: For me the thrilling thing is that parents would come up and say, "Do you know that my child plays Dinosaur Rock, they pretend to be Professor Jones, they pretend to be the dinosaurs," one friend said you are entirely responsible for my child's fantasy life. Every show we've done, we hear that they play the show. Now THAT to me is the biggest thrill of all.

MV: We're very contented with what we've done.

BONNIE DUNCAN

JB: Let's talk about where you started. You're based in Boston, but a re you originally from New England?

Bonnie Duncan: I'm actually not. I'm from South Carolina and Georgia, and I moved to Boston to go to graduate school. I went to Lesley University and studied Creative Arts in Learning. I had this want to integrate the arts into classroom curriculum and so I moved to Boston for a year and that was twenty years ago. So, I stayed. I loved it.

All through my childhood I was in involved in dance and sports. I was a swimmer and runner. From there, I got into theater in high school and college and studied that through college. And then when I was in Boston, I saw this dance company called Snappy Dance Theater and I loved it. It looked just like what I wanted to do. It was acrobatic. It was athletic. It was funny. It was theatrical. It was dancing. It was everything.

So, I auditioned and got into this company and stayed with them for eight years. We were a collaborative company. We toured the US and abroad, performing these sculptural, humorous, dance theater pieces. While I was doing all of the dancing, I, like most children of the '80s, grew up with the Muppets and decided I wanted to see if I could build one, so I got a book. I got The Foam Book by Drew Allison and made a puppet. His name was Egan and I took him to my classroom where I was teaching drama. He had these giant orange dreadlocks -- he looked a lot like me. And he mesmerized my students. I had never seen anything like it. They completely forgot I was there and were totally invested in him. And I went to the Boston Area Guild of Puppetry and showed everyone my puppet. Bonnie and Andrew Periale and all the other members of the guild just kind of took me in and encouraged me and introduced me to other artists my age. I started working with Dassia Posner and we made shadow puppet shows for adults. It was also the beginning of the puppet slams, so I just experimented and played with different styles and types of puppetry. Not using language, using music. How could I put everything I loved into one thing? And it just morphed from there. I continued to explore that. We used puppetry in my dance company.

JB: So, where'd you meet Dan?

BD: I met Dan, my husband, in 2000, around the time I got to Boston. He was running a theater company and I went to see his show and loved it. But I felt it needed better costumes, so I said, "Hey, can I make costumes for you?" so I started designing costumes. I designed costumes for at least 10 of his shows. His company, Rough & Tumble Theater, made original shows, often in gibberish. There wasn't a lot of language. My creative life tumbled out -- it all makes sense when I look back. Yes, so Dan and I worked together as director and costume designer. And I did perform in a few of his shows, but all of those things were happening all at once. And then we got married and the dance company was around for a few more years and then the dance company folded and I had a baby. And I made a show, with one of the dancers in the dance company, that we loved, and it was great and people were excited by the show, and so were we, but then I got pregnant with twins. My older son was a toddler at the time, which was working fine until we had twins. And then my dance partner went to medical school, which is an eight-year-long project. So, when all of this happened, it was really tough on all of us because this was our identity, this is what we did. I had to quit my job as a theater teacher because it was all just too much. I couldn't keep up with anything and I felt lost. Who am I, what am I? And I went to the Hatchery at Puppet Showplace where they just get together. Sometimes you talk about a show you're working on or you need help or you need advice. And Roxie Myhrum invited me in and I met everyone. I had kind of been away from the puppetry community for a few years. So I came and I met Brendan Burns, who now is a musician with the Gottabees. I was talking to Roxie and then with Liz Joyce and she was like, "Do you have a show for kids?" And I said, "No, I don't. I don't make shows for kids." And she's like, 'Well, you should. If you do, I'll book you." So, between that and Roxie kind of pushing me to make a show for their Incubator Program, I said yes. Dan helped me shape Squirrel Stole My Underpants and we got a Jim Henson Foundation grant. We kind of made the show on a whim and people loved it, and we realized it kind of fit everything we had done up to then.

JB: The first time I saw Squirrel Stole My Underpants, was it in 2014 at Puppet Homecoming at a campground called Ramapo for Children.

BD: And the gym was so hot. It was like a hundred degrees!

JB: I remember reading the blurb on it. I just thought to myself, I don't see how she could possibly sustain this for more than 15 minutes. And I kept thinking that throughout the show, how can this last? And it did. And it just kept getting better. And obviously that was the intent to some extent really, but was squirrel conceived as a full-length show or did it start a something smaller and grow?

BD: It was conceived as a full-length show. I tested things out at slams, but it was not a slam piece. I think with my husband's background in making nonverbal theater shows and my background and making nonverbal dance shows, between what I do visually and with my body, and what my husband does with the narrative, we knew it could work. It was not an easy process because you answer the entire show in the title, which is great. But like you said, how do you sustain that? How do you keep turning left? How do you keep surprising your audience?

JB: Well, I came away from the experience being able to answer that question. And the answer is brilliantly. I was very taken by both of your shows that I've seen. Let's talk a little about you as a physical comedian. Are you influenced by any of the great physical comedians like Carol Burnett or Lucille Ball? It's usually men doing that stuff, but when you do it, it is unmistakably feminine. It is not male slapstick. It is something that's yours. How did this come about? What were you influenced by?

BD: Well, I think subconsciously I am influenced definitely by both of those women, by Lucille Ball and Carol Burnett. The Carol Burnett Show -- that was one of my favorite shows. I just turned it on and I felt like I was there, you know. So, I think without realizing that, I think that they're an influence because it's just part of my childhood memories. I'd say I don't think about it a lot in terms of direct influence though. I think silent movies definitely have an influence on us. My husband is a huge Buster Keaton fan and we always return to his work.

JB: You were an Emerging Artist at the O'Neill puppetry conference in 2017.

BD: I've been to the O'Neill three times and it's been just amazing every time I've been. Doing the Emerging Artist felt like the right thing. Making Squirrel was so fun. I mean, it was really hard, but I didn't have any expectations of myself. I was making a show that might be seen by a few hundred people, you know, whatever. I was redefining myself. It was like it came from a different place. I also had at the time children who napped during the day and went to bed really early and so I would work when they went to sleep and at night my husband and I would rehearse in our living room while they were sleeping. It was great. When we made our second show, Lollipops for Breakfast, we tried to do that, but our kids did not nap as much. They went to bed later. We had to rearrange how we worked. So, we were trying to find like once a week, at night, at Puppet Showplace where we could go and be away from our family. And that worked okay. It was a really tough process. At each stage of our family's development, how we work has changed. With Go Home Tiny Monster, our kids didn't go to bed till eight-thirty or nine and we're exhausted. My husband works a full-time job and I'm trying to make work while the kids are at school and the late-night rehearsals were not working. And so, for Go Home Tiny Monster, I knew I wanted us to have uninterrupted time, like true, uninterrupted time and so the O'Neill made perfect sense for us. We actually just had the germ of the idea and went with two objects, we had nothing. And it was so amazing to have a space to experiment. We had some of the resident company with us. We had Austin Costello and Kaitee Tredway with us and they would step in and we would rotate through improvisations. We were just experimenting and trying to understand our theme. For this newest show, we knew we wanted the audience to be a big part of the experience. And so being at the O'Neil with their "risk, fail, risk again" motto, I was like, we have to push ourselves to use the audience in a different way. And so, we really experimented with that and I think found the heart of our show with that. And over the course of the rest of the development of the show, we actually did three other residencies. That was a real gift so that we could sustain focus and unplug from everything else.

JB: So, you had been building and rehearsing shows out of your home, in limited space. You now have a separate space to work in.

BD: We just moved in the fall and I have a space where we can rehearse, it's just totally amazing.

JB: Let's talk about being an Associate Artist at the Atlantic Center for the Arts in 2005.

BD: I worked with Paul Zaloom for three weeks. I have always been a person who does three jobs at once. I'd be dancing in a dance company the morning, teaching in an elementary school in the afternoon, working on puppets in the evening and designing costumes on the weekend. I was always doing so many things at once, I could switch very easily. The Atlantic Center for the Arts was the first time I think in my whole life it felt like my only job for three weeks was to make stuff. Like that was it! And it was a gift and it was also terrifying to really just have to focus on this. So, I felt like in the end, I made a bunch of different stuff. I wanted to experiment and learn from everyone there. I met so many amazing people there. It was great.

JB: You were a Resident Artist at Perishable Theatre or 2007 to 2009.

BD: That was actually the home of one of the first puppet slams, Blood From A Turnip. Vanessa Gilbert ran that space for many years, and she had a resident artist program. Tim and I, my dance partner, we used that residency program to get our show, Poste Restante, made. Once a month, we would go down and meet together as a group. Everyone was working on totally different things, and we would experiment. We'd talk about the process. They were basically supporting us in developing this show. They also gave us rehearsal space. We would drive down to Providence and use their rehearsal studios and use the car time to talk and develop the work. We performed there while we were developing the work. So, it was just this really supportive space with these really interesting playwrights and storytellers and visual artists, coming together to help each other support that.

JB: When you really devote yourself to an artistic career, even though it might not be the only career you enjoy, it's consuming and usually you have to concentrate on just one or maybe two aspects of all the different things that inspire. You seem to have pretty seamlessly combined all of your performing interests. You've got a lot of artistic background in a lot of different things.

BD: Well, performing for families, that's just been in the last six years and I think the shift made sense to my life in terms of--- there's a market, I get to perform, because that's what I love, and I have a captive audience! I think it was the synthesis of everything I've ever done that made sense. The shows and the business of performing these shows is what has been consuming in a way that I don't know how to balance. Balance is the wrong word, because it'll never be balanced. But how to capture it…where I want it to be.

JB: And when you're saying business, you're talking about the meetings, the promotion, the licensing, all the stuff that has nothing to do with the actual writing, building and performing the show. You're talking about all the other support things, correct?

BD: Correct.

JB: You're are still doing all that yourself?

BD: I do that all myself. I try to keep the cost as low as possible, so that I can pay my designers and other artists and pay myself. And I do see it as a business. That, I think, is kind of exciting, because a lot of times you make shows for adults and you don't make a lot of money, but it feeds your passion. Or the money's there and it's a lot of pressure, so performing for families made sense, on a scale I could hold on to. I think it goes well when I'm not making a show, but making Tiny Monster and then booking two other shows, and coordinating, and scheduling and marketing, and all those things on top of also trying to carve out the time to make a new show has really defined what I make. I know that after we made Lollipops for Breakfast, we kind of wanted a pallet cleanse, so I just made two pieces for adults, these like slam pieces, and I spent way, way long time on these things because I wanted just to make something for myself that didn't have the same criteria as our work does for families. Because that's where it feels like performing in the way that we do for families, definitely steers how our process works, what our content is, what drives us. And so, I still want and still have this desire to make work for adult audiences.

JB: Adult audiences are difficult things. One of the things that I hear talked about a lot is improving the quality of puppetry. And one of the things that I've noticed is that this is only important really to an adult audience and adult critics. You could have an absolute terrible puppet show, on all fronts, that an audience of children goes nuts over and you're left sitting and thinking, "Why did they enjoy that?" Adults are more difficult to please because they bring their own filters, they bring their own neurosis when judging a work, so I think a show for adults is a different thing altogether than building a show for children. Children tend to accept things more openly, I think.

BD: I think you can take more risks, well, you take different risks for family audiences. I want everyone in our audience to feel confident that they know what's going , so the puppet has to make sense to the story or image on stage. They may have a different picture in their mind of exactly what's going on, but they're comfortable in the audience. If they don't get what's happening, I try to answer that question within a few beats within the piece. That said, I made one piece for adults that's very abstract, a piece that I was totally 100% okay if only 30% of this audience gets this or is connected to it and the rest are like, whatever, it's not for me.

JB: Were you successful?

BD: I was! I think I got more than 30%, but there was this sense in my mind that I gave myself permission not to go after every seat in the house. With my shows for families, I do go for as many seats as I have. Our shows aren't just entertainment for children. What are we wanting for the audience as an experience? And I think that's something as a performer and creator I very much want to understand and think through. And you know, when you perform for family audiences, half your audience is made of adults, because they bring the kids. And so, you're playing to both minds' eyes and that's the biggest challenge -- that's also the most exciting thing. We expect a lot from our audiences. This morning, I performed Squirrel at an elementary school, and I had 130 kindergartners to second graders and it was a reminder that a lot of these kids had never seen a show like Squirrel Stole My Underpants. What I love about it is that they're processing what they're seeing verbally without realizing it. They are working out the story in their head and you could hear little sprinkles of chatter of like, "Oh, this is what's happening!" And it makes me so delighted that they're engaged and they're figuring it out. Like they're trusting themselves to understand what's going on. It's just this reminder of why we make theater. Why we make shows for families, why we make shows for kids in particular, is that you don't know where one of those kids is going to be in 20 years. And they're like, I saw this thing and it made me think about this or it started something. And there's something really magical about that that you can't quantify.

JB: As far as how your collaborative operates, are you the leader of The Gottabees or just a rank-and-file Gottabee?

BD: Yeah, I'm definitely the leader of The Gottabees. I have the most hair of all of us, so I'm definitely out in the middle of the stage, for sure.

JB: You definitely have a great creative team.

BD: I feel so lucky.

JB: Brendan, Tony, and Dan of course. I was looking at Marte's [Johanne Ekhougen – puppets for Hand to God] things earlier today when I discovered that she had made the puppets for Go Home Tiny Monster. And then I went to her website and found out I couldn't actually purchase any of her puppets.

BD: I think she sells sometimes in coffee shops. If you follow her on Instagram, [www.instagram.com/doctorsuperhelga] you'll find out where. I met her at the O'Neill while developing Tiny Monster (which had no name at the time). And in the pitch circle they do the first night, to talk about your participant pieces, she was crocheting and she dumped out this bag and she said, "Well, there are some monsters if anyone wants to play with these." And I had gone there without a puppet, any puppets at all, and I knew I wanted little creatures in my world. That's all I knew. I saw those monsters and I was like, "Those are my monsters." And I say, mine, like they belonged in this world we were exploring. Over the course of development of the show she would come up to Boston. And we did a lot of talking and designing and drawing and sketching. And then she would come to rehearsal and make puppets -- she improvises them without a pattern. Then I would retrofit them so that they would move in a way that I liked, for the function for what we needed. It was a fun collaboration because I've never worked with a builder to make the puppets.

JB: You've always built them before yourself?

BD: Yeah and building is not my strength. I like it and I figure it out. I ask a lot of questions, but that's not necessarily "the thing" that I do best.

JB: Bringing in other builders just gives you this wonderful look outside yourself and even if you've done a sketch or something, a builder brings something new to it that you likely wouldn't have thought of yourself.

BD: It's totally great. It's been the same with having Brendan and Tony. I used to always just find music and use it. And then we've been working together so long now, we kind of mind-meld. I can do what I do on stage, because of them. And I think the audience is like, "Such a simple show!" and it's like, no, actually the complexity of what is happening with the music and visual and narrative is really rich and complex.

JB: It's concise. What I heard was concise but not simple. Being a musician myself, a concise score, musically speaking, is very important. It's very easy to overblow something.

BD: Yes, it makes such a difference for us right now. We're still working on Go Home Tiny Monster. We always keep working on our shows and for this show, I will only perform it with live music. That is going to be amazing, but also poses challenges for scheduling and budgeting and all of that. But we felt like it was totally worth it to really have a bigger experience with our audience. It's wonderful that we're at a place where we are getting booked to perform together because people are understanding and we're understanding that it's all of us together. That's what The Gottabees' magic is.

JB: You've been performing your new show, Go Home Tiny Monster, a great deal lately. How has that been going?

BD: It's going really well. It's interesting because we premiered it and then we've been performing it and between the performances, we're still continuing to work on it. We dive deeper, because once we get to know a show, it changes and grows.

JB: What kinds of changes?

BD: So Tiny Monster is a very different show from Squirrel and Lollipops, because of the emotional depth that we go to. It is a show about the main character losing her home and we see that happen on stage. So, the balance of understanding sadness and fear, balanced with humor and community, that felt really challenging. And part of what we've been working on is the musical tone, because the music guides our show so dramatically and when it comes to showing these big emotional shifts, we need that music to guide the audience. Not hit them over the head with an emotion, but let the emotion be there or spice it up or guide us a little bit away from it. I feel like that has been our biggest challenge, our biggest try-and-try-again, in terms of the changes in the way the show works.

JB: This all must resonate deeply with you since you and your family recently went through this yourselves. What happened?

BD: In the winter of 2015, Boston got, I believe, 109 inches of snow in three weeks and in that time our house developed ice dams on our roof and the water poured into our walls and our entire house was sick, from the outside in. When we went to get repairs done, thinking they were going to put some holes in our interior walls and dry the walls out, we packed up our stuff thinking we would be gone for a couple of weeks. We came back after demo was done and all of our interior walls were torn out because there was so much water inside of our condominium (we were in a three family house). We were out of our house for six months and in that time we stayed everywhere.

We were out of our house for six months and in that time we stayed everywhere. With friends and on tour and we rented a house and we borrowed a house and we were in a hotel and all the while fighting with our insurance company while keeping our cool for our kids who were four and six. Brendan and Tony also have their own experiences with displacement --- right before I met them, they were roommates in a three-family house with two other musicians and they had a house fire and their entire apartment was damaged. They left with maybe their clothing off their back and very few possessions. The firemen went back and were able to save their instruments, not all of them, but most of them. These experiences deeply informed this show.

JB: I imagine that it's difficult to write a story that was so deeply felt. But you know what this experience is like.

BD: It was a difficult experience and there's a scene that we call "The Hotel," and no one else knows it's a hotel, but for my husband, who directed the show, and I, that's the hotel we stayed in with our kids and we can go back to that experience as we work on the scene to make sure the heart of the scene feels right. That's what we're going for. It's been amazing that we can turn this experience around.

JB: I know you went to India this summer. Let's talk about that.

BD: We did three cities in eight days and we had six performances. We did Squirrel there and it was a really amazing experience to share our work. It always is, but with this one we felt we really came across big ideas and thoughts and conversations about life and the world. It was just an amazing experience, especially having the community of puppeteers and theater being in the audiences around us. It was a festival called the AHA! International Theatre Festival for Children. There were eight other puppet companies there. There were people from the UK and from Switzerland and Peru and Germany and India.

JB: What's coming up?

BD: In January we start touring again. We're touring Go Home Tiny Monster. We're at the Strong National Museum of Play for their Day of Compassion. And we'll be at Sandglass (Theater in Brattleboro,

VT), Cabot Theater in Beverly, MA, The Eric Carle Museum in Amherst. We have a lot of performances coming up.

JB: You came to the puppetry community as a dancer and actor, and not as a puppeteer. I too, came from the outside. I've always loved the art, but my professional life didn't include puppetry. Becoming part of this community has been one of the most enriching things I've had the pleasure of doing.

BD: I would say that the puppetry community is been the most supportive, open, welcoming art community I've ever been a part of. I have this amazing network of amazing people who are all over the country, now all over the world. Everywhere I go, I meet all these puppeteers, which makes the world feel smaller, and we all immediately bond because of puppetry. And that's a rare, amazing thing. It can't be taken for granted.

JB: I have also enjoyed the same experience. I don't tend to find very much ignorance in the puppetry community.

BD: I love that about the community. I love the National Festivals. I love seeing these generations of artists. When you step back and you look at it, every decade, we're all there to visit and party and celebrate and it's just really great. The puppetry community has embraced me and I am so grateful -- I love that I get to bring everything to life on stage in my shows -- that I make the world bigger than it seems.

BONNIE ERICKSON

JB: You did not start out in puppetry at all. What led you to that part of your career? Was it costuming or was there something before that?

Bonnie Erickson: It was theater. When I was in college, even in high school, I had done theater and also taken art courses. When I was in high school, probably my junior year, I started getting the Village Voice just so I could see what was going on in New York. I finally got a job upstate at a camp as the drama coach. Leslie Gore was my Gigi and crooned her way through the whole musical. Who knew she would soon find fame with "It's My Party and I'll Cry If I Want To." We followed that up with West Side Story. It was one of those camps that lasts the whole summer. When it ended I kept postponing going back to Minnesota. I enrolled at the Arts Students League [of New York] and met a lot of people who were involved in the art world. I also started doing accessories for a small dress store. A costume designer, Patricia Quinn Stuart, saw my work there and hired me to help her. I had been sewing everything by hand because I didn't have a sewing machine, so I did a lot of hats, belts and things like that. The first day as I sat at the sewing machine she came by and said, "You know you're sewing backwards." And I said, "Oh yeah, I know, I always do" [laughter]. She laughed! And she kept me! I did finally learn how to maneuver that machine and I worked with her off and on doing any kind of costumes she needed. We did Cry of Players at Lincoln Center, we did an Off-Broadway musical called The Me Nobody Knows, that went to Broadway with Northern Calloway who became a cast member of Sesame Street. It was a real learning opportunity. I had been in theater at the university, but this was a really valuable work situation. I loved it. I loved New York. I did go to a few auditions. I found I didn't take direction well and realized backstage was much more interesting to me.

JB: But you did have some desire to be onstage…

BE: I did, but then I decided that acting was just not for me. I wasn't very good at it and it didn't satisfy me the way making things did.

JB: So, originally you hadn't intended to become a costumer, it was something that you were doing to make ends meet and to make connections.

BE: Well, I love clothes and I would have focused on being a fashion designer in a heartbeat. But it's one of those things where you never know which direction things are going to go. I was open to opportunities. so when Patricia Quinn Stuart asked me to work for her…well, I learned an enormous amount from her. The portfolio with work I had done for her as well as my own work, got me my first job with Jim Henson. Actually, it was Fran Brill who first told me that Jim was looking for a costumer. At first I didn't believe her. I knew Jim's work. At that time he was doing some really abstract stuff on the Ed Sullivan Show, the morning shows, the [late] night shows. "Sesame Street" wasn't even on air yet. They had just finished shooting it when I started at Muppets. I wasn't really sure what this job was going to be, but I knew I wanted to work with Jim Henson because I thought his mind was incredible and concepts he'd come up with really hilarious. I started with a freelance job doing the costumes for The Frog Prince…the beginning of working for Jim. When he asked me to stay on and run the shop, it was a little daunting and a bit intimidating because of the talented people working there before me … Caroly Wilcox…John Lovelady, Faz Fazakas. But it was Don Sahlin who really became my mentor. Funny, sweet, darling Don Sahlin. He taught me about puppetry and puppets because I had no idea! It wasn't part of my training. What especially appealed to me at Henson Associates was the fact that we did everything – we did sets, we did costumes, we did props, we worked with the writers, the performers. At the time there were probably only seven people on staff including the receptionist. Kermit Love and a number of other people came in and out. Faz would work on electronics project by project. As there were more projects, the staff got larger…and larger!

JB: And you started in 1970 with Jim?

BE: Yep.

JB: How many years did you spend in New York City doing costuming before you started with him?

BE: I did costuming for almost eight years. But when I came to New York in 1961, I started doing other freelance jobs…oh, I had a lot of wonderful temp jobs! I worked at 505 5th Avenue. It was an office where I would answer about twenty phones in the name of the company it was supposed to be. I would set up conferences in the little room where we would pretend it was the office of anybody who booked it. That was an education! I worked for Kohler Bathtubs, I worked for Modell's Shoppers World downstairs in the office. I thought I was Judy Holliday, because at lunchtime I got to give a break to the girl who actually answered the phones and I got to do the "Judy Holliday" switchboard. I had seen the movie [Bells Are Ringing]. I thought it was such a great thing to be able to do for an hour, and not have to do it the rest of your life [laughs]!

JB: Lots of jobs are like that! They're fun as long as you don't have to do it the rest of your life!

BE: Right! I lived in Greenwich Village until I couldn't afford that anymore and then I moved to the Lower East Side, where I stayed until I moved to Brooklyn.

JB: It must have been very interesting to be living in Greenwich Village at that time. There was so much going on then. Bob Dylan was there and Joan Baez.

BE: It was wonderful! Bob Dylan and I knew each other from Dinkytown in Minnesota and he was playing at the Gaslight [Café], just downstairs from where I lived. It was a very exciting time, there were a lot of interesting art and music scenes going on in the Village.

JB: Let's go back further. Tell me about your "growing up" period in Minnesota.

BE: I had a little bit of the best of "both worlds". I had a grandmother in North Dakota and a grandmother in Minnesota, both on farms. So I would spend the summers with them. I would take a train to get there. When I think about it, it was a really very special time. They taught me to embroider, to crochet and to knit. I would walk up town to get the mail for my Grandma Minnie and I'd stay maybe three weeks with her and three weeks with my other Grandma Hilda in Minnesota on a very different kind of farm. I did that until I was well into my teens and had my friends in the city. But those summers were really wonderful - and it was funny, being from St. Paul, to have people think of me as a "city" girl, because I hadn't really thought of myself as a "city" girl before.

JB: Let's talk more about the period before you were hired by Jim.

BE: I started college at a really active time for students. The '60s were amazing everywhere - the literature, politics, space, art - it was a very exciting time. A whole group of us at the University of Minnesota were protesting about civil rights and worrying about Cuba. We were all progressive and left-leaning. I think my parents thought everybody at the U of M was a communist. [laughs]. When you get to the 1970s, I was in Washington still protesting. But in the 60's I really had my sights set on getting to New York.

JB: How did you get to New York? Train?

BE: I drove out. There was another student from the university who was going to be the tennis coach at the same camp. We bought a 1951 Buick convertible. It was yellow and red, and we had painted "New York or Busted" on the back. It took us two and a half weeks to get to New York. Well, we stopped a lot. The car died on State Street in Chicago, so that delayed us a little bit. We just had an adventure. It was really fun. When we drove up at this camp, I'm sure they couldn't imagine who was coming in this car! The kids were really fascinated. I'm not so sure that the owners of the camp were as fascinated, but in the end we all got along very well and I enjoyed that summer. I came with this Minnesota trait, so that when the parents came on Parent's Day and offered to "tip" me, I didn't understand and I said, "Oh no, it's my pleasure to take care of your child." When they all went home and all the camp counselors got together and said, "So, how much did you get?" I said, "You kept that money?!" [laughs] I had no idea! But the summer was a good experience. I'm really glad I did it. It got me to New York. It was a road trip! That car, by the way, died the day the insurance ran out on our way back from camp. The rear end literally fell out of the car onto the road in New Hyde Park, New York. We sold it for $12 junk. A friend of mine from back home came and picked us up and brought us into New York City. He knew of a place to stay in the Village with six other people in a small apartment. The parents who leased the apartment had moved back to Minnesota and their kids were living out the lease. So all these "strays" ended up living in this building. One of my best friends, who now lives in Paris, was the first person I met when we were living in that apartment.

I got on the bus the day after I arrived in the city and saw Saks Fifth Avenue. I had worked from high school through college at a dress shop so I went in, interviewed, and they hired me. I loved that job. More interesting people. I would come home from there and work as an usher at the 5th Avenue Cinema where I got to see all these fabulous movies. Well, not all that many of them, because each one lasted forever at this art theater. If they had a movie, it wasn't there and gone in three days. It was there for a month. I saw Wrong Arm of the Law, I saw Macario, I saw Shoot the Piano Player…all became my favorites, well, not Macario! I posed for a portrait artist in my building when I finished there. I got fired from the theater because I fell asleep behind the retaining wall! And they caught me!

I worked for a bunch of commercial artists. Several were wonderful car illustrators. Another one did "family" kinds of things. So, I sort-of learned what it took to be an commercial artist while I was going to the Art Students League. I was taking commercial art there. So it was an education every day. The '70s, which are supposed to have been some of the worst days in New York, I felt were wonderful! I didn't have any money, neither did anybody else I knew! The people that I met and the fact that New York is constantly changing was something really interesting to me. I still like to go back to the old neighborhoods. My first apartment on the Lower East Side cost $25 a month.

JB: Was it a fifth floor, cold water, walk-up?

BE: No, it was second floor, had hot water, but it had no heat. So I had a pot-bellied stove. It was a tenement and you used to have to go out the door, down the stairs, and around the hallway to go to the bathroom, but somebody who lived there didn't like that, so they cut a hole in the living room floor, and there was a trap door! I mean, where do you ever get that? I would have never found these places anywhere else!

JB: These places kind of don't exist anymore.

BE: No! Now they're in the Tenement Museum! That's the problem with New York. It's lovely when places get gentrified, but they put a lot of people out of homes when that happens. New York has some pretty strong housing laws, but when you got an apartment for $25 a month you could pretty much do whatever you want, because everything was an improvement!

JB: Let's talk a little bit about the weeks leading up to your first interview with Jim. You said Fran Brill told you about the opening. What was going on before she told you about it?

BE: My friend, designer Bob de Mora was headed to California to work on a film and he asked me to go with him. But I had a son, Christopher, who was only two and I didn't really want to pick him up and relocate. I was trying to figure out how to deal with that when I got the second call saying they really do want somebody to make costumes for this special, so that's when I called Jim. I made the appointment and then came down with a terrible cold. I was so tempted not to go. First of all I didn't feel great, and second, I thought I'd be sure to give it to him. But I didn't want to miss the opportunity and was afraid I might blow the chance if I didn't go. So I went. (I hope I didn't give him the cold.) I talked to him and Diana Birkenfield, who was the producer at the time and showed my portfolio. I was building these muslin, life-size, female figures and clothing them in antique clothes that were part of a collection I had. I showed the work I'd done with Pat Stuart. One of the things we had just finished doing was this production for the Manhattan School of Music. It was the opera Dido and Aeneas and we had done it all pretty much in plastic. I think Jim may have been impressed that we had used "new" materials, since Jim was very much involved in anything that was a "new" and in the exploration of "new" things. He said, "Hmmm, this has been interesting. Call Diana tomorrow and we'll let you know." I called from a phone booth and she said, "Yes, we'd like to hire you to do the special." My quandary was solved, I didn't have to worry about leaving for California. Later on I wondered, so what would have happened if I had gone to California? I'd probably live in LA. I'd probably be in the film industry. I don't like LA. I'm very happy things worked out the way they did! Worked out very nicely.

JB: I think we're all very happy things worked out the way they did.

BE: Well, I am! I couldn't have worked for a better person than Jim. He was really incredibly confident and inventive and the people he had around him were such fun. Jerry Juhl, Jim's head writer, for instance. We met at the workshop when I first started, because he was working on Frog Prince. And he said, "So, where are you from?" I said "Minnesota," he said, "Oh, me too!" And I said, "Well, where in Minnesota?" "Oh, St. Paul." "Well, me too!" "Where in St. Paul?" "Well, Falcon Heights." "Me too!" Well, it turned out that my parents knew his parents. My father bought the big old house that I loved, from the superintendent of his father's nursery there in St. Paul. And my mother knew his mother. He was a couple years older, so we probably didn't meet because at that time, two years made a big difference. But we all went to the same drugstore after school. It was really weird to have this connection! Wayde and I spent a fair amount of time with him just months before he died.

In fact, Jerry and I were working on a book …I always wanted to call it Hired Hands…about all the people who worked behind the scenes with Jim, the people putting it all together. Jerry and I had talked about it a lot. We made lists. The time has passed, but it was an exciting idea. There were so many wonderful people. Caroly and I are still friends. John Lovelady, I just talked to him. I miss Donald (Sahlin) every day.

JB: And I guess Dave Goelz is on his way here, now. [He had just called and we'd overheard one side of a conversation her husband Wayde had just had with him]

BE: Yes, right! Recently we were neighbors in New Zealand. I should explain. Nicola Marshall produced The Jim Henson Retrospectacle, an almost a month-long celebration of Jim Henson in Wellington. Wayde calls it Muppet Woodstock. There must have been about twenty of us, from Sesame Street, from Henson, from Disney, from Puppet Heap - all together in the same hotel. It was just extraordinary. Dave and I have been good friends since he first came to work at (the) Muppets. And here we were…next door neighbors! I was always a little upset with Jim for taking him away from the shop and making him a puppeteer. He was a puppeteer to start with, but he was a fantastic (puppet) designer/builder. He built Zoot from my sketch. He's a multi-talented human being.

JB: Most of you trained the next generation of puppet builders at the Muppets. People who came and they already had skills, but it was Faz and Don and Dave and you who trained the next generation, right?

BE: Yes, and Caroly. Faz did all the mechanics and remote-control. It became such an important part of Jim's work. And Caroly trained I don't know how many people when she was overseeing Sesame Street. So many people who went through the workshop learned their skills from her. Now, Rollie Krewson, who was the first intern in a program that I'd started at Henson Associates, is training even more. But everybody who worked there brought their own skills and came from different disciplines. All the people who loved craftsmanship, who were problem solvers, who were process oriented, got great satisfaction from the work. It was a engaged shop but at first our safety habits could be pretty relaxed. At first we had no idea of the toxicity of some of these materials…

JB: Barge Cement!

BE: …until I got a book about health hazards for artists. Barge IS the best contact cement. We thought that must be the reason we all were so happy all the time! We were using hot wires to carve foam, you know how toxic that can be. So, at a certain point, when I realized the dangers, first, the windows got opened, but then we got real exhaust systems in the shop. Initially we were just doing whatever was needed to get things done. Now people are much more aware of it, which is a good thing. I wonder what problems there are with 3D printing. I keep thinking, oh my, if we just had 3D printing back in those days! I saw an extraordinary exhibit of 3D printed furniture.

There was no way to do this work any other way. I know Jim would have been the first to buy a printer for us to use.

JB: Let's talk about how Harrison/Erickson, the company you founded with your husband Wayde, evolved. How did that start? How did that get going?

BE: I did some costumes in 1970 for Twyla Tharp [choreographer]. Kermit Love designed them and I built them. I was freelance, and I wanted to stay freelance. But after I had done Frog Prince, Jim called me up to his office and said, "I'd really like you to run the shop." And I said, "I really like being freelance. I like taking different jobs because I love being in the theater, too." And he said, "Just try it." Well, I did. It was a great fit for me. But several years later, I was divorced and had left the Lower East Side and moved to Brooklyn with my son. I met Wayde through a friend in the neighborhood and when I'd take my son to nursery school, I'd go past his building. We fell in love walking Christopher to nursery school and riding the same subway to work every day. Lucky me! Wayde was a biologist doing cancer research and ready for a change. It was perfect timing for both of us. As much as I loved working for Jim, by that time The Muppet Show was a big hit and I knew it was going to be done in London for four more years. Christopher and Wayde lived there for part of the first year. I had been living there longer. But I really wanted Christopher to go to school back in the U.S.

JB: When was this?

BE: It was late '76. And when we came back, Wayde resigned from his job and I told Jim I was leaving. I cried, but he said, "Don't worry, we're not going to lose touch." Well, Jim became one of our first clients. We worked out of here [their apartment] to begin with and took any job we could get. Then we found this fabulous space on 17th Street and 5th Avenue in Manhattan. We had 24 windows. It was 110 feet long and anywhere from 11 feet wide to 21 feet wide. We got hold of Hardy Holtzman Pfieffer, a very hot, new architectural firm. They had just finished redesigning the Brooklyn Children's Museum and they were around the corner. We had very little money but we saw this article in the New York Times about the museum and said, “What have we got to lose?” So, we went over there and asked them to look at the space. I think they liked it because it was so weird. They built this most wonderful studio for us. There were little ‘buildings’ all along one side, one of them was a kitchen, one of them was a dye facility, and we had a dressing room and shower for performers coming in for rehearsals or fittings. We had a conference room in the front with a garage door that was clear glass. We had a traffic light at the elevator. It was everything we ever wanted. And Jim, as I said, became one of our first clients. I oversaw the build for Fraggle Rock. I spent a year overseeing new projects and scouting new talent. For thirteen years I did creative direction for Henson and the domestic product group at Sesame Workshop as well as product concepts for licensees. Those sketches and all that work has been donated to The Strong Museum of Play up in Rochester, NY. Like Jim, we had people in and out as we did projects. We found a lot of interesting people. Ronnie Burkett was one of the first people we hired, dear Ronnie, brilliant then, brilliant now. We were lucky to have so many talented people around.

We started out doing toys, puppets, and commercials here and in Europe…Burger King…Budweiser. We did the first talking Happy Meal! Fran Brill and Erin Ozker, a puppeteer for The Muppet Show, and I went out to California to do one of those commercials. I did puppeteer for our commercials. We were under a mound, green with flowers and on top, our talking happy meal puppets and Ronald McDonald. All of a sudden, it's very quiet and Fran peeked her head out. They'd forgotten us under the mound and gone to lunch. It's such a puppeteer story. When the Phillies [baseball team] came to Jim to ask if he would create a mascot for them Jim said, "No, but Bonnie Erickson is the person you need to talk to." (Thank you, Jim.) They came to us. So I was thinking, we'll do a character, give it a back story, and we'll do merchandising if they want it. We'll set it all up so that they're ready to go. They liked my design. We offered to sell it to them for a very reasonable price, copyright and all. But they said, no. They thought it would be just a one year thing. Well, the Phillie Phanatic is now 40 years old. At first we leased it to them for personal appearances around town and on the field and we did the merchan dising and paid them a royalty for the use of the logo. We gave the team the back story, a mascot manual, and information on setting up personal appearances. The first year of merchandising, we did $2,000,000 worth of retail sales. We were amazed. We designed all the merchandise. Soon, the Montreal Expos came to us and asked for a mascot. We did Youppi! the next year. This time, we didn't offer to sell it to them. We just leased it to them. We did the licensing and did the same thing - another $2,000,000 in retail sales. In the end we sold both to the teams.

In all we've done sixteen mascots. There are still six of them that we created that are running around. We became known for mascot design, which we did not expect. We even had our own mascot for more than seven years. “Sport” traveled around doing personal appearances and an act at these minor league clubs across the country. So, we have this whole history in sports, something I knew very little about. Wayde would say, "Don't talk about sports when we're there. Just leave that part to me." It became a very reliable business for us.

JB: So when you design one of these characters, how much of it is your design? Do the representative of the teams ever come to you to specify specific things, outside of the Jersey?

BE: No, but we would ask about the fans and make a presentation of our ideas. The Phillies wanted a super fan – a Phanatic. That’s how he got his megaphone snout. We’ve only worked with national sports teams. We knew colleges probably couldn't afford an experienced performer. A performer would be in costume for a while and then graduate. We wrote bits and sketches for these characters to do. We did costumes for the costume! The merchandising potential was a big part of it. We got to the point where we didn't even lease any longer. We just made the copyright part of the sales to the team along with the costume.

JB: So, this is still ongoing. Do you still maintain a shop?

BE: No, we don't. We haven't done any new ones for a long time.

JB: Are you still responsible for the maintenance of the characters?

BE: Well, we’ve maintained the Phanatic and Slyly, our mascot for

The Carp baseball team in Hiroshima, Japan for many years. Others use other people. But we have people who've worked for us for a long time. They have their own studios now. While I do most of the sourcing of the materials and any sketches, the people we work with are very experienced craftsmen.

JB: Talk about your work for toy companies a little.

BE: Well, we did a number of toys for others. We did the original toy patterns for Maurice Sendak's Wild Things. But we did two of our own lines of toys. One of the lines was for Applause called Central Casting. It had animals from all your favorite fairy tales. The other line we did with Nolan Bushnell whose first animatronic toy was Teddy Ruxpin. For his company we did a group called Party Animals. They were puppets with a solar chip that made the sound of the animal when you opened their mouths. We did a gorilla, a frog, a turkey, a goose, a dolphin, and I forget what the last one was. Oh, mosquito! How can I forget the mosquito? Because Nolan said, "Oh, nobody's going to buy a mosquito." I said, "They're going to sell out." And they were the fastest sellers because they were so annoying. Everybody wanted them for gifts. I still get letters from people who had them in the '80s. When Wayde and I started donating our toys to the Strong Museum, one of the women at a meeting brought a dolphin that she'd had since she was a child, and her brother still had the mosquito. I thought, this is crazy. It makes me feel really good that somebody cared enough to hang on to these animals!

JB: Let's talk about your work for The Jim Henson Legacy a little bit.

BE: Of course. By 1992, there were so many awards coming in to Jim posthumously, there was no way the company had the time to deal with them all. So Jane Henson set up The Jim Henson Legacy with colleagues Arthur Novell, Al Gottesman, and Dick Wedemeyer. Arthur became executive director and initiated projects to fulfill The Legacy's mission. He was responsible for getting the stamp done, the US Muppet stamp, that was all Arthur. There was a Legacy exhibit called Designs and Doodles. The exhibit became a book. There was a Jim Henson concert in Carnegie Hall. There was Jim Henson's

Fantastic World touring exhibit that traveled for six years and reached almost a million people. And there was The Legacy's oversight of the Henson family 's permanent donations to the various museums. More recently in April, after trying for almost ten years to reach out to Jim's audience in New Zealand, The Jim Henson Retrospectacle took place there. People were so touched by Jim and his work that they wept hearing stories about him. The support of the founders and all who have served on the board of The Legacy have made these things possible. As you can see, The Legacy has been lucky that Jim started keeping things early on. Bob Payne was one of the first puppeteers with Jim in Washington, D.C. and when he came to New York, he began saving things in a more organized way. I remember getting a call from Al Gottesman asking if I would return the sketch I made of the two old men. Since they were my sketches, I had kept them. I was happy to return them. So, the company was always thinking about keeping things for the archives. And of course, the shop, when they were finished with something, would put it in a box if it wasn't going to be used for a while. It would go to a warehouse storage, until it was needed. So, there was always an archive of precious stuff that had been used and maybe not going to be used again. All of that was part of the storage The Legacy took on. Around 2001, the Jim Henson Company gave The Legacy responsibility of overseeing the warehouse collection and really reviewing it. Rhoda [Cosme], our collections manager, and I went to the warehouse and looked at just about everything. Karen [Falk] had looked at a lot of storage as well. Rhoda and I put together the database that eventually encompassed everything that was in the archives and in the warehouses in New Jersey and London. We went to London and looked at everything there. I believe it was around that time Jane and the Henson family became interested in making donations of some of these objects.

JB: Who was involved in deciding where all the physical items would go?

BE: I was really responsible for recommending where a lot of it would go. Jane, Karen, and several other people would look at the lists Rhoda and I would prepare. But it was often obvious where things should go. That became The Legacy's responsibility for all the years until most everything was distributed. Karen did the works on paper that were stored at the company. I did the three-dimensional things from the warehouses - puppets, props, sets. Every box a surprise! The database was huge. It took us probably two years to get it all together. We had to include categories like color, female or male, puppet, costume, dates, loans, projects. And by the time we finished it, there were over 6,000 items in that database. Plus, where does it go? Where has it been? Is it out on loan? Because we did loans, we had to know when something was out, where it was and when it was due back. It was set up to kick in and give us a notice when we needed to get something back. It was a pretty big job. Rhoda was indispensable.

JB: This must have been a giant task. Were you doing anything else during this period? Other creative work?

BE: Well, until 2000, Harrison/Erickson was under contract to Sesame Workshop. For over a year I traveled to Hong Kong each month to work with a Sesame Street product staff there. I continued doing concepts and product designs for Harrison/Erickson clients and we continued to do the maintenance for our mascots. And then, once the museums began installing the Jim Henson exhibits, I became a stylist or sort of Essence Checker, a role inherited from Don Sahlin. I've also helped with traveling exhibits. But much of my time now is spent organizing donations of our own work to museums. Toys to the Strong and puppets to The Center for Puppetry Arts.

JB: Karen told me the physical objects have all been sent out. Almost all the puppets and props, that there's almost nothing about left. The only thing that hasn't been given away is the historical paperwork.

BE: Pretty much. Works on paper are still there and they go out on loan, but works on paper are much more delicate than anything else, which is sort of interesting, since a lot of materials we used for puppets just turned to dust. But props, costumes, everything either went to The Smithsonian, The Center for Puppetry Arts, the Museum of the Moving Image and The Academy in Los Angeles. There's a

Fozzie Bear in England, but the bulk of the exhibitable things are really (at) The Center for Puppetry Arts and MoMI. The Smithsonian has probably 30 puppets there. Jim gave them, I think, a Bert and maybe an Oscar, but the family gave them the original Sam and Friends from Jim and Jane's early days in D.C. And I have to say, I'm so very proud of both MoMI and The Center for Puppetry Arts. They've both done beautiful shows. They both continue to do exhibits using alternate puppets because they have more than one exhibit's worth of puppets, and now MoMI is doing traveling shows. So, Jim's work continues to draw big crowds.

JB: Karen told me this wonderful story. I asked her the question, what was the most amazing thing you found when you were digging all this stuff up? And she told me that she got to take the original Kermit home with her for a night. Do you have a story like that? What was a truly wonderful moment that happened to you?

BE: It's a small thing, but it was so Jim and it's something I never forgot, and it sort of set the tone for my whole life working with Henson and with Jim. I came in to do the costumes for Frog Prince and I always did a lot of shopping first. I lived on the lower east side, so I was always on Orchard Street and I knew all the people who sold fabrics there. I was very careful about prices. I found this great fabric for Jerry Juhl's favorite character [Taminella Grinderfall]. Anyway, I was doing her costume for the Frog Prince and it was this wonderful fabric. It was sparkly, and it was perfect for her. I'd written down all the yardage and how much we'd need and what the prices were. At that point Jim was involved in everything, so I went up to his office and I said, "Here's what I've got, this is what I'd like to do, here's the sketch." He looked at it and said, "Hmmm, that's fine, that sounds good." When I went to buy the fabric it turned out to be twice as expensive as I had told him and I was petrified. So I had to go tell him and I said, "Jim, the fabric is twice as expensive as what I thought it was." And he said, "If you think it's right, you get it." And I know it's a little thing, but if that was your judgment, he was behind you, he had your back. And so, I bought that fabric. I want to tell you that we unpacked that dress in Atlanta after more than forty years in storage and put it on Taminella, it looked like it had been made yesterday. He held himself and us all to a high standard. Quality and details mattered.

JB: You're pretty much retired now, at least as retired as someone like you can be. I'm sure you can't stand still. What's on your horizon?

BE: We have plenty to do. As I said, we're archiving our own stuff now. That's why I have Rhoda here, because we've saved everything too! I learned a lot from Jim. Wayde and I both feel we owe him a lot. I've always been a keeper. We have collections, so now it feels like the time to be sharing things. From time to time I appear on a panel. During Women's Month, Fran Brill, Sonia Manzano and I were on a panel moderated by Karen Falk at The Center for Puppetry Arts. We all had such a good time. We learned things about each other we didn't know, and we've known each other for years. So it was… it was great fun. That's what I mean about the people that you meet on the street…

JB: …the people that you meet each day. Thank you for such a wonderful talk. Let's finish with one last fun story. Just a fun memory.

BE: It has to be the mice! We had mice at Muppets. Wayde would free them from cancer research. And Donald loved making houses for them out of different materials to see how fast they could eat them. Well, I decided that a line from Fraggle Rock came from Don's experiments. And when somebody, I think it's Mokie, is worried that the Fraggles were eating all the Doozer's constructions, the Doozer says to Mokie, "We feel architecture is to be enjoyed."

I think that's what Don thought about all the houses he built for the mice. making houses for them out of different materials to see how fast they could eat them. Well, I decided that a line from Fraggle Rock came from Don's experiments. And when somebody, I think it's Mokie, is worried that the Fraggles were eating all the Doozer's constructions, the Doozer says to Mokie, "We feel architecture is to be enjoyed."

I think that's what Don thought about all the houses he built for the mice. So, when we had our studio on Fifth Avenue, we continued the practice. We had parties…even a wedding for the mice when we realized that one was pregnant. Cause for celebration! We had a great group of people partrying with us through our lives. We're still in touch with many of them. It was just wonderful because of the people that you meet along the way. They have made our lives very, very rich. Yes. Yes. Been a good, good, good run.

OLGA FELGEMACHER and CRAIG MARIN

JB: I'm with partners Olga Felgemacher and Craig Marin and we're going to talk to them about their life and career. We're also going to talk about the new live show they're doing, which is Hans Christian Andersen...

Olga Felgemacher & Craig Marin: "Tales Real and Imagined."

JB: Let's go back as far as we can go. You were born in Queens.

CM: Just over the 59th street bridge.

JB: How did this all get started for you? How were you attracted to puppetry? You're also a musician.

CM: Well, my father was a cartoonist in vaudeville and my mother was in his act. They were billed as "Paul Marin The Chatterbox Cartoonist and his Blonde Georgia Model." Then after the war, rather than keep touring with USO's and things like that, they settled into Fort Tilden, New Jersey, while housing projects were being built in Queens for returning veterans. My sister Marcia was born in Fort Tilden, then they moved to Queens and I was born. My earliest memory is my Dad drawing bedtime stories for me, and then he would do the voices for the story. "So, the giant says BRARARA," like that, and he would do the voice. Now flash forward till I was three, sitting in my room watching my little black and white TV set. There were a bunch of kids there surrounding a sliding pond. Suddenly this man comes sliding down and he has a kid on his lap, and the kid started talking and everyone started laughing and I had no idea what was going on! What? "That's not real, but that's really real and everyone's laughing, and that man is doing it!" That man was Paul Winchell, with his wooden sidekick Jerry Mahoney. I remember saying to myself, "I want to make other children feel the way he makes me feel right now." And that was the beginning of the spark. So, as I was learning to talk, I was learning how to talk without moving my mouth. I would take socks and my father would draw the eyes, so I suddenly had a puppet. Then when I was about five years old, after two years of being a ventriloquist already, we went on vacation to Atlantic City and while waiting to go out to the Boardwalk and visit Mister Peanut, I was watching TV, Channel 5, and on came this little elf on top of a roof singing about the weather! Then there were more puppets. And that turned out to be Sandy Becker, who was one of the first great kid show hosts in the New York City area. And by great, I mean, not only a great puppeteer, but a great storyteller, with great puppets, and great voices, and a wonderful personality. So, I thought, oh, that's great! Greatness all around! There's a picture of me at about five or six years old at Christmas, surrounded by two Jerry Mahoneys, a Knucklehead Smiff and three Jingled Dingles. That's all that mattered really. I was just fascinated with that whole art form. Then about 1959 or so, WPIX Channel 11 started showing Laurel and Hardy films, but not just Laurel and Hardy films, Laurel and Hardy films introduced by Laurel and Hardy puppets. I discovered that those marvelously articulated hand puppets were by the incredible Paul "Rootie Kazootie" Ashley, with voices and animation by the phenomenally brilliant Chuck McCann (you might remember him as the "Hi Guy" in the Rite Guard mirror commercial). Everything came into focus for me right then: Laurel and Hardy/Chuck McCann/ puppets/comedy. Before long, Chuck had his own show, "The Chuck McCann Show" which broke through the Laurel and Hardy format and it became this wild vaudeville, set in a make-believe TV studio called The Little Little Theater, with this whole repertory company of puppets, and characters, cartoons, stuff, and Chuck McCann. Well, my life began to revolve around Chuck McCann and Let's Have Fun (which was the aptly named title of his 4 hour Sunday show). In fact on Sundays if I be out in the court yard playing with my friends, I'd have my father call me from the window of our 6 floor apartment at 12:50 when the show was going off, because at the end of the show Chuck would take the puppet off his hand and put it on a stick. No one made fun of me because that's who I was. That's what I did. And the most vital thing was that Chuck and I shared the same initials! So, I kept making puppets. And then when I was about 12 years old, I got up the courage to subway into Manhattan to WPIX Channel 11. I put my puppets on my hands and announced to the receptionist "I want to see Chuck McCann." She chuckled and said, "Well, he doesn't have an audience." And suddenly I heard a big voice from behind, "What have we here?" And I turned and there was Chuck and I said, "My puppets!" He said, "Oh. Come with me." And he put his arm around me, led me into the studio, and he said, "Sit here and I don't want you to do anything except laugh." And I said, "OKAY!" I sat there the whole time with the puppets on my hand. What a Wonderland!!! Everything was there – and in color! These beautiful puppets in vibrant col-or! Red back drops that looked gray on TV. Brown was actually bright gold lame! And Chuck McCann bigger than life! At the end of the show, he had a few minutes of live TV left, so Chuck called me up and put me on the air with my puppets. I went home a hero to the neighborhood kids and painted a big 11 on my bedroom door. I turned it into the TV studio. I started going down to WPIX as often as I could and they just kind of accepted me there. I observed and I observed. One day Chuck signaled me from behind the puppet stage and said, "Pull this string when I nod my head!" And with that, I sort of started an unofficial apprenticeship with him. I would bring out the puppets, hang them up before the show, that kind of thing. Very low profile. I really didn't make a big splash. I just wanted to observe what it meant to be in that type of work – a television puppeteer. A few years later Chuck moved over to WNEW Channel Five, and I sort'a, kind'a followed him there. That's when Paul Ashley introduced me to Sandy Becker and Soupy Sales. This was a whole crazy thing: the station would do one kid show, turn the camera around, and do another kid's show. Live, like that! And I just knew that that's how I wanted to spend my life.

JB: This was an exciting period. I got to meet Chuck at UCONN at the national festival a few years back. He was there because he was being honored there.

OF: We arranged that.

CM: We were the liaison between them and Chuck.

JB: You got the wonderful experience of knowing these legends. They were not real for us. They were invisible people who appeared on the TV.

OF: Yeah. Just to tell you what a special human being he was, I didn't grow up here, I didn't know Paul Ashley, or Chuck McCann, but when I came to New York, all the people I met, you know, before I even knew Craig, would talk about Chuck McCann, Chuck McCann. Then

I met Craig and knew how really special he was to Craig and we were doing a show at National Studio right on 42nd street. It's no longer here, and this man came on the set. I had never seen a picture of him. I had only heard of Chuck McCann, and I don't normally do this. I ran to him and threw my arms around him and hugged him and THEN realized "who is this and why are you doing this?" This is the presence that Chuck McCann had as a human being. He just radiated this warmth and love, and love of puppets and kids and…

CM: He was a heart with legs.

JB: You and Olga had not met yet, so you kept work-ing with him. What else was going on?

CM: I was mostly performing my own puppets on all the local shows, like Wonderama and Sandy Becker and all that. My mother died when I was fourteen, and without Mom I was forcing myself to go to school. I began to flounder somewhat (thankfully I had the puppets to keep me sane-ish). In high school I auditioned for Theater Workshop and was put into the technical side of the theater instead of the acting side and I was really pissed off. How dare they do that to me? I'm fifteen and I know everything, you know? As fate would have it, it turned out that my drama teacher was not only a brilliant teacher, but he was also the co-founder and artistic director of the Classic Stage Company, which is now one of the top repertory companies in New York. It was just beginning then. The CSC (as it was also known) were doing Man and Superman by George Bernard Shaw. I guess my teacher saw something in me and asked if I wanted the unenviable task of being the stage manager for this show. And I thought, again with the technical, you know? So, I'm hanging lights. I'm painting walls black. I'm running sound. I'm handing props. I'm calling the show – in a real off-Broadway theater! It was a remarkable experience.

OF: At fifteen.

CM: And everybody else was a grownup. You know, twenty-four, twenty-five years old, real professional actors, you know, and they all treated me well. My teacher's name was Harris Laskawy. I mean, if I had one mentor, Mr. Laskawy would've been that fellow. After school we'd drive together into Manhattan, eat, go to the theater, rehearse/

perform, then drop me home at night. All I had to do was get passing grades in school, which I did. After Man and Superman, they were doing the New York premiere of a play by Jean Anouilh called The Cavern. And I got the role of the Scullery Boy, who was like the one ray of hope in this Upstairs/Downton kind of story. I got great reviews in all the papers, and I was acting and smoking cigarettes and eating yogurt and all that cool, actory stuff. So, I didn't do puppets for those two years. After my tenure with the CSC ended, while still in HS, I became friendly with a fellow named Dug Cohen. He loved lighting and when I met him he was at one of those great old plug ‘em in lighting boards. I went backstage one day and there was Dug with two prisms in his eyes. “You got to see this man!” and he screws the prisms into my eyes as he starts flashing the border lights and I go, “What the hell is going on here?!?!” Needless to say, we became fast friends. Dug turned me onto the Grateful Dead. We went to the Fillmore East, and it was like, I see it all now. Eventually I thought “wouldn't it be fun to create a real light-heavy puppet show?” Wow. It was puppets plus a light show. So Dug and I formed The Marko Puppet Theater (Marin and Cohen, but “K” is always funnier than “C”). Dug would be going away to college in Binghamton the following semester and we created a show to debut there. It was called “Hal Lewis Nation in Kingdom Kum.”

OF: Hallucination in Kingdom Kum!

CM: I guess this was 1969, maybe like that. We used Grateful Dead music and some original music as well, because of the Grateful Dead I started playing guitar and composing. Rhythm guitarist Bob Weir was my hero. I would watch him play and memorize the way his hands looked as he played, then at home I’d sit in front of a mirror and try to make my hands move like his. That's how I learned how to play guitar.

JB: Being a guitar player myself, I can relate to this.

CM: Right? Because no one played like he did. He created a way to fit be-tween Jerry Garcia and Phil Lesh. Their music was the spirit of the magic of the timing of the transcendence. The songs were launching pads to take you places. At the same time there’s Zap Comix. Thanks to my Dad I always thought in terms of cartooning. He and Max Fleischer were my cartooning heroes, Max Fleischer's gritty, psychedelic stuff. You know, New York. Because that stuff doesn't happen in Looney Tunes or Disney. So, putting the Zap Comix aspect together with the puppets made it all make sense.

JB: I was going to ask about Max Fleischer. I can definitely see the more psychedelic design aspect in your work. Even the Jukebox Band from Shining Time Station; everything's just a little off kilter.

CM: The Marko Puppet Theater took off! I had a girl-friend at the time (Holly Smith) who became a puppeteer because of me, and then the other two fellows and us decided, "Let's tour the country next summer playing colleges and eventually meet the Grateful Dead." That's a plan. So, the four of us took off in two different vans, go to Buffalo State, to Antioch College, the whole hippie loving college tour thing. Really no preplanned trip, pre-internet. We'd roll up to the college and say, "We do a psychedelic puppet show." And they'd say, "Yeah!" And we'd go, "Okay!" And they'd pay us: money, food, a dorm to sleep in, having wonderful energetic spiritual hilarious unbelievable experiences traveling around the country and cosmos. By the way, all us puppeteers were also musicians, so when the show ended the music began. The stage turned into a light show. It was a puppet theater/dance experience as we played Grateful Dead-Jefferson Airplane types of songs. We went across the country doing these shows, settling in San Rafael, coincidently, just down the block from the Grateful Dead. Marin comes home to Marin County. One day we finally got up the nerve to go meet the Dead, and Dug says, "I'll do the talking." We rang the bell and Rock Scully (the Dead's manager) leans out and goes, "Yes?" And Dug freezes. Homina homina homina..

I jumped in and said "We're the Marko Puppet Theater," and Rock says "I just read about you." There was some story in a San Rafael paper about us that we didn't even know about! He said, "Come on in." We went in, and Bob Weir was there. We talked about our show, Dug found his voice and rhapsodized about "lighting cubes in space." We showed them our color slides in a little wooden hold-it-up-to-the-light viewer. "Oh, far out, that's freaking great," they said. "So what do you want from us?" I said, "We just want you to know we exist." "Okay, cool." We went home, half-hour later the phone rang and Rock Scully says, "Do you want to do your puppet show at Jerry Garcia's birthday on Mickey's ranch next Saturday?"

JB: Well, that's an easy yes.

CM: And we cleared our schedule. We went, did the show for them and they loved it and it was great. They ended up booking us at different places, now and again. Then we moved to the Sierra Nevada mountains, North San Juan, Nevada City. Holly and I were living an idyllic life in a tent. But after awhile our ambition to create puppet art over-whelmed the quiet solitude of mountain life. So we disbanded Marko as those fellows kind of put down roots and Holly and I spread our wings. We came back East and settled in New England where she was from. We lived in Shirley and Leominster, Brockton, Dedham and Westwood. We kind of owned the whole school circuit while we were there. Changing from the psychedelic shows to the children's shows at schools was a beautiful transition because we could bring the same thing that we did in the psychedelic shows, but now we just had to look through a child's lens. We flourished.

JB: This is all happening in the early seventies?

CM: The school show years were like 1974 -76, yeah. Holly and I were just partners by 1975 and my actress girlfriend Janet was living in New York City. She called me and said she read in Backstage that "puppeteers were needed for a show outside the tri-state area. The audition was at 59 Barrow Street." Now I never worked for another puppeteer in my life, but 59 Barrow Street was the home of the famous BIL BAIRD MARIONETTE THEATER!!! I drove down from my farmhouse in Littleton, Massachusetts, met Bil, auditioned, he liked me a lot and hired me on the spot. I moved to Williamsburg Virginia that May and worked for Bil Baird at Busch Gardens. The show was called "Once Upon a Dragon," we did 10 half-hour shows a day. Five days a week. Wow! Talk about slinging hash. It was rough, but there were lots of girls, so that was fun. Dancing girls in different shows, tourists, and stuff like that. That was really fun. Everyone seemed to enjoy the show, which always makes the work worthwhile.

When the run ended in November '77, I could go any place in the world. I knew I was not going to go back to those guys in California. And I'm not going to go to LA, because I don't want to break into the movies and I didn't think I could round up my own work in LA. Whereas in New York I could probably hustle a mountain of work. So, Janet and I got a place in Manhattan Plaza (first tenants on the 31st floor) and I started trying to find work. One day I met my friend Marty (Robinson), who worked at Busch Gardens with me. He was shooting a Bil Baird TV special. So, I'm standing on the corner of Barrow Street and this beautiful blonde person walks up and says "Hi" to Marty. And a lightning bolt went off in my heart. He said, "Oh, this is Olga Felgemacher." She was famous. Her name was whispered about Busch Gardens all the time. So, this radiant woman whom I knew was Bil's star, well, they went their way and, and I went my way. But I never forgot her. You never forget anything like, well, Olga Felgemacher, once you can say it right,

OF: Once you learn it!

CM: [to Olga] …Then you can take over, you tell your story, then that brings us to where we actually met.

JB: Where did you grow up, Olga?

OF: Cleveland, Ohio. My parents had a sweet shop and so I did, you know, performing and making things. I did backyard performances and I was able to bribe all the neighborhood kids with five cents admission, plus free refreshments from my parent's store. So, I had an audience.

CM: Her mother said one of the earliest things she did was that people would be leaving the sweet shop, she'd be handing out free bags of potato chips. That's really her heart. That's where she is.

OF: Sometimes I think getting to puppets, was like picking a bouquet of flowers in this beautiful garden. Because so many pieces had to come together before I discovered puppets. One of my earliest memories on television was Susie Snowflake. Before it was animated, it was this little cut-out thing on strings. You know, "Here comes Susie Snowflake, look at her snow-white gown, down, tap, tap, tapping at your window pane…" and I was enchanted, so I made little things like that. And I made costumes and clothing for my dolls and they were always part of the shows. But Cleveland was fortunate enough to have Serge Nadejdin who had been the artistic director of the Russian Imperial ballet. And after the revolution, he fled with Balanchine. They were best friends. Balanchine stayed in New York and Mister Nadejdin came to Cleveland and opened a ballet school. So, I started, my mother took me to ballet class. I guess I was six and I was going to be a ballerina. I loved when we had costumes for things, so costume design turned me on. I also was one of the kid actors at the Cleveland Playhouse and I got to see backstage, with real stage costumes and it was all fascinating. Puppets had never entered my world yet. Never dawned on me that you could make a living with Susie Snowflake! Then I went to Northwestern University and I got the lead in "Anna Christie," one of their big theater productions they do a couple of times a year. I liked acting and apparently, I was good enough at it to do that. I also loved the costumes and all my best friends were the set designers and the lighting kids. And I just loved that. So of course, I came to New York. I went back to dancing for a while and Mary Anthony asked me to join her company, but I knew I didn't want to do that. And at the same time, I did an off-Broadway play, and I did a TV episode of Camera Three, with James Earl Jones and Robert Earl Jones. It was about the Mississippi Freedom Riders. Some-thing possessed me, I don't know, at one of the first rehearsals I went up to meet them and told them my name was Felgemacher Jones. I had no idea why I did that. I thought it was really funny! They didn't get it. Anyway, I did costumes for a dance company whose name I can't even remember. And then a friend was working with a company called Nicolo Marionettes. I'd been in New York maybe a year and a half, so I went with her to see a rehearsal and I walked into Nicolo Marionettes and there were all these beautiful puppets and marionettes hanging all over and was like, TAH DAH!!! All of those different pieces of that puzzle came together and was like, YES!! THIS IS WHAT I WANT TO DO FOR THE REST OF MY LIFE. PE-RIOD. END OF STORY! So, Nicky Coppola, bless you. Nicky, and dear Pady Blackwood, taught me how to work a marionette. And I got hired by Nicolo and toured nationally with them. One of my best stories is of Ruth

Waxman, who owned the company. We were in Colorado and there was a blizzard. You know, one of those Colorado blizzards, and we had to get across this mountain pass to a show the next day, and the Rangers had closed the road and they said, "the only way you're going to be able to go there is one of you walks in front of the van." And since I didn't drive (I still don't) of course that someone would have to be me. So, I called Ruth, crying and fearing for my life and said, "What am I gonna do?" Taking a drag from her ever present cigarette she rasps "It'll test your mettle, honey!" Fortunately, the blizzard suddenly stopped. The roads opened and we were okay!

CM: You're the Moses of puppeteers!

OF: But I always remember Ruth, "It'll test your mettle, honey."

CM: We've used that phrase many times when we got our mettle tested!

OF: Oh, yes. My mettle has been tested many times and I hear her words. Um, um, and then, uh, I worked for Dorothy Zaconic. I did the Snow Maiden with her and she was wonderful. She was in Czechoslovakia learning to carve puppets at the outbreak of World War Two in the forties. She was a little Jewish girl from America doing that and she refused to leave. I don't know the story about how she got out or anything, but she was a wonderful character and a puppeteer who should be remembered. She had a company called Suzari. Then I read that Bil Baird was having auditions and it was just like, no, I'd seen his stuff on television and loved it. But at that time, I just loved it. It never dawned on me that this is what one could make a living at, most of the time. And so I thought, I'll go to the audition and I got to the subway station, paid my fare, got on the train and got so scared, I went back home. And then I thought, what are you crazy? Are you F/N? So, I went back down into the subway, paid another fare, got to the theater in time for the audition. There were 300 other young women that auditioned and I got the job. At that time my stage name was Olga Lisa, because Olga Felgemacher didn't sound like a stage name to my friends at least, who advised me to change it. So, then I've got the job. And on the first or second day of rehearsal, Bil came up to me and said, "What is your real name?" And I went, Olga Felgemacher and he said, “That's a puppeteer’s name!” So ever since then I've used my real name.

CM: When Bil met Olga, Cora [Bil’s wife and partner] was just two, maybe three years gone and all of a sudden, this Olga one appears with her toy voice and all that skill and stuff like that. He must’ve recognized it because this began the Renaissance for the Bil Baird company.

OF: Yeah. And I worked with people like Leonard Bernstein doing music and Sheldon Harnick who wrote Fiddler on the Roof and Pinocchio for us...

CM: ... which won the New York state council’s Gold Medal for the Arts. Pinocchio was written, for Olga by ...

OF: Jerome Cooper Smith and Sheldon Har-nick.

CM: Then they did Alice in Wonderland by Joe Raposo.

OF: Then the theater closed, though Bil did not want it to. They were going into production for Busch Gardens. I help build Busch Gardens, but then I was off. Busch was not an Equity company, and there was a PBS television series called Vegetable Soup, and I got offered to play two of the lead puppet children on the Outerscope II segments. Bette Midler did the music, and sang the theme song. Through the years at Baird’s, Jim Henson would offer a job. He would come to the theater and say, you know, if you ever think about working for me that would be wonderful. And so, I finally called him and said, “Is that job opening still open?” “Oh, yes.”

So, I did Sesame street and played all kinds of differ-ent characters. Let's see, Lady Photographer, the people in your neighborhood, vegetable cart owner (with The Count). Yeah. Once early on when I was puppeteering a meter reader with Oscar, for some reason my blonde hair kept showing, you know, my arm was as long as it could be! Kermit Love came over and he had this black beret and he plopped the black beret on my head and patted me on the knee and walked away. That solved the problem. I worked in the first Muppet Movie but I really by then wanted to do my own thing. I just thought I would be at Bil’s my whole life. And the Muppets were a wonderful experience, but it wasn't exactly what I wanted.

CM: Because you couldn’t build as well.

OF: Yeah. And Faz, Franz Fazakas, advised me not to do it anyway. Jim asked me, do you want to work in the shop? Faz told me that I better pick one or the other cause I'd be stuck there. I would either be in the shop all the time or perform.

CM: Actually, what he said was “you can always build puppets in your bedroom.”

OF: Yeah, which I did.

CM: Which we still do, sometimes!

OF: I love performing too and I could always build the puppets on my own. Absolutely. That made good sense. And then I puppeteered for The Adventures Of Slim Goodbody on Captain Kangaroo. Puppets by Danny Seagren, who is our son's godfather,

CM: He was also Spider Man on Electric Company (Shhhhh).

OF: Then I met you (Craig).

CM: I had just moved back to New York and I hustled up my own live family show for Christmas down at the Greenwich Mews Theater on West 13th street. Alice Tweedie (SNL) showed up and she really liked my show. She said, “I'm always looking for puppeteers. Can I have your number?” So, I gave her my number. Meanwhile I’m still look-ing for work, trying to figure out how was I going to fit. I knew they didn't have kid shows on TV anymore like I wanted to do, I didn't want it to tour schools in New York City, so what am I going to do? I did some commercials. I did this and that, and I get this call in April from Alice Tweedie who said, “I'm doing a film. My puppeteer cut his thumb on a bandsaw. Can you come in tomorrow and meet the other people I'm working with and then do the film the day after?” I said, “Of course.” So I went up to Alice Tweedie’s apartment, and she [Olga] was there. It was really serious work. An industrial film for Met Life. Had a lot to do on-the-fast, you know? Next day we met on the set, put the puppets up on camera, and BOOM the studio big-banged into a thousand million stars. The lens couldn't hold it. That relationship. Our first scene together had the puppets under a bed, which was kind of cool, and set the tone for the future, you know? The puppets interaction with each other was of such a high nature that we thought we should get together, play with puppets somehow.

OF: And it was the right time. Both of us were look-ing for the next thing.

CM: But that didn't happen right away. So, we got like through that year somehow. My birthday is New Year's Eve and Olga and I independently found ourselves at a Christmas puppet party out in Long Island. I was there with my actress girlfriend and Olga was there with her musician boyfriend and stuff like that. We sort-of talked to each other, but then we all shared a car ride back into the city, courtesy of that gentle master of all things balloon, Allynn Gooen. Olga and her boyfriend in the front. Marty Robinson, my girlfriend ȧnd I squeezed in the back. We are taking this normal car ride back from Long Island but in that bubble of altered reality there really was nobody else in the car 'cept Olga and Me. It was like a flying carpet zipping down the Grand Central.

OF: Talking about puppets the whole time.

CM: Everybody could feel it, could sense something cosmic was afoot. So we decided we're going to get together and play with puppets for reals.

JB: And this was what year? 79? And you were married in '82. So you guys got together and...

CM: We formed a partnership, "Craig and Olga, The Puppeteerz" - trademarked with a Z. We decided to go on the road somehow, so we could spend time together. I wrote a quick show and we toured malls. It was really great fun, plus we got a chance to be together. One day Danny (Seagren) called again. Do you know the comic strip Miss Peach? We brought it to life with Danny's puppets. Martin Short debuted his Ed Grimley voice as the intellectual Turkey in the Thanksgiving Special. We shot it up in Toronto, with scripts by Mel Lazarus, who created the strip and Ed Scharlach, who created Mork and Mindy

OF: And I told Danny that I couldn't do it because I have this new partner and, and you have to see my partner, we have to do it together. And when Danny met Craig, he was blown away with how good Craig was. So that was no problem.

CM: He said, "You'll be my Frank Oz." I said, "I can't promise you that, but we'll have fun." And we did. We hit it off really well. We did four half-hour specials for syndication and one NBC After School special with the Miss Peach puppets. Right after that, Danny did another season of Slim Goodbody and I joined him and Olga – and Alice Tweedie! Side note: when I was a kid, my friend Paul Rubin and I used to dress up like Laurel and Hardy and do Laurel and Hardy acts.

OF: Chubby little Craig looked just like Oliver Hardy.

CM: And it was a lot of fun. Paul and I met at the Chuck McCann show. Paul was very sophisticated for a 15 year old, wore a suit, looked nice. Smoked cigarettes. Me? I looked like Wayne Newton. But we hit it off well. We put out a newspaper called Celebrity Post Magazine, which was really just an excuse to meet our heroes. One of the famous people we met was a voice actor named Bob McFadden (editor's note - https://en.wikipedia.org/wiki/Bob_McFadden).

Bob McFadden was Cool McCool. We told him we loved his impression of double talk artist Al Kelly. So, for the next 20 minutes or so, he answered every question like Al Kelly. We must've touched his heart because he was a grown-up and we were kids and were on the floor laughing hysterically. Just never forgot him. Well apparently, he never forgot me either, because in the second season of Slim Goodbody, he was doing most of the male voices for the puppets; he was off on the side and I went over to him and said in Al Kelly's voice, "Bob McFreilman!" He remembered who I was! And then we was pals, tightened up our friendship just like that. While we were on the set of Miss Peach, Danny was very good friends with a woman named Sandy Kavanaugh who was starting a new network and wanted some mari-onettes for this TV show she was doing. Danny tells her, "I don't know anything about marionettes, but I've got Olga and her partner here and they do marionettes." So, we went and met her and she really liked us. It turned out to be something called Pin-wheel for something called Nickelodeon on something called cable.

OF: Nobody knew what it was when I'd say now we're doing a show on cable with Nickelodeon.

CM: In fact, even the union said, "What it is that? Public access?" I said, "I don't think so." They said, "Well, get scale."

OF: They let us do it, as long as we got scale.

CM: Before we did that though, we did a TV pilot out in California for Don Kirshner Productions (remember Don Kirchner's Rock Concert?) The pilot was called Roaring Doughnuts, starring Stubby Kaye. Oh, it was so much fun. All about van racing, but right then the FCC stepped in and said you can't do any kid shows that have a product on it that you have to get, in order to enjoy the show. And they were giving away free booklets, like scavenger hunt stuff, because the whole show was like a scavenger hunt. But because of that, even though it was free, they couldn't do it. It was a sweet show. As we were flying home we designed Herbert and Lulu the Hobo Bugs, Silas Snail, Molly O'Mole, and the Admiral Bird. That began our Nickelodeon career, where we did 260 one-hour shows over two 32-week periods. We were on 10 hours a day when Pinwheel first started, so much so, the kids called it the Pinwheel channel!

JB: Both of you have done so much interesting work like The Muppet Movie, Pinwheel, and of course Shining Time Station. And you were DJ Kat.

CM: DJ Kat was interesting too. But let me back up a little first to like 1985(?) We had already done Pinwheel when an inventor named Dr. Michael Freeman, who was the actual inventor of interactive television called ACTV, was working out of Port Washington, and he hired us. It was a really fascinating system where four channels run simultaneously and you could have these different branches in the show. So, you can say, do you want to go to the firehouse, or do you want to make a cake? If you make the cake, then that branch would kick in. And it would remember that stuff. And at the end the puppet can say, "You wanted to go to make a cake, so next time, maybe we'll go to the firehouse." That sort of thing. We did multiple series for the network, from preschool to preteens.

Then came Shining Time Station, which was just the greatest thing at that time. On a Friday afternoon, we get a call from Sean Kelly, who's one of the original editors of National Lampoon. We had hired Sean to write a TV pilot called Cartoony Vision, and Sean and I just hit it off like that! Rude, funny, child-like, you know, really funny.

OF: Very rude and funny.

CM: Real good, creative blend in writing. And he called us up and says, “Look, I'm over at Channel 13. They're doing a show, they need puppets and they need your puppets. They just don't know it yet. Get over here.” So, we threw Herbert and Lulu and a Dracula puppet – things that weren’t Muppety - - in a bag, and ran down to WNET where we met with creators/producers Rick Siggelkow and Britt Allcroft. We pulled out the puppets and puppeteered them and they just said, “Oh, very interesting. Okay, well, let us think about it.” We went home on a cloud. But it was a very long weekend when you couldn't check cell phones or anything like that, so we were sitting there willing the phone to ring, or, if we went out, every 10 seconds running to a pay phone to check the answering machine.

OF: That was like the point that like we needed the next job. Like we really needed this, you know. We had a kid.

CM: And we wanted it to be something that mattered. Not just a one-off or that sort of thing. STS was immediately going into production on 20 epi-sodes. That Sunday afternoon we took our little boy Gabriel to the park. He was four, I guess. There was a big slide on the East side. And I said, “Olga, I'm gonna go find a payphone.” Several long blocks later I did, and finally a call! The woman left a message saying, “Everybody else said they could bring something special to the party, but you're the only ones who proved that you could. Would you like to do the job?” So, I ran back to Olga as fast as I could. She was coming down the slide with Gabriel. Well, we were just so happy. We got to work building all these Shining Time Station Puppets and it was a dream come true. But no marionettes. Yet.

OF: We had to convince them to do the marionettes.

CM: We shot the first 20 episodes up on 116th and Park Avenue East in a studio there. Those are the ones with Ringo.

JB: All of Shining Time Station was done in the same studio?

CM: Puppets first, then actors, then Mr. Conductor.

OF: Thomas was separate. [Shot in England]

CM: The show debuted to universal acclaim, when few months later Rick called and said they were doing a Christmas special, starring Lloyd Bridges as Mis-ter Nicholas. I said, YAY and okay, and asked if we could build marionettes for the show, and suggested shooting the musical numbers single camera film style. I said, "I'll draw story-boards and cut it that way." Rick, bless his dear heart, said "Okay man." So, we did Jingle Bells with storyboards. A camera shot here as the Rex Boy Brother marionette jumps off the piano/cut/next set-up he lands across stage with the camera dutched. A week or two after the shoot Rick calls me up and says, "I gotta tell you, we were cursing you out when we started editing this, then we started following the storyboards, and now we say, bless you." Amazingly, they parlayed this wonderful series into 45 more episodes, plus five home videos! That translated into six weeks in Toronto. It was wonderful. We sub-sequently shot four more one-hour family specials. I think it's 1990, right? And then I get a call from a director we hired for STS and he says "I'm working over at Channel 5's on The DJ Kat Show. Want to be DJ Kat"? That's how those karmic things pay off. Not only was it Channel 5, but that was the exact same studio where I used to see Sandy Becker and Chuck McCann do their shows!

OF: And he'd always dreamt as a kid that he would do something in that studio.

CM: It was like I was remembering the future. Seriously.

JB: You were both involved in the film Strings. What was that like?

CM: That was a complex show and we were called in for the last month of shooting.

OF: Very complex. And, uh, in the middle of it, the Danish crew quit and they brought in a Swedish crew. Some of the puppeteers left.

CM: And very physically draining and emotional. The studio was actually converted army hangars because they didn't need to study war no more. A core group remained, and we were brought in to do other stuff. A lot of B unit stuff and all that. This was Peter Baird's last show. Peter was Bil's son, who puppeteered Grace The Bass for us on Shining Time. He called Steve Widerman and Steve couldn't do it. Peter was funny when he called us and said, "Can you leave Friday?" I said, "No, we need until at least until Tuesday or Wednesday." He goes, "Yeah, so you guys have a life. I don't!" Peter was the funniest person in the world, who died way too soon. He is always and forever in our Karass. So, we went to wonderful wonderful Copenhagen, met the people, and it was delightful. There we were, in the land of Hans Christian Andersen, and we got along great with everybody. I had a lot of downtime though, and the back walls, behind the set, all naked plywood and what not, looked at me seductively like she needed cartoons on her nekkid wood. It was just this incredible blank canvas. So, Magic Marker in hand I started drawing all over, drawing, drawing, drawing. And then the producer came up and said, "Oh, like Storm Petersen." "Who's Storm Petersen?" "You don't know Storm Petersen?!" I felt so provincial. "You know, he's the greatest cartoonist in Scandinavia."

OF: The most beloved. And there's a whole museum.

CM: So, we had a day off and we walked to his beautiful home that was turned into a museum and there were all his drawings. He drew exactly like my father! It was as if my Dad's drawings were there. And she saw that in me. I don't draw like my father, but she saw that thing. We bought a poster of his that comes out every Christmas. We did the film and saw the Little Mermaid statue and the Hans Christian Andersen statue. The days on the set were long.

OF: Some of the sets were like, three story stories high for some of the scenes. We have a lot of rules here for the safety of actors and puppeteers. They didn't have those. We were up in one of the three-story-highs bridges with the ice crystals and stuff. And if you're up high and something at the bottom moves an inch, it sways a foot at the top, you know, just that pivot point. And at one point somebody bumped the set and one of the puppeteers, Libby, who fortunately had been a trapeze artist for a while, went tumbling forward and was able to grab onto a lighting pole. She would have fallen to her death, be-cause to get up there, we had to climb on a rope ladder, like a trapeze artist, toe, heel, toe, heel, toe, heel. And they realized that this is dangerous and thank goodness, they gave us all grappling hooks so we could hook up there, and you wouldn't tip forward and plummet.

CM: The thing about Libby, she and her brother were also sort of famous puppet-eers in England, and their parents were the Grangers. The Granger's were one of the best marionette acts in England, who also did all the puppets on Planet Patrol, which was sort of like Supermarionation, but not. One quick thing about Strings, they were showing it at a film festival here in New York, and we went in and it was packed. We sat down and before the show starts, someone says, “We were just told that two of the puppeteers from Strings were in the audience and maybe they'll talk to us afterwards.” So, we were like, hey, okay. We spoke about it afterwards. Then the Smithsonian who happened to be there came up to us and asked if we would we like to speak at the Smithsonian on behalf of Strings? So, we put together a whole slide show and did that.

OF: We had pictures and got pictures from some of the other puppeteers that were there.

CM: But Strings was beautiful.

JB: An amazing and mythologically potent story, full of life, death, loss, impermanence, and you just don't find out elsewhere. Strings isn't just a puppet show.

OF: It’s Hamlet.

JB: It is Shakespearean in nature. It is a fully realized piece of art that just happens to be rendered with puppets. What other insanely fun stuff have you done?

OF: We made The Talking Stain for a Tide-To-Go commercial. It is one of the Top Three Super Bowl commercials of all time. Our

Flexitoon Films have won Official Selection Laurels in several film festivals including LA SHORTS and KIDS FIRST.

CM: We produced a live show that toured all around the country and internationally as well. We opened the International Festi-val of Puppet Arts in Taiwan. Our show was called HAMLIN. It was a modern retelling of the Pied Piper. For us really, it was the ultimate, most terrific two person show we could do. It had lights and sound and music and all these new puppets and sets in it!

OF: It was the most that the two of us could do by ourselves!

CM: With a four-hour set-up! It was nuts! But we were passionate about it.

OF: It was a good show.

CM: And it took us to Romania for the…

OF: …Luceafarul Festival of Children's Theater.

CM: We represented America. We were the only American company there. Another cool thing was when our exhibit "Art That Moves - The World Of Flexitoon" opened at the Greenwich Arts Council. We had over a hundred of our puppets props and sets on display. Every weekend we did two shows and they were packed all the time. Until people saw the show no one recognized us, so we could lurk as people looked. They would come up and see the Pinwheel Puppets on display, start singing the song, and some would start crying at the memories the puppets stirred. In October 2018 we built and performed puppets in a horror film called "Separation." It stars Brian Cox, Rupert Friend and Mamie Gummer.

OF: Scheduled for release at Christmas 2019.

CM: It's a supernatural story of divorce, and the puppets play a very prominent role. When we got the job, the main criteria was that we had to do this shot at the end where all the puppets are sitting on the child's dresser, and as someone walks across, they all have to turn just their heads to follow him. So, we built them knowing that's what they had to do, and the simplest solution is the one that's going to work. Why use robotics if you can pull a string, know what I mean? So, it was the next to the last day on set, it's like two o'clock in the morning when they finally got to this shot. The crew had been with these puppets all the time, looming, for months already, at this point. The exhausted stage manager schleps into the bedroom set and looks at the puppets and says, "Okay, show me the magic." He's sitting there sleepily when all of a sudden the puppets sloooowly turn their heads. He jumps up and cries "Holy Shit!" They loved it. It did its thing, you know. Green screen guy goes home early. Felt so good.

OF: You know, analog! CM: So, this past April we get a call from a fellow who says, "We're doing an Off-Broadway show about Hans Christian Andersen, but not the Frank Loesser version. The Ensemble for the Romantic Century is the name of the company." We had done Ugly Duckling at Symphony Space when they did the Wall-To-Wall concerts of Frank Loesser. We love Hans Christian Andersen, but we didn't really know his real story. They sent us the script by Eve Wolf which we read and, as with Shining Time Station, knew we have got to be part of this beautiful painful story. Hans' tales were born from deep, deep hurt. This company proved to be amazing. We have two, nine-foot pianos on stage and a full percussion set-up. It uses Benjamin Britten's music and Stravinsky and has counter tenors. It's just remarkable to tell his magical story this way. And she's [Olga] also onstage playing Hans' mother, who in this iteration is the inspiration for the Little Match Girl. The designer, Vanessa James has fashioned the set to look like a large Toy Theater with life-size cutouts of different characters called dummy boards.

OF: Which were popular in those days.

CM: The amazingly talented Jimmy Ray Bennett who plays Hans, walks over to the dummy board and says in an imperious voice "So, Hans Christian Andersen, you think you have this job?" Then Jimmy as Hans responds, and so forth. He's exploring his memories. The puppets interact and intersperse throughout the play. I perform a short-strung Pierrot marionette who is Hans alter ego. I even made the Pierrot look like Jimmy/Hans. The story we really bring to life is that of the Little Mermaid, which is a very tumultuous tale. You know, it's not that happy-go-lucky thing. She gives up her legs, you know. So, the Sea Witch casts a spell and tears her tail off eats it. Then knives swim out and hook onto her and then she has to walk on her knives.

OF: I remember so vividly as a child, being a dancer and reading it, when she gets legs from the Sea Witch and every step was like walking on knives. I remember that.

CM: We do it visually. Then when she gives up her legs and goes to the shore to join the Prince, she sees he's getting married, realizes her love will remain unrequited and dissolves into sea foam right on stage. That's pure puppetry out in front on the stage as well as behind the proscenium on the puppet stage. It's remarkable. The director, Don Sanders, is brilliant. He has a deep handle on the multidimensionality of what the show is and gives us latitude within our puppetry to bring it to life. It is a beautiful collaboration, and Olga and I look forward to working with the Ensemble again.

JB: What does the future hold? What's coming up?

CM: We're in development for a ...

OF: I don't think we should say yet, but it's been something we've wanted to do forever.

CM: Olga is right again.

JB: And you'll let us know as soon as it's a deal?

OF: We'll let'cha know!

HOBEY FORD

JB: Hobey, it's a pleasure to be here with you and talk about your career. Let's start with your childhood. Where did you grow up?

Hobey Ford: I grew up in Rowayton, Connecticut, about an hour from New York City. My dad commuted into New York. It was a quiet little new England town growing up. When I got to be about 18 years old, I decided that New York was beginning to swallow it up. Traffic and everything. So, I moved away from New England. 1976 was the year that I moved away. I was going to State University of New York at Purchase, Purchase College, the school of the arts up there, and I was going to be a visual artist.

I had no thoughts of puppetry at all. My experiences of puppetry before that were in the late sixties. The Sound of Music came out and I was just enchanted with the Lonely Goat Herd scene (Bil Baird) and I went into New York City and saw it at a big theater. I think I saw that movie nine times in the theater. Then in the fifth grade, I had gone to a boarding school and you had to finish your homework or you couldn't go home on the weekend. I was the most homesick kid in the world. I went from a flunking student to being a straight "A" student and I always had my homework done. So, when they asked who had finished their homework, I raised my hand. (They asked me), "Could you help the Marionettist set up?

So, it turned out to be David Syrotiak! Now, I didn't know that at the time who we was, or what it was, but I helped him set it up. And the show was Ali Baba and the 40 Thieves. And it was in an athletic building that we were doing it and the ceiling was low and there was a beam that doing it and the ceiling was low and there was a beam he was afraid he'd hit. He was worried about it. And I went and got him a lacrosse helmet that he could wear just in case. And then sure enough in the middle of the show, he hit his head with the helmet, but it caught him in the little air pocket on the side. And he passed out in the middle of the show and they had to bring him ice and finally he finished the show. It was him and a young woman. He had red hair back then. And I never forgot that, although I didn't know who it was at the time. It was New Year's Eve, 1975. And I said, I've got to come up with something different to do. I don't understand the art world. It's all modern art. I like representational things. It was all just abstract and seemed a little BS to me. Although now I think differently about that. I just didn't understand it.

HF: A lot of the students did get it and did understand it. I had been like mesmerized by the Renaissance. Of course, I knew the Renaissance had ended, but I didn't really think about it that hard when I got to art college. I just thought, oh, we'll learn to paint and draw and sculpt and all these things. So, I felt like I had to figure out something else and I closed my eyes. I'd been reading about Yogis. Autobiography of a Yogi [Paramahansa Yogananda] had just come out. All of a sudden, I imagined Paramahansa's face. And I thought, maybe I'll paint the portraits of Yogi masters or something like that. And then in my imagination unbidden I noticed there were two lines along the side of his edges of his mouth. And I realized, No! I'm going to make the marionettes of them and do a show about Autobiography of a Yogi, Paramahansa Yogananda. I got back to school, did an independent study on puppetry and then a bunch of students were going to go out to San Francisco Art Institute. And I thought, well, maybe I'll do that. Maybe I'll stick with art for a little while longer and I can do puppetry out there, you know. I didn't know about colleges that would have puppetry at that point or anything. So, I landed in a little town in Nevada and needed a place to camp out. And I met a native American family and I ended up living with them for two years, on the Nevada desert. They were building a community on the desert, a traditional community, and they were going to build traditional lodges and they had just gotten the land. The Grateful Dead had made the down payment on their land. And one day a puppeteer and his wife arrived from North Carolina and he had a little leather, 1950s, 1930s or '40s leather doctor's bag, smaller than a briefcase. And at night he would pull out little rod puppets, miniature rod puppets, and he would entertain us for an hour and, and be able to do another show the next night and improvise something else. And he was brilliant. It was Clyde Hollifield. So, I decided to get out of there and I moved back to Asheville, North Carolina area. It was before Asheville really was on the map. It was a ghost town. Basically.

JB: What year was this?

HF: It was '78. I got a little cabin for 25 bucks a month and we'd go hang out with Clyde and tried to convince him to show me how his puppet controls worked and eventually, you know, he saw some promise. So, he started showing me how to make things. I played guitar in a little coffee house once a week to make rent, because it was very cheap. So, it gave me about three years to just experiment with puppet making and build puppets. And then I started bringing them to the gigs, and then pretty soon the guy at the gig said, "Leave your guitar at home, bring the puppets." And then that jumped into, oh, there's this little festival in town. Why don't you come and be in the festival over here? There's a little school here. And then it just started picking up. And that was about 1979 or so.

JB: And then you started Golden Rod Puppets.

HF: Yeah. 1980. My first marionette troupe in College, it was just me and a friend, it was Golden Strings, Marionettes. I changed it to Golden Rod Puppets since I was going to do rod puppets. And that year I went and visited the workshop of the Dark Crystal in Manhattan. A friend from out west from the native American community, her sister did some set design for them early on and she got me an appointment. But then my neighbor who worked in advertising knew this guy, Lee Donaldson who was one of their new engineers. He spent a lot of time with me and showed me all the K and S Engineering stuff. I was getting my rods from piano strings and he said "You can order these new, you know, you can get this material." And he showed me all these tricks and he encouraged me. And so, I dove into all this new engineering material and continued experimenting.

And then around that time, when I was up at the Muppets, I had seen they were carving foam rubber. And I asked, how do you do that? And one of the craftsmen was carving on a puppet and she said, I'll show you. She's making a big bird foot. And so then I started experimenting with the foam and then I heard on NPR an interview with Bruce Schwartz, who Jim Henson had discovered. And he was one of the people who did the six parts series of, you know, Albrect Roser, Richard Bradshaw, etc [The World of Puppetry series]. Bruce

Schwartz was doing Bunraku style puppetry. And, and so I put that together with the foam puppets that I was starting to make. And that inspired moving in my own direction that at that point I felt like 1980 I began to go in my own direction instead of like following Clyde's work.

JB: What kind of foam do you use? The plain white stuff, right? Not the reticulated foams with very small pores, right?

HF: It's not the expensive reticulated foam. What I use is upholstery foam. North Carolina, back then it was still the heart of the furniture industry and it still is to a degree, but it's spread out, moved away to Asia, things like that. I would go to the foam factories, not where they made the foam, but at the next stage where they were milling it and cutting it into sheets and into blocks and different things. I'd go through their scrap area. I was looking for a medium density foam, but on the soft side, and there was a grading system of four-digit numbers, but I would go in there and just squeeze and say, oh, this is good. The medium density that would be used in a couch cushion is too firm for what I do. And I want the movement in the foam. There's a super soft foam that I don't use, but this is a soft medium density foam I get. I'd go there every year or two or as needed and buy blocks of this foam.

JB: Are you dying it or painting it?

HF: Well, some people dye it, like Grey Seal. Drew Alison and Donald Devet. They would dye their foam. I think in the washing machine. They were using sheet foam. I was using blocks of foam. And what I was doing was spraying it with water, lightly, and then staining it with acrylics. I get the acrylics out of the tube, not the bottles and it comes out like toothpaste. And I mix it down to more like heavy syrup with water. Not to where it was too watery but get it a little less pasty and then spraying the foam with water spray bottle, wetting it down to maybe an eighth of an inch deep or so, and then rubbing it to distribute the water. And then, I would pick up the paint brush, get rid of any big globs (of paint on) it and then try to get it on (the foam) very evenly. Then after I covered the whole thing, if it was all going to be green let's say, then I would massage it with my hands just to get it smooth. And then if there was a lighter area, I could mix, you know, adjust it and when it was the right color, I would get a hair blow-dryer and rubbing it with one hand and drying with the other hand, I would dry the foam thoroughly and press and make sure there's no water, no color came out. Let's say I'm doing an Orca whale and I have very precise boundaries. Those are hard to do. With this, I would start with the foam without wetting it and just establish that edge, and have a kind of watery paint, but not too watery to spread. Then I would spray the area beyond that, that I wanted to fill in with the same color and then do all of that and then completely dry that, being very careful when I'm rubbing it as I'm drying it, not to spread it into the white area where I want to paint another color. An orca would be black and then these white patches, and I could keep them very distinct. But I dry each one before I move on to the next color. Okay.

JB: Does the foam actually absorb the dye?

HF: Foam rubber actually will absorb the color. You can snip through it and it'll be solid. Whatever color you're painting.

JB: What are you using to shape the foam with? Razor blades? Scissors? Let's talk about the actual tools you use. You take these large pieces of foam and you chop them up into sculpted animals. And of course you have to cut away large sections in some places and then you have fine work in other places. The tools must vary.

HF: Well first, some people do use straight edge razor blades and it's a way to do it. Well I learned woodcarving, where if you want to carve a bird, (you) learned from a bird carver. Appalachian bird carver. You draw a profile of the bird and then you cut that out on the band saw. When I visited the Muppets, they were using jigsaws that were like industrial electric meat knives, so to speak. And I think the one big regret that I have in my career now that I'm 42 years into it, is that I never invested in a good one of those. I thought, oh, that's expensive, I'll just buy a $20 meat carving knife. So, I use an electric meat knife and at a certain point the blade gets dull and you just throw it away and get a new meat knife. It was hard to get the blades and it was kind of a disposable tool. So I cut the profile out and then I would cut the front view. And so, if I had a five-foot blue whale, I'd have that carved down looking pretty much like a whale in about 20 minutes, all with the meat knife. What the Muppets used were little Fiskars fine points (scissors). I would get Fiskars fine points. Now I buy other scissors that just have the adjustable screw and then I'll file my own fine point on to them on a belt sander or something, when they become dull. Those are fabric scissors and carving foam's a little rough on them and you're compromising a Fiskars fine point eventually. You know how you would rub two butcher knives together and that actually sharpens them up? I do that with cheap scissors, and you can sharpen up a scissor really quick. Now, some would be horrified if they were fabric scissors, but this is foam carving scissors! Now at this stage of carving a five-foot whale, I'd carve for two days almost, to get it down to where it was fairly smooth. I have a good belt sander and so I can do a little bit of belt sanding, but for the most part, the puppets are carved 99, 98% with scissors. I could do a little foot and a half long dolphin in about four hours, finish the whole puppet. The carving could be like a couple of hours. A larger fancier puppet, with a lot of detail. It could take longer. I took a little six-inch piece of foam, about an inch by an inch, by six inches, and spent two weeks carving on it, just carrying it with me wherever I'd go. And I carved a little dragon with every scale on it, in detail, and I still have that. So, you can put a lot of detail in the foam. I don't cover it. Most people cover their foam with a fabric, but that defeats the purpose of what I'm doing. Most of my puppets would be animals, not always, but they'd be animals. The beauty of the foam was because it has a matte surface. It doesn't reflect light. It moves really nicely. As soon as you put fabric on it, you're putting an adhesive in there, the movement's going to (suffer), then you get wrinkles and crinks and creases in it. But at the same time, these puppets get torn uneasy. They can get dents in them. That will come out usually naturally. I can repair them to a degree, but they are disposable puppets. A little butterfly might last me a year or two and then I'll need to make another one. A Dolphin will last me five, six, seven years. An otter will last me ten, twelve years.

JB: You've gotten to the point where the stuff is not precious. It's a work tool. It's a work tool and tools degrade over time.

HF: Disposable. And it's worth it to me to get that effect and when this puppet has just had it, I'll then repair it, repaint it, get it just pristine looking as I can and then I'll use it. I'll put it in in my shop attic and I'll save it for exhibits. Or if one gets damaged and I don't have the time. I can grab the other one and go perform with it. But generally, they wear out and they're done.

JB: How do you go about mounting the rods? There must be different techniques for different puppets. How do you mount and secure a rod inside something like a large whale?

HF: There are two orientations that I use, vertical rods coming up from the bottom or horizontal rods. We'll talk about that differentiation later. So, on the whale it's a vertical rod going in a third into the whale, sort of at the back of the crease of its mouth, let's say it's a blue whale. I get a [wooden] dowel. For a five-foot whale, I would use probably a ¾"inch dowel and I would cut it vertically in half, for about four inches, so it's a half round and it has a flat surface. And then I'll get a piece of Luan [¼" plywood] and I'll glue and screw it onto that, like a ping pong paddle. So, I've got a rod with a ping pong paddle on it. Then I'll cut a slice in the whale as deep as I want it. And then I'll use a foam rubber spray adhesive.

JB: What are you using? Super 74? Super 77?

HF: Yes, I think it's 77. There's some off-brands that I use more now, because they're just cheaper and they work well. Then I'll glue that in there. You really have to kind of open it up and get it down in there. I make sure I get it all the way in. Once it sticks, it's hard to get it undone. There's a little play in that. Then the back rod will go toward the last third of the puppet. It will come up vertically through the puppet, before the tail, the fluke. Then I need a wire to go up to the fluke, to pull it down a little bit. I need a little more pull, so I'll go down the rod, about halfway down, and attach a wire that's going to go up diagonally toward the tail. And where it's glued in the tail, I'll make a wire loop, forming a two-inch circle and I'll wrap that with gaffer's tape, because it's just more stable. And then I'll just glue it in the exact same way. Then that it has that gluing surface. You need a gluing surface, just a stick is not going to do it. And if I'm doing a little foot and a half long dolphin, I'll do something really similar. I won't just have the dowel glued in there. I'll make a little paddle on the to where it has some gluing surface area. So, getting to the horizontal Rod. Instead of coming up from the bottom of the dolphin, like with the rods into the bottom of the whale, I'll come in sideways horizontally. Something I discovered. Originally, I did them all vertically and then I experimented one time where I needed it to come in sideways for sightlines and I found out that it worked better for some animals to come sideways. I found that I could make a more realistic movement. Imagine drawing two circles in the air, a foot diameter circle with your fingers in the air. Bring both fingers up to the top of the circle and then bring one finger down to the bottom of the other circle. The other fingers at the top of the circle, and now keep rotating in the same direction. And now they've changed places. That ratio of movement is in every mammal. And I discovered it kind of kinesthetically and then I heard on NPR a story that all mammals have that ratio of movement in their body, all four-legged animals. We had it when we were apes. When we stood up, that changed it. When I go to operate a human being [puppet], everything is different. And that's because we stood up and I find that kind of interesting. On a dolphin, a whale, an otter, um, a lion running, the body, the spine is moving in that same way. So, if you take a little piece of foam and do that same sort of carving, except instead of making a foot and a half long dolphin, make it seven inches long and use bamboo skewers instead of dowel rods and go in sideways, about halfway through. Just hot glue it in there. And put one rod a third of the way through the body horizontally and then one back toward the tail and do that movement, it works perfectly. If I made a cat and I put one rod in at the base of its tail, one rod in its head, one rod to each paw in the front, and then in the back I can just put one rod through one leg, all the way through it into the next leg, and glue all those points and then hold them like two sticks in each hand and do that same movement, but now kick out the legs a little bit as they're going, twisting my wrist as well as going in the circles, it will make an animal lope along like a lion would walk, you know, bounding.

JB: Have you studied any of the Eadweard Muybridge stop-motion films that showcase movement?

HF: No, I learned just by accident. It was just 42 years of puppet making and making the same kind of puppet.

JB: Some puppeteers' movements are more natural than the others. Your work is particularly fluid.

HF: I could spend a half an hour with a puppeteer doing animals and get a lot of things cleared up.

JB: Many of your shows feature stories about the natural world that seem to be about our lack of awareness of the part we play in its health. Even though your show Sea Song is about a little boy, really it's about the little boy's rediscovery and integration back into the natural world. A world that had been lost to him because of his dependence on his cell phone.

HF: When I was growing up, my mom was a bird watcher. And we would go on vacation to Florida, we'd go to the beach for an hour or two, and then we were off to a swamp, out in nature. And we camped out most summers. We'd spend a good half of the summer camping out. I had a real good exposure to nature and then synchronistically in 1978, when I started getting interested in foam rubber, I was listening to the music of Paul Winter and his music is inspired by nature and even has animal calls. I love the album Common Ground. And, and so my first show back in 1982-or-3 was a show called Wizard of the Wind. It was basically about pollution and how it's hurting animals and the planet and whatnot. I used that music as my soundtrack and got permission from him. Then I branched out into other shows and experimented with other things and there was usually an animal or two in them, but eventually, I got into folktales and whatnot. In the last ten years, the whole issue of cultural appropriation has really come to the front. And after I moved away from Nevada, living with native Americans, Jim Henson gave me a Henson Foundation grant and I did native American stories. It was called Turtle Island Tales. It was shadow puppetry. I just did the last performance of it. I phased it out a long time ago, but I stopped performing it this year. I decided I wasn't going to do that anymore, because the bar had changed of what we can do with other people's cultures, ethically. And now there's a higher standard about borrowing. You know, we as puppeteers do everything ourselves. So, we're always doing external things. It was different because I was a white person telling native American stories. I'm not native American. I'm trying to do less and less of that. So now in the last several shows, I've gone back to the natural world as my basis because there's plenty there to work with them then I'm not right. You know, I'll still do folktales here and there, but I'm trying to veer away from that and just do the natural world.

JB: This is an issue that concerns many in our community. Being a practicing Buddhist, I've often thought it would be nice to do a puppet series of the Jataka Tales [a series of children's stories about the Buddha's pre-enlightenment lives). I've wondered if this would be controversial as these stories originated in south-eastern India. Where and how do we draw those lines? And who gets to draw them?

HF: Well, here's the issue. My wife is a music teacher and her expertise is Zimbabwean music. She's a white woman. Their private school got an equity director. And part of what they did was talk about cultural appropriation. In an educational setting, every teacher must teach native American history or native American culture. They have to cover it. You know, maybe it's just Thanksgiving and you know, uh, we're at November, you know, this native American month and they've got to teach that. And so you can't expect them not to teach history. But here's the thing, if you can give it first a context saying I'm going to tell you a Buddhist story or a native American story and I'm not native American. and we're going to tell the Cherokee story and this is where the Cherokees lived here. And you would probably be using a book and you're giving it context, but if you go 30 years ago to a puppet festival, you could see a white guy get up there with a little crepe paper headband and a feather coming out and be very offensive dressing up like a native American. That's not right. I can tell an Italian story. I can tell an Asian story. A black man can dress up like an Indian in New Orleans because they're not oppressing that other culture. We're not oppressing the Chinese. It's not an issue with them. But it is an issue with Native Americans. They do not want us telling their stories. They want to tell their stories themselves.

JB: It's good to see these issues being raised in the community.

HF: John Bell posted this very issue. He said, does anyone know of any academic papers on cultural appropriation in the world of puppetry and no one did. But we all started a conversation and I said, I'm doing my last show of Native American stories tomorrow. And there were two puppeteers who got very upset, very upset. What do you mean, why are you doing that? But he's coming from a place of privilege. They have not read Howard Zinn's (A People's) History (of the United States).

JB: Talking about these issues is something that actually we should do in a larger context in the field of puppetry, at another time, with more people because as performers, as people who carry culture, especially to children, we bear acute responsibility for helping to make a better world, if only through the spread of ideas.

HF: That could be, in the puppet world, somebody creating a puppet piece that is very sensitive, very inspiring, very positive, but deals with the issue in a way that people could hear it. I will perform for very conservative audiences and I know that if I do it the wrong way, they're going to pigeon hole me. If I do it in the right way, I come in sideways and I influence them and they feel open, because you opened them up with art and then you slip your message in. And then with a Cathartic story, it affects people. It has the power to change people. But the first step, it needs to almost be like a movie that everybody watches, you know, a movie made about this topic or a series that really addresses it in a way that people can hear it and, and just to where people get it because half the problem is they don't get the problem.

JB: This is true.

HF: First, they have to understand the problem and most people don't understand the problem.

JB: Talk about how Peepers came about.

HF: Okay. So, around 1986 I came up with the concept. Nothing comes out of a vacuum. Okay. So I had seen Yves Joly, his hand in a glove, with two ping pong balls on it, in George Latshaw's book from the Mid-Seventies. And that was, essentially, what a Peeper is. I've since seen a 1950s movie where an actress had rings on that had gems on them and did it. I contend that probably 10,000 years ago, sitting around the caves with walnuts on our hand or acorns and did it, because we were puppeteers, you know, before we had the wheel. Later, when I was challenged by other people who said they'd come up with the same, they didn't have patents. One had a really good utility patent. There's a guy named Mariotti, an Italian illustrator who would paint his hands. He had a book called Humands and he painted his hand like an orca whale, and they get a little plastic eye and slip it right in between a couple of fingers. Illustration after illustration, there was a conductor and a whole orchestra. And they're painted onto their fingers. I was fascinated with not just the Kermit the Frog "position" of using a puppet like that. I was interested in all the myriad ways that your hand can become a spider, could become an elephant, could become, a snake. And when I invented Peepers, my daughter wouldn't let you wash her hair, because she hated the shampoo dripping in her eyes. She was about three. I made a puppet to wash her hair with and it was a Peeper puppet. I made it with Friendly Plastic [https://www.amaco.com/t/mixed-media/friendly-plastic-pellets]. I made them not big, like ping pong balls and made them small. Then, I started experimenting in the different hand positions that you could use. And then, a friend would want one. I went to a festival in Oklahoma in late eighties and I brought 20 of them. And I took Jane Henson's manipulation workshop. I got in there and she was handing out ping pong balls on rubber bands. The Muppets would use that as a rehearsal tool in the board room. And I don't know where they saw that or if Jim came up with it or whatever. So, I put on my own Peepers and put my hand up and she just cracked up when she saw it. A friend of mine, Regina Marscheider who was doing puppet shows, anti-child abuse shows, really intense shows, she saw the work and she said, "Hey, you should do something with this." And I said, "Look, help me do it and I'll make you my partner." So, she went about getting a mold. We got a lawyer and got it patented, split the costs. And then we licensed it to a guy in Baltimore. He had a factory to make the puppet. And then before we even went into business, he said, "You know what, I've done some test marketing,

I'm not comfortable with this. I'm not going to do this." And I said, "Let me buy you out." So, I paid him $10,000. (I) got the mold and about 6,000 Peepers and went into business and I had it paid off in six months. So I bought it back and we had a patent and about six months after I got it, someone said, go down to the grocery store in Weaverville. Your puppet is in a gumball machine. And I realize I've been knocked off. I got lawyer, I got nowhere. And a guy called me up and said, I can get this under control, no upfront money. And he said, what we do is get you out of your contract with your lawyer. And he did that artfully and then said, we will sue every last importer in the United States. The other lawyer was going after the Chinese and he said, no, go after these big corporations. They do not like uncertainty. They will all settle with you. We'll split the money. And I never met the man. Everything he said he was going to do, he did. He got the thing under control. Then, about the time that my patent was expiring, the child safety laws just came in full on strong and the Chinese manufacturer pulled back at that time and now I'm just quitting peepers. I'm still selling the inventory I've got, but I'm not going to produce any more because the sales went down. I wasn't making enough of them to make the manufacturing of them affordable. If I were still making 30-40,000 of them a year, I'd be in business still, but it just no longer affordable. And it's a burden now as arts funding is going down, it's gotten harder to get that money together in a lump sum to have them manufactured. So I'm just done with it. Yeah. You know, I'll always have some, you know, the puppeteers could get some few of them, but yeah.

JB: You've gotten three Jim Hensen Foundation grants and received two UNIMA citations for Rainbow Bridge.

HF: No, I got one for Turtle Island Tales and then I got one indirectly when I built Jim Gambles, Peter and the Wolf show for him and it won a citation, so it was listed, but I only really got one citation of excellence. I don't think my best work got citations. It just frankly doesn't bother me. I have a funny relationship with UNIMA. I'll just say that I think only in the United States it's oriented to adult puppetry and they don't consider children's puppetry viable. 90% of the stuff they write about in the journal, it's all adult work. I felt like, I do children's work. I'm just not concerned with it anymore. Right. And I liked the people. At first, I made a big Brouhaha, but I'm over it.

JB: You are known as a mechanism master. You're often spoken of in the same sentence with Jim Kroupa. And you don't have a mechanical engineering background. This is all stuff you've learned in the real world. Many of your mechanisms seem very intricate, they're delicate. Is all of this self-taught? Oh, and they're beautiful, too.

HF: Okay. I learned a lot of the principles of engineering from Clyde, in a very shade-tree sort of way. Things like metal and wood rub against each other and reduce friction. The metal starts to polish the wood, things like that. I learned a lot. Wood against wood is not great, if there's a lot of tight friction. I learned a lot of those principles and I learned how to carve. In my education work with the Kennedy Center, we'd look at multiple intelligences. What are your particular (type of) intelligences? I happened to be a visual/spatial learner and so sculpting is quite natural to me. Even before I knew how to do it, I had the potential to do it. Whereas another person who is an interpersonal or linguistic kind of learner, it might be like Mars to them to do engineering or sculpture. I feel like I have that natural ability with teaching. Those are three strong areas that I just happen to have naturally that make puppeteering really a great fit for me. I've noticed it in Geahk Burchill, out west. It comes natural to him. My grandfather was an engineer. He built the first sea-plane. He got the first license from the Wright brothers to build their patent. Starling Burgess. He designed three America's Cup boats. He built a Buckminster Fuller's three-wheel Dymaxion car for him in the 1930s. So, I did learn it and I did study it, but a lot of it came naturally. A lot of these controls, if I'm sitting around thinking, "how am I going to make this little fairy move?" I've got to make the control work and take a right-hand turn. Usually you just go straight down vertically from the puppet. Now I want to come in at a 90- degree angle. If I pose that question to myself, within 24 hours, the answer will pop into my head. And I've even dreamt controls that I was able to build the next morning, came in three dimensions. Yeah. It's just because that's the way my mind, the creator gave me that gift, so to speak, which is made for creating stories and plays.

JB: You've done two videos for the Avett brothers.

HF: They discovered my daughter in a coffee house playing guitar and said, "Get a band together. We want you to be our warm up band." So, when they came back east, I was her roadie for a week or so and I met them and showed them puppets. They put Peepers on their mics that night at the show in Atlanta. So, they needed some skeleton marionettes to do an homage to a Grateful Dead music video that had skeletons of the whole band playing. So, they called me a week before and said, "Can you make four skeleton marionettes next week?" I bought factory seconds of anatomical skeletons, took them apart and rejoined it. We couldn't determine how high up the bridges we're going to go because there was some communication issues, so I made the controls where you could wind the whole thing up on a fishing reel and make them three feet from the puppet or make them eight feet from the puppet. The video's called "Another Is Waiting." They ended up not building bridges. For a marionette bridge they said, "We have this tower, you can do them from there." And I said, "Yeah, and how are you going to make that tower disappear in the shot?" And they went, "Oh…." So everything had to be compromised. Grayson Morris, a puppeteer from Asheville, was my intern then and I got her a paid position to come with me and do the video. And she said, "Hobey, I know you're mad. Let's go with it. Say we'll try and we'll just do that." And we figured out a way to do it, but it was a huge compromise. I had to re-do stuff on-the-spot and they realized how hard we worked. So, Scott Avett said, "Pick a song, deal directly with me." "Bring Your Love" was the song I chose and I did a shadow puppet music video of that. We shot all the shadow puppets on a screen and then we white screened them. We selected out the white and made it disappear and reversed it, plucked the shadows out and then plugged them into a software to where you have a virtual camera in the computer that can change angles and, and things in the background and foreground, middle ground and things will overlap as you move the virtual camera. So we did a live performance, then spent three weeks behind a computer with a motion graphics artists who then animated them into a virtual 3-D shadow world. And that's how we filmed that.

JB: You've been putting photos and videos of gorgeous puppet mechanisms on Facebook, is a book forthcoming?

HF: Yeah, so it's a book about rod puppet mechanisms. Mostly for smaller rod puppets, but it'll apply to larger ones. I started it in April and it's going to be ready for the July National Puppet Festival and I'm going to self-publish it. My deadline is to finish it by the end of May or mid-June. I'm going to make a digital book first. I thought I'd make a soft cover book, but now I'm going to do an affordable digital book. And then I'm going to make a really nice hardcover book, a small coffee table kind of book. When I posted that I was doing the book about 500 people said, "I want a copy," but all over the world. The digital book will be a solution to sending it to India or to Uzbekistan or something. Lulu, which is the company I'm considering, publish in Asia and then Europe. And my understanding is the shipping will be cheaper. It will come out of Europe and go to Europe and then we won't be sending it overseas, but I will bring probably 300 books to the national festival this year. That's my goal. It's all illustrated instead of photographs because I feel like I can be clearer with an illustration. Where does that little hole go to? It's hard to do with photos. Yeah. And, and, and more expensive. I go into it and spend most of the time just making that drawing beautiful, but also understandable.

JB: You're giving a workshop at the national festival this year. Tell us about that.

HF: Okay. The workshop will be basically what the book is about, rod puppet mechanisms. That's the name of it. The workshop's going to be directly supporting the book. It's just drawn from the very same material. What are the principles involved in making a mechanism? There's a control, there's linkage, there's return springs, there's friction. It's how to deal with all those things, materials for a puppeteer that work really well in solving those problems. Cable systems, whether it be a roto-rooter cable from Lowe's with a cable going through it or whether it be a plastic drip tube with nylon going through or a cable for model airplanes, all of that kind of thing. So, I'll be showing them the principles and really how to think about making mechanisms. That's a big thrust in the book, how do you even approach a mechanism? I want something to happen way over here, but I'm over here and I can't be seen and it's got to go down here and then take a left hand turn and go that way.

JB: We're going to really be looking forward to the book. Thank you for your time today, Hobey.

HF: Thank you.

OLE and INGRID COWAN HASS

JB: Let's talk about your early education in music because both of you are fine musicians. You both have a Master's Degrees in opera. Ingrid, could you go first? Talk a little bit about your childhood and going to college and getting your degree.

Ingrid Cowan Hass: So, I started piano lessons when I was seven, maybe six, can't remember. And I had violin when I was 11 and played those two instruments throughout high school in the orchestra. In college I also played in the orchestra and started voice lessons at the end of high school. As a young person I was mostly outside because I grew up in a very rural area in North Carolina.

JB: Where'd you grow up in North Carolina?

ICH: I was born in Rutherfordton, it's sort of the foothills near Asheville, and I spent a lot of time outside listening to the music of nature. But I was also involved with our community arts council and did a lot of musical theater with them and singing. And so I was always performing as a child and a young adult in my teenage years, did a lot of Shakespeare. And when I discovered singing, like taking lessons, the thought of doing opera was very exciting because it kind of combined all that. The violin was so tedious, and I love drama, but then to sing and do drama together was really, inspiring to me. And I started taking voice lessons seriously in college. I went to Smith College in Massachusetts, which is not known for its singing necessarily, but it was a great school, great music school there. I was in Germany my junior year abroad.

Ole Hass: You majored there in visual arts.

ICH: I majored in painting, so I have to say that my entire life has been kind of a pole between visual and music. And Smith didn't have a core curriculum, so I was able to study as much music and art as I wanted and that's what I did. I majored in studio art and I minored in music and I studied lots of German and I went abroad to Germany and I went all over Europe. And saw all the art I wanted to see and went to the opera and the symphony all the time. And that's where I met Ole. I also started really studying with a teacher there that I liked and had told my parents of course that I wouldn't stay long. It wasn't all about Ole. And I went back to get my Master's at the North Carolina School of the arts in opera. Turned out that I wasn't really that great of an opera singer. I was kind of mediocre, but I was great on stage. So I ended up, when we moved here doing more, you know, like Operetta, like with The Washington Savoyards and kind of Avant Garde opera with the In-series. So there was a lot of English translations. My debut opera role in DC was Cherubino, but it was set in the late sixties in Las Vegas. And I played a hippie. It's quite a physical role, because the Cherubino is a "pants" role [editor's note: also known as a trouser or breeches role, in which an actress appears in male clothing, usually playing a younger male character]. I sing a lot of young boys because I'm tall and I'm a mezzo soprano. That's kind of what I did. And it wasn't lucrative by any means. It was a lot of fun. We didn't have kids at the time. We had a church job and we pulled stuff together that way. When we had kids, it got hard because you would just rehearse and rehearse and rehearse at night and not get paid much. On top of that, to be a good singer, you have to have a coach and a teacher and they're expensive when you reach a certain level. So a lot of our money that we were making was going right back out into getting really good coaching so that we would get hired again. It just didn't make much sense to really be an opera singer anymore. Besides opera, we did a lot of church gigs and there's so much chorus work, not singing the chorus, but doing solo work for chorus. So, you know, it's more like a classical singer. Opera is what we did somewhat, but not completely. We made most of our money not doing opera. And also I taught piano. I've been teaching piano for 20 years and that is an income I can count on. Little kids coming once a week and it's fun. And I love the one on one work. This is a wonderful thing. I love it. That's basically it.

JB: And Ole, you have a doctorate in musical arts from UMD. Tell us about your early life.

OH: I grew up on the somewhat outskirts of Hamburg in a former working class environment, right close to the metro station. I'm from a working-class family. My father was a boat builder, but worked most of his life as a carpenter because there was more money in that.

I think more than half of the men in my family were plumbers. My mother was a tax advisor. She had been put on the intellectual track by her father and so I always had this dual thing going on in my family. Have a very word oriented and a very hands-on oriented view of life. There was no music in my family at all. I mean, my father sang at work and my mother sang songs with us sometimes, but there was no sense of, you should be taking music lessons and you should be learning this. And you go to school and you come home and you play and you don't get into trouble and then you're fine. But in second grade a classmate invited me to join the boys choir. He was already a member and he took me to an audition. We took the metro downtown to Saint Michael's Cathedral and I auditioned by singing some children's song. And from then on, sang four times a week at St Michael's Cathedral. I got to sing mostly the Sunday services, but sometimes also with the adult choir, with soloists from all over Germany, Hermann Prey, (Dietrich) Fischer-Dieskau, Christa Ludwig, it's… incredible. But I never had any music education even through that and it was just the exposure and just doing it there. I didn't decide to study music seriously. Oh, I played guitar actually for a while and through that learned more and more what it actually meant to do daily practice and really tried to hone a skill. And you know how hard it is to get to actually make music on a guitar once you get past, you know, strumming a few chords?

JB: It is a discipline. It is a practice.

OH: It's really something that you just have to get through it, and have you taken care of your fingernails? and all this stuff. I originally planned to study biochemistry. I was going to be a gene technologist, but then decided to study voice and become a singer, not necessarily to be an opera singer. I was really thinking of the big German Lieder repertoire and of all the church music that I had been exposed to already, I was going to be an evangelist. Singing the evangelist part and Bach's big oratorios. Then I met Ingrid and decided to come with her to America to get my Master's in opera because that's where you get to learn every aspect, you know, from makeup and stage combat and acting and how to dress and how to walk and how to take care of your body.

ICH: We once had to duel in an opera and it was pretty cool cause I was a boy. He was trying to take my girl!

JB: Were you successful?

OH: Do you mean did I die or no?

ICH: I don't remember how it ended. It was like a four hour opera! No, did you want her?

OH: No actually, you [Ingrid] were interested in the woman I was betrothed to, but then the woman who I had tried to kill showed back up and she was the one who I was really in love with. It's written by a twelve-year-old Mozart…

ICH: …and the plot was not the strength. Keep going. Sorry, didn't mean to interrupt.

OH: So, we were in North Carolina for a number of years, got married during that time and then decided to come up here to this area for me to study at the University of Maryland. They gave me a full ride. They paid me to be here for four years. It was fabulous. We found this lovely little town home right around the corner from here. Then a few years after I finished the degree, found this place, which is so much nicer for evening practice because we don't scare away the neighbors when we open our mouth.

ICH: On Sunday morning, we had to get up really early and warm up and that was not good for our neighbor in the town home. Singing opera scales and stuff.

OH: I think he actually had a bit of a nervous condition. He was a musician himself ironically, but he would play his saxophone into the closet. Nobody could hear him, but as soon as you made any kind of noise, he would leave the house. Yeah, that was too bad, but this has worked out really well.

JB: I know you both love gardening by the raised beds in front of your home.

ICH: There are other houses that have raised beds that are just not right in the front.

OH: Ingrid's parents are both great gardeners. Ingrid's mother is more into flowers and her father more into vegetables, but they have a vast knowledge of native and non-native plants and both have green thumbs, no question, so there was a lot of nature appreciation, of knowing the bird songs and knowing what the snakes and the frogs looked like and what they are and which ones to leave alone and which ones to play with. That's something that I didn't get at all as a child. I rode my bike a lot and I liked nature, but that's different from actually putting your hands on everything and walking around barefoot.

JB: How long have you been married?

OH: Twenty-three years this year.

JB: When did you start working with puppetry?

OH: After we had children, [Felix and Cecilia] because that somewhat changed our perspective. We got married while we were in Grad school, so through that and my doctorate and then a number of years after that we were really, really focused on having a career as singers and exposing ourselves to the scene and auditioning everywhere and getting better. We were both rather well known in the area, not nationally, but in the area.

ICH: And famous for our German pronunciation.

OH: So, once we had children, we connected a little bit more to our neighborhood here, which is a beautiful community that we had somewhat insulated ourselves from, being so focused on our career. And suddenly we met other people, other parents our age and other little children. There was a little German group. They were four or five families of Germans or at least half Germans like us. And we would organize these meetings where we would then put on shows for the children….

ICH: ...play dates in German...

OH: …two little puppet show for these little children and they were the version of the mitten and the Grimm fairy tale about the shoe maker. And that was a beautiful experience.

ICH: There's also one other thing, because I'm a knitter too…fiber works, obviously. And I made dozens of hand puppets with crazy yarn that I had spun, and I gave it to all my friends who were having babies, right? So, we ended up with three or four and we called them the monsters. We had names for them, and they only spoke German, because I didn't want to speak German in the house all the time. It was too hard for me to think in German when I was living in English. So, my mother tongue is English, but the monsters would speak German with my kids and we would play, read books and do all sorts of games with the monsters to practice German when he [Ole] wasn't home. And so the puppets became part of our family.

JB: Do you still have the puppets?

ICH: I do. I can get them out of the freezer.

JB: In the freezer?

ICH: It's just that they just got eaten by moths.

OH: Yeah, they're still around. Felix said that he would not speak German unless required, "I'm in America, I'm an American. I speak English, but the puppet is German and I will speak German to the puppet."

ICH: And then once his [their son Felix] little sister was a toddler and I got the puppets out, he would start speaking to the puppets in German as a five year old or four year old or however old he was and the three of us would talk in German with the puppet. My mother's Latvian. And she never taught me a word because she said, well, I came here and this is my new country and we speak English. Why would I teach my children my mother tongue? I grew up listening to my mom talk on the phone to her mother in Latvian and not knowing what she was talking about. But if I heard Latvian anywhere, I would know, because of that.

JB: So, it was that first little puppet show that you did in German, for this group, that eventually inspired the creation of Beech Tree Puppets.

OH: I think that was a very, very important experience towards that.

There were a number of people, when we were in this classical singing world, who knew us well and we're very involved in opera and were thinking about what people were doing and talking about opera all the time and networking, and we weren't quite into that. But some of them would say to us, “You two. You are so good at so many different things. You're going to have your own opera company at some point.” And in a way, we don't like to tell other people what to do. You know, we like to stay on our own turf and do our own thing. So, having a puppet company allows us to do the whole gesamtkunstwerk. We are in charge of the text, of the music, of the set, of the staging of the…

ICH: …the timing…

OH: ...the timing, the stage movements…

ICH: …the jokes…

OH: Everything! And when our performers are done, they get put back in the box! They don't get paid much!

ICH: They don't have to be fed or talked to, there are no contracts! And so that's really special, doing this just between the two of us. I'm looking at this cow that's half made here. We're having trouble with how, with four hands, how are we going to get a cow and Jack walk across without the cow falling over? And you know, I'll look at it, I'll show Ole. We have so much back and forth. I could never make anything without him. Although he says I make everything, but without his input nothing would be made.

OH: She does make everything.

ICH: Yeah, so it's very fulfilling. We performed together a lot before we became puppeteers. We would put on recitals, joint recitals, and we would even stage them like a cycle that usually one person would sing, with however many songs. We would split them up and make it into a scena [mini opera] and a story. And by the end of the twenty minutes, you know, there was some sort of conclusion. And we would make props. We made a big clock once, I don't even remember why! You were serenading me at midnight or something. But anyway, we have a lot of experience working together and I think that's also what would appeal to us about doing the puppets because it was fun. I know when he's going to breathe. If I forget a line, he knows that I'm going to say something that will somehow get us through and I know he'll pick me up. I can trust him, we breathe together and not just because we're sung together, but because we know how we think.

JB: Performance does that, it tends to entrain the mind, if you're performing with a group of people and if you've done it enough and you trust, it's like an organism. If the organism is not working correctly, the performance often fails.

ICH: I can remember in The Gondoliers we came on to the stage and we're doing this big number, with really complicated choreography while singing, but we needed the sofa and it was not there. Somehow it didn't get put on stage. And the scene had started and I don't know how Ole did it, but he got that sofa on stage in time.

OH: I was also playing the servant. So you know, I could

say that was my job in the first place.

ICH: I wasn't looking at him at all the whole time and suddenly there's this sofa! I'm just saying that I trust him. I mean, he makes things happen.

JB: How long did it take for you guys from the point of starting with the initial idea until you actually had your first full-blown show? What was the process of going from point A, which was that first show for the kids, to point B, which would be, you're actually working on your first professional show and you're serious about taking it someplace?

ICH: Okay, so this is what happened. Our children went to a preschool where they did puppetry in the classroom and it was very artful, and we got to see a show or two and we were really inspired by that particular type of puppetry. Then Ole quit his job, which was a great thing, and I said, “Let's start a public company!” Like the day after he quit his job. And he said, “okay.”

OH: I want to say that we did our first show the winter after Cecilia was born, I think she was a little baby. This would have been in winter of 2008 or early 2009 and I quit my job a good three years after that. Felix was starting first grade at our local elementary school in 2012 and on the first parent meeting, the teacher reached out and said, "We have a third or a quarter of an art teacher for our school. There was one art teacher who visits three or four schools and your child will have an art lesson four times a year and if any of you is willing to come in and do art with the children, I will make time and space for that in this classroom."

ICH: Which started a whole other career for me.

OH: That was also part of the thinking. What do we have to give here? And I think that also leads us in this direction of why are we trying to do so many school performances, especially in Prince George's County. Because that's really what we think we have to give.

ICH: Well let me just say that I had been doing projects in the school for a few years and I teach. A mentor who had been doing art in the schools for many decades taught me how to write grants, so I wrote a very small local grant and I won it for our puppet show that we were going to do - we didn't have a puppet show and there was a deadline. So that was when Felix was in first grade. And I actually made two shows. We did Butterfly Wonder and we did The Crystal Ball. The Crystal Ball was the first.

OH: Felix started first grade when he was seven. And the fall of 2012, that's when you were applying for the grant. That's when we were starting to plan the show. We performed it at the end of that school year in May 2013.

ICH: And that was our first show. And we performed for every single grade separately in the library. It was like a scientific experiment. I remember the very first performance. We set it up and there's like a hundred little bodies coming in and they're all sitting down on the carpet. And then this teacher says, "It's okay if the preschoolers come in too, right?" And then 40 more. And we're like, what have we done? What were we thinking? I mean, I remember the fear that just shot through my body. Like there are too many little children in this room and we don't know what we're doing. Anyway, we started off with a very calm song and the chime and as soon as I did the first chime and started singing, they didn't move for 30 minutes and we thought...

OH: …it's amazing, yeah.

ICH: How did that happen? It often happens and we try to create this mood and pull the children in. We don't do loud performances, so they have to participate and come to us. And we're like, okay, there's something to this, and we were hooked.

JB: You've received grants from other organizations to build your shows. I want to talk a little bit about the grant process. Let's talk about doing grants and building shows.

IGH: That is a little boring. I mean writing a grant is really not practical with the amount of time you actually spend writing a grant and the amount of money you get, it's not really worth it. Let me back up and say that's not completely true. It's not like it's not worth it, because we definitely get credentials and we build our grant history. The more little grants you get means that eventually can get a bigger grant because you have proven yourself. Look, I won this, this and this and I followed through and they kept giving me money because they like my projects.

OH: So, to go back to the first sentence, the first number of grants often have a really bad relationship between the number of hours you put into applying for the grant and the money that comes back out of it. There are certainly big grants that can really fund you for a whole year, but we're talking about three-hundred, four-hundred, five-hundred dollar grants for which you spend two weeks in the basement writing.

ICH: I'm obviously much better at writing grants now, than I was at the beginning. So, you get better at it and you also learn. You make contacts with certain people and you know that they're going to get you money, most likely. I don't reinvent the wheel now. When I write for certain grants, there are certain projects that are very popular at the school and I know that they want it, I'll write a grant for it and I'll get more money. It's also strategic. You can't always ask for the same thing. You have to kind of rotate your projects.

JB: The way you're explained it is very good, because I think people should know that the process can be a little daunting in the beginning. Even if it is a lot of work for a small grant, it does set you up for getting better grants and more money.

ICH: And the grants enabled me to go into the school officially, and it was in a way, my laboratory, because I kind of started developing these similar projects where there would be a performance and then directly after, making puppets with the kids, so they got to tell the story after seeing a professional do it. And then I started interweaving curriculum, like metamorphosis for example, (where) the kids are studying the life cycle of the butterfly. So, I do my twenty minutes show in the classroom, then the kids make their little butterfly and caterpillar and cocoon and leaf, and we all practice making them come to life and growing. And we tell the story again with puppets, simple puppets, but the kids are so excited about it. You can teach anything with a puppet.

OH: Yes. There's also a follow up to that. When we officially formed Beech Street puppets, we were wondering what kind of a legal entity that should be. And a friend of ours who used to be a lawyer pointed us to some literature and we ended up forming an LLC, limited liability company that also had something to do with the meeting we had with Michael Cotter from Blue Sky Puppets who said, "You know, a nonprofit 501(c)3 is all fine and good, but what I decided to do in these thirty years, twenty-five years," that he's been doing Blue Sky Puppets, was to (form an LLC and) just sell (his) shows and just do them and, and go full for-profit and, I think he probably got some grants at some point, but for the most part, he just does not do grants. (He's) developing a product and selling the product, and to a great extent that works for us, too. Because that's what we want to do. We want to take it to the schools. So we kind of have that perspective of us being a for-profit organization. On the other hand, it's also clear that it's life and it's bread and butter, right? We live in Prince George's county and we really would like to take our shows all around here. We make most of our puppets multicultural, so that this very diverse community here in Prince George's county has a chance of recognizing themselves in the puppets when they see the show. But we also realize that the budget for extra-curricular activities is much smaller here than it is in Montgomery County or other counties. And most of the work that comes to us is outside the county. So, in that respect I would love to see some kind of grant money allowing us to do these shows for less here, but we haven't figured out how to word that and set that up and what kind of money to fish for. And I think that the money is there and I think the interest is there. But we're just happy that we're getting our shows together at this point.

ICH: Someone once told us about a grant opportunity for the Baltimore school system and it was something like $75,000 and we were thinking we'll contact Head Start and we'll do shows for every single preschool in Baltimore County and meet with them several times and make puppets or something, but we were just not ready for that size grant. And I think now we're getting more ready for that.

JB: You have six shows with a new one on the way. The Crystal Ball, The Giant Turnip, The Hollow Stump, Rainbow Crow Brings Daylight, The Apple Tree, Butterfly Wonder. You like to highlight relationships in the natural world.

ICH: Well, nature definitely is my main source of inspiration and I do also a lot of workshops with gardening with children. So, I just can't get away from growing things. I mean look, Jack and the Beanstalk's the next show! There's going to be a beanstalk number where we make music while the beanstalk grows!

OH: And just to support that, Butterfly Wonder and The Giant Turnip are the two shows that are 90% Ingrid that she really put most of the work into and was the main visionary of what that would be like and what that was about. Not saying that I didn't have a ton of fun building the set for The Giant Turnip and of course I'm a 50% participant in performing it, but this whole idea of what this is actually about and how this will all be set up and in writing the script. Usually I have much more of a hand in the writing the script and writing the music. This was all Ingrid and this is the nature thing that she just has this big connection to.

ICH: Well, there's also a garden sprite in it too, but we don't plant the seed in that show until 15 minutes or 20 minutes into the show. I mean, we're preparing the garden. There's a whole song about planting the seeds. We meet the worms.

OH: Change of seasons. Change of weather.

ICH: There's a rainstorm.

OH: And then the other half of that is relationships, right? I think that's a big item in our shows too, of how people treat each other. There's a certain civility that we try to establish, which maybe just expresses us that we are usually civil with each other. If you do plot writing without conflict, there's no plot. You know, you have to have some obstacle to get over to have the story be about something. But that doesn't mean that you have to fight the person standing next to you.

ICH: I feel like kids aren't outside like they used to be and it's so important to me. So I like to show them and celebrate even just a rainstorm for example, or the change of day to night, we make that into a number, and we make the moon go away and then the stars come up.

OH: And that's the way that we pay attention to it happening. So, here comes the prop sun and it's - did we honor it as it happens? Because if we don't, then how can the audience?

ICH: But for me, it goes one step further and that that's my inspiration. Then I want it to be beautiful. Not Saccharin beautiful. I just mean beautiful colors, rich. Something that feeds the soul of the audience. So, I see it as the story or the subject matter being a wholesome story, nourishing image and sounds. We want those children who are taking it in so deeply, they're like sponges and I feel responsible to give them beautiful imagery that nourishes them.

OH: For children, all sense perceptions are food.

JB: Do your shows ever get dark or scary? Do they venture into that territory?

ICH: From my perspective, if we're discussing Jack for example, how scary is the giant going to be? How ugly is he going to be? I want him to be ugly. I mean, he represents greed. He's not the hero and I'm not afraid of evil. I don't want the evil to be watered down like Disney often does. You know, kids think in black and white. So, it's not that I'm afraid of ugly, but the way I make it, he's still is, I don't want to say beautiful, but yeah. I don't know how you feel about it.

JB: Let's talk more in-depth about how you go about developing your ideas.

OH: First thing is always find the right story. Which means we kind of figure out what subject or what cultural realm and it just involves reading lots and lots and lots and lots of stories. We usually use a preexisting story. I think part of Butterfly Wonder is the only exception to that. Then we talk about different stories, like eight different stories or so. Then we talk about whether we like the story, what aspects the story he has, what it means to us…

ICH: …how are we going to do that part of the story physically…

OH: …if it's actually possible for us to turn that story into a puppet show…

ICH: …with four hands! And so some that we like may be on the back burner. And then we finally, finally pick one that we're going to work on and then what do we do? Find different versions.

OH: Then we decide what kind of a show it's going to be. If it's going to be marionettes, if it's going to be a rod puppets.

ICH: We talk in the car when he's driving and can't get away. And I take my notepad and I'm like, okay, let's talk about this show. Like, so if we do it like this, how big will the cow be? How big will the puppets be? How big will the house be? To just get simple dimensions, cause I'm not gonna make anything until we have some basic things in place and agree on them. We usually talk for about six months to a year after we've chosen a story.

OH: We often say that it takes us about a year to make a story and it's probably only the last two or three months of that, that are really building and working, and making it happen. The first nine months are conceptualizing and just agreeing on the proportions, on the concept of how this whole thing can actually work out. Making rough drafts of a script, coming up with what scenes we're actually going to have. Are we going to write our own music? Are we going to just find folk songs and write new texts for it?

ICH: Then I'll say, "So, this is the way we're going to set it up." And he'll say, "Oh, okay." Then we draw another picture after we talk and then I'm like, "Ole, are you going to write the script? You gonna write the script, you gonna write this script?" And so, I learned that I have to write the script even if it's terrible. Like from what we've talked about, I sit down and I write whatever, stream of consciousness. And then I give it to him and then he writes it. Because the first show, he wouldn't write it and he wouldn't write it, and I got so frustrated waiting! I thought it would be better to just write a script and then of course he changed it and it was all fine. I learned, oh, that's how I do it is to write at first, so he'll have something to react to and of course it's modified, edited even after we've performed it.

JB: If you write original music for it, how does that come together?

ICH: He does it, mostly.

JB: Do you write on guitar, piano?

OH: I mostly write in my head. Since we are busy, holding the puppets. I don't even have to do four-part writing for the most part. It's just melodies that I write, with some concept of harmony in the background of that. We don't pre-record anything. The main two shows I've actually written music, The Hollow Stump and The Apple Tree. And for The Hollow Stump, we have seven animals that come to the stump and find shelter, the idea was to write a two-line melody for each animal that could be sung together with any of the others. And so, they all have a different character, but they all follow the same harmonic progression, sung in the same key, that could be all sung at the same time. You can sing it as a canon so that they interweave, and I thought even if there's only the two of us, we can show that the animals can all be there at the same time. And so, I came up with a two-liner for each of them and that worked pretty well. And for The

Apple Tree we decided to have only for those songs that I wrote, only pentatonic melodies. If you just play with those five notes you get a sense of the leading tone being missing and that helps that child not being pulled into this world quite as much.

JB: There's something fundamental about pentatonic scale structure that rings deeply in us. So many civilizations worldwide have used pentatonic scales.

ICH: We have a pentatonic recorder. And we also have a, what is that big one? Is that Pentatonic? [she picks up a large flute and begins to play]

JB: Wow, that's really beautiful. Where did you get it?

OH: Ugly Boy Flutes, North Carolina. [http://ww.uglyboyflutes.com]

ICH: This is a cedar stick and we can tell the students, the fifth graders or the fourth graders in the Q and A after, we bought this from a guy who loves Native American history and the forest was cut down and he went and made 200 flutes out of the trees, so the forest could sing.

JB: Let's talk about your new show, Jack and the Beanstalk. When did you decide to do this classic story? When did the process of Jack and Beanstalk begin?

ICH: I know that for several months we couldn't decide if we were going to do Jack next or a different one.

OH: By last summer, we knew.

ICH: When we go on vacation and we decide finally what we're going to do. I pack a whole suitcase filled with supplies and ideas, because the only time I get most of my work done is when I'm not a mother feeding my children and taking them to flute class and x, y, and z.

ICH: So, in Germany, I worked on the puppets and I wrote the script right before we left, so I would have an idea of what I was making.

JB: Are there any surprises in this Jack and the beanstalk?

ICH: I really don't like the "Disney-fication" and we actually looked at so many versions. We want it to be as original as possible. So we've spent a lot of time saying, "What is the original?" A lot of time was spent deciding how we were going to structure it and what we were going to add and what we're not going to add. Cause many of them have castles in the sky. And it used to be Jack's castle and his father was murdered. And then there's this new one, like Kate and the Beanstalk, which I really liked, but she also is restoring what was taken from her family, (but) we didn't want that. That's not in the original.

OH: There seems to be a discomfort in the adult-thinking-world that Jack seems to be stealing stuff.

ICH: And he is. But you could also see the castle world as the heavenly spiritual world or whatever, that he's (seeing that) the ordinary folk are able to get the gifts.

OH: Like a very low-class Prometheus. He's such a prototype human. The Jack tales are so much about the low, the downtrodden, grabbing fortune by, you know…

ICH: …but also happy go lucky. He's witty, but he's not smart. He's just ordinary. We have a teenage boy, so these decisions have to do with how does it ring true. So these decisions we don't take lightly. I think it's more about the gifts. The first thing that he takes is a bag of gold. That sustains them for not very long. His rite of passage, the second visit, he gets the hen that lays the golden eggs, so there's a more sustaining quality to that. And then the third thing he gets is the harp, which is about culture and arts. To me, the higher level of what we need to eat, again, nourishment. So that to me is what the core of the story is, and I don't want to mess with that and I want it to speak for itself. I'm not into this witty change of plot. You could call me an old fuddy-duddy. I don't care.

JB: The stories that have meaning are perennial. The cheap stuff that we do to make a quick buck never lasts and to do that undermines the basic ideas we're trying to share.

OH: I think that's a really good thing to keep in mind. And that also makes it the more important for us just stand back as much as possible. That is actually a beautiful experience for me. I'll just make that about me as a performer because as a singer, the training is always: you get onstage and you say, “Hi, here’s me, look at me.” And regardless of whether you're in an opera costume and you're portraying something completely different, or you are singing about the life and death of Christ and the Church or some romantic song cycle, you always have this moment of the person coming out saying, here’s me. Here’s I. When you come out and do a puppet show, in all our puppet shows, we are visible as performers. We never hide ourselves. But at the same time, I'm standing on stage (introducing the show) and I might share twenty, thirty words with the audience before we get going. But then I disappear (and) we tell the story through the puppets and it's not about me anymore. I feel that children, especially when they are being told something have to get past the adult relating the information and if there was a puppet they can go straight to the story and I'm not in the way anymore. It's such a beautiful thing and it's actually quite redemptive for me to not have this pressure of being up there and always being ME.

ICH: I was thinking of something a little different. I agree with him. We did choose Jack because it was a famous story. It's like we don't have any stories that are recognizable. Jack was chosen because it's famous and we looked at a Cinderella version with the crocodile Godmother, which we might do, too. I love that one. So, there was an aspect to it of, what do the libraries want, when we chose it. We had to find the story we liked, but also one that maybe was a little more recognizable. I find being an opera singer was very stressful for me because every single note was so scrutinized. Is the high note good? Is the conductor going to be happy? (Is) the person out in the audience going to critique me and put me in the (Washington) Post? It was very stressful and the high level that we were striving for, not that we don't do that with the puppets, but it's just, I don't feel that pressure and the kids love us no matter what we do. And it's much more fulfilling.

JB: Children tend to enjoy art in a way that adults can’t or at least can’t anymore,.

ICH: There's just not this pretense. However, I have to say that we are very surprised by the adults. They bring their children. But I've had older men and they're sixty-five, seventy years old, crying after the show, like finding their inner child. And I don't mean like bawling, I mean like just really touched and, and I have to say, I wasn't prepared for that, that there would be so many adults that would say to me, “Whoa, I feel like I've been on vacation. You took me away from the fast pace of the world. I've had a moment where I could watch the show through my grandchildren's eyes, and I was so touched by the truth that you're revealing.” Because I don't believe in preaching. I don't want to preach a moral, I don't want to say, don't do this, don't bully. I'm not saying that people shouldn't say don't bully, but I want the story to say it without saying it. I feel like there are these truths that come down that the puppets somehow show and all we're doing is “ensouling” the puppet. I pour myself into the puppet and yes, I'm thinking, why would you do that? I'm acting, I'm like an opera singer, but I'm putting my, my acting body down there. I don't know if that makes sense.

JB: Thank you, Ole and Ingrid, for a delightful talk and inviting me into your home. Thank you so much for the gift of your time and insights.

JOSHUA HOLDEN

JB: Let's start with your childhood. You're from Peabody, Massachusetts. What was it like growing up there?

Joshua Holden: All sorts of emotions went into growing up in Peabody. I had amazing parents. My parents are absolutely incredible. They're so supportive of everything I've done in my life and have done very little to hinder anything that I have wanted to pursue, even though it might not have made sense to them. So that was incredible. I'm thirty-five, so I was '90s kid. I discovered theater when I was about six. We went to a place called the North Shore Music Theatre, which is a big regional theater up there, and I had never seen anything like it and I fell madly in love with it. I said, "I want to do that!" My parents were like, really? I was like, yes, yes, yes, yes. And so they signed me up for acting classes in Salem, Massachusetts at this place called Studio One. It's no longer there, but this woman, Cynthia Marnik, was my acting teacher and she was kind of grumpy. But um, I loved it. I absolutely fell in love with it and that's where my love for performing began.

JB: And for High School you went to Walnut Hill School for the Arts in Natick. Was Walnut Hill a goal or did it just kind of fall in your lap?

JH: Fell into my lap. After my sophomore year of high school, I sat my parents down and I said, I'm really serious about this. I really don't want to do anything else. I don't. I had a hard time with my academic classes because all I wanted to do was be at the theater and the theater department was, it was okay. And the culture of the school in Peabody, Massachusetts in 1999 was not a positive experience for me, I did not feel very comfortable or safe outside of the theater when I was going to school, and so I just wanted to get out. I had a friend who went to Walnut Hill and we went there for a tour and I just knew stepping onto that campus that that's where I belonged. It was going from a school where I was in a class of thirty kids, the majority of which were mean to me. And then going down to a class of twelve students maximum at Walnut Hill. The education there was incredible, like really individualized. The respect they had for the arts and understanding that these kids have a passion for the arts and they were there to support that, was, yeah, it was a dream and I got a full scholarship to go there because we couldn't afford to pay tuition to Walnut Hill. But yeah, at sixteen I sat my parents down said I want to move away from home and go to a boarding school. They were like, oh my God. Oh, okay. They said yes to pursuing this opportunity. And so I moved out of the house at sixteen.

JB: You went in your junior and senior year. And then then you went off to Roosevelt University?

JH: I did, yes. Chicago College of Performing Arts.

JB: What was that like going to college in Chicago like after being up in the northeast for your whole life?

JH: It's interesting. I mean, to be really honest, that was my safety school. Artistically, I got into all the schools that I applied to and academically my grades were not good enough.

JB: What was the Chicago experience like in theater for a young college student?

JH: It was amazing. I went to Chicago expecting to be there for a year with the understanding that I was going to transfer to another school, I had no interest in staying in Chicago. I'd never been to Chicago. I didn't know much about the school and I got there and the very first thing that we did as freshmen was my acting teacher said, "I'd like all the freshmen to write a three-minute piece of their own," that was, "now that I have your attention, this is what I have to say," and she said, I want you to make a piece based on that phrase and you're going to present this to the rest of the conservatory.

And so right off the bat, for the very first time, I created a piece of my own and this was as a freshman in college. I'd never done that. And, I was eighteen years old. And I never even considered the idea that I could be a creative artist. I always imagined that I was going to be a chorus-boy on Broadway and then eventually work up into being a character actor on Broadway. And that was it. And working for other people. And so that was incredible to me. And the more explored

Chicago, the more I realized that that is a community of artists. The people are making their own work. There are so many theater companies out there and they're looking for people like me to come be part of their shows and so I was able to be part of workshopping a brand new play multiple times. I'm given the creative freedom to take the writers work and create a full character from this and step back and say, yeah, I can see my footprints all over that. That was very exciting. And so, I didn't leave Chicago. After my first year, I said, this is where it's at, this is what I want to do. I love this creative atmosphere.

JB: Is that when puppetry started to come into your life?

JH: No, that didn't happen until after school. I pursued musical theater for freshman and sophomore year of college and then switched to regular acting with a focus on physical theater. And then it wasn't until after college that I got a call from the Chicago Children's theater asking me to understudy Blair Thomas in a production of The Selfish Giant that he was writing, and I had never picked up a puppet before in my life or even considered that there were people underneath the puppets that I'd ever seen. I was like, oh yeah, puppets are a thing! Like I never really, never really had interest in it. I liked The Muppet Show as a kid and I love Sesame Street, but that was it. Like I was not a puppet person at all. At all.

JB: Many people in theater also don't take puppetry seriously.

JH: Yeah. I just think they just don't really know. I think a lot of people don't know the potential of what puppetry can do. We have a relationship to Sesame Street and we have a relationship to The Muppets. And that's fun, even though it's such a small slice of the world of puppetry.

JB: After that, did you start taking puppetry more seriously saying, well, I can create a show with puppets?

JH: Well, I thought I was a total hack! I thought I was terrible. And I had to do a one-man show. So, it was myself and a live musician and I had to go on these performances and I was terrified and then people thought that I was good, and I really had no sense because I couldn't see what I was doing. I just took everything that Blair taught me and just went with it. And then people started hiring me afterwards as a puppeteer. I just said, oh boy, someone's paying money, which I needed, and I hope they don't find out that I have no idea what I'm doing. Like I really felt like it was a true story of fake-it-till-you-make-it. And then eventually, I remember standing in a room one day amongst a bunch of people and explaining something having to do with puppetry and feeling, yeah, I actually know what I'm talking about. I mean, you know, by no means an expert. But I started to really get the knack for bringing objects to life in a truthful manner. And I had this very extensive background in acting and that's what I was bringing to puppetry and I think that is what really got people excited about the work, and that's what excited me, because then it was like, I'm learning! I'm learning this new vehicle to do exactly what I was always doing, which is telling stories and connecting with audiences to emotionally effect people. And that was thrilling! Once I made that connection, it was like, oh, the sky's the limit, really. And then I moved to New York from Chicago and I booked the national tour of Avenue Q and I was on that, the second national tour, for about a year.

Then from there, I toured in a couple of other productions and then I did a production called Peter Pan 360. And I entered that process and they rolled out the red carpet for me and treated me like I was just the king of it all. And I just thought, oh my God! They loved my audition and they just had such a respect for what I did, and I was so touched and so excited. And for the first time, that was the first time that I started calling myself a puppeteer, before that, I was an actor, "I'm an actor, I'm an actor and I also do some puppetry." But then in Peter Pan I started saying, "I'm a puppeteer", and that was really exciting and when that tour ended, it ended abruptly, and I had no place to live. I thought the job was going to last for another two years, but the show financially went under. Huge multi-million-dollar touring production in London.

Then I went traveling across the country. I was on a road trip with a friend and was asked to do a puppet slam in Chicago, I was traveling through Chicago. And I said, what is a puppet slam? She's like, "It's like a little evening where you create your own pieces and you and I are going to do something together, okay?" And last minute, her name is Casey Foster, and Casey said, "I'm sorry, I have to back out, but you should still do it on your own." And I said, "No, I can't, I don't make my own work. I don't make puppets, that's not something I do. I work for other people." And she said, "What do you daydream about?" I said, "Well, I want to be the next Mister Rogers and I want to make content that makes people feel really good." And she said, "Well then you should do that. It's ten minutes. It's going to be forty people in the audience. You have nothing to lose." And so I did. I pulled some stuff together. I made Mr. Nicholas. He came out of nowhere. He introduced himself to me when I made him. And I made this ten-minute little piece with my theme song. I was the only song in the show. And this ten-minute piece was the start of it all. People just went wild for it and I expected to throw the puppets away and move on, on my road trip. And that thankfully did not happen.

JB: Mr. Nicholas is certainly a force to be reckoned with. When I go out and I teach a workshop at a high school or something, and I go to show them someone other than myself, you're one of the first people I pick, and Mr. Nicholas has to be one of the most expressive sock puppets I've ever seen in my life. And the puppetry work is some of the finest I've ever seen in my life. So, we have the birth of Mr. Nicholas. Did he start out the way he is now? Or did he go through a period character development? Has he evolved much in the way you want to present him?

JH: That's interesting. He has been the same. My friend Casey gave me this sock puppet with these two-little beady-eyes - had no arms, no hair and this crude little hot-glued, mouth-palette. And he didn't really look like what he looks like now, but I wrote this little poem about being grumpy and how you trick yourself into being happy on days when you feel sad and blue and I knew I wanted to make a little puppet that expressed his grumpiness and so she has a whole bunch of sock puppets and I found this one and I said, "Yeah, he looks grumpy. I can take him." So, I clipped his nose and I did some color on the eyes, just fuddling around. I fixed the mouth palette and I put him on and instantly, instantly, instantly, I just started making him breathe and I was looking at him and I, I remembered my training from Blair and from past mentors. You let the puppet tell you who they are, and you let the puppet show you how it wants to move. Opposed to you imposing things on it. And he started making some sounds and then he said, “My name is Mr. Nicholas.” And I said, “Oh my gosh,….okay, cool.” This cute little British voice. And then he did this lovely little poem. And yeah, he was always very, very grumpy and very pessimistic. So over time, the thing that's really flourishing is his vulnerability. The ways in which I think he really wants to fit in, but he is just too scared. He's such an open and vulnerable soul, with so much worry, that that is like, that has been a really exciting part of him, too. Really, that's really developed since the beginning. And also the love that we have for one another, and his love for me, because there was a period in which Mr. Nicholas was just, he's just grumpy and it was a mood. He just put the fears up, the little brush strokes of this grumpy little guy. And the tenderness and the real companionship has come in with the two of us in a way that I just, oh, I am just so over the moon that I have in my life, because I've traveled all around the world with him and it has affected people in such a deep way that I just, I'm so touched by it. Whenever it happens.

JB: Well, I have noticed that no matter how badly Mr. Nicholas feels when he starts out, you, Joshua, can always make him feel better and calm his fears. We live in a very frightening time and to see someone take a fearful character like that, a character that really wants to shrink into not just into his own shell, but to shrink away from existence entirely, and to bring this character back out into a world of living beings, into a world where happiness is possible. That’s a powerful thing to show people. You know, I should ask you how much has changed from episode one to episode two of The Joshua Show?

JH: Well, the structure is similar. It still feels like you are at this episodic children’s show. Like, there's a wonder of the day. There's still the theme song. There's a word of the day.

JB: Did you get that from Pee Wee’s Playhouse?

JH: Yes, absolutely. One hundred percent. I got the tap-dancing, out at the beginning from, Pinky Lee (editor’s note: Pincus Leff, better known as Pinky Lee, was an American burlesque comic and host of the children's television program The Pinky Lee Show in the early 1950s). At first it was supposed to be parody of all these iconic children's television shows all mushed into one and it's sort of, you know, I pay homage to these people that I had such a great effect on my life. In the first episode, it centers around the word authenticity and the importance of being true to who you are and the things that make you different are the things that make you great. And Mr. Nicholas, he discovers that he's a puppet and he wants to be anything but that, and he just loses it. He wants to just go away and never be seen again. And through the show we teach him that being an authentic sock puppet is really actually a wonderful thing and he should be proud of that. He expresses that even though he knows that that's the case. he still can't help himself from feeling horrible on Sundays and we talk about that that's okay. That not every day is going to be great. It's important for you and everybody else to honor those feelings and know that yeah, some days are going to be rotten and you just to let yourself feel that way and then when you feel that and then eventually, we'll move past that and you'll be in a place of joy again. Turn to your friends in those times. And also don't pressure yourself into feeling anything else. Just be authentically how you're feeling. So that's what the first episode was and that really is like a big part of my life and like how I conduct myself. I mean it's no secret to me. I'm not trying to keep it a secret that Mr. Nicholas is absolutely a part of who I am. I have a lot of feelings similar to his and I'm learning that most people do too. There's something about it when we all say, Gosh, I hear you man. I totally hear you. So, I'm a very emotional being and so that's what that show came from. The second show comes from my completely overwhelmed feeling that I get when I turn on the news and feel like this is doomed, we're doomed, we are just doomed, we need to get outta here, we should all move to another planet and there's nothing we can do about it. And then you just take a breath and you say, actually there's a lot of good things happening and there's a lot of good people out there and we've got to focus on that and we got to find ways for us to be that. So, I want to be part of that change. I want to be part of that sunshine and that light to remind people.

JB: Jeb played a smaller part in Episode One and now…

JH: Yeah, he had a small little scene where he plays a character, otherwise we didn't sing a whole bunch together. The second episode was written with Jeb, bearing in mind that the two of us have a great musicality together. We really built that into the show and so he's more heavily involved in the second episode. The first one (Episode One) feels a little bit more like a one man show.

JB: Well, it was certainly a wonderful show. I enjoyed it immensely and every time I get to tell anyone about it, I tell them to come see it. It's just pure fun. Let's talk a little bit about your becoming the president of the Puppetry Guild of Greater New York (PGOGNY). I guess what I would love to know because of course, you know, this is going to go into a little bit over the discussion of the future of puppetry guilds in our country and stuff. And especially on the east coast here. Peter Lewis had been basically doing this for I think sixteen years. All on his own.

JH: Yes.

JB: And you show up in December of 2016.

JH: Two years ago, yeah. I joined the guild in December 2016. Liz Joyce told me that it was my duty and I had to join the guild, and I was just a member, just observing it. No one came along with me. I was just there amongst whomever was there for like half a year.

JB: Then September of 2017, that's when it really turns around. You bring forty or fifty new members in. What prompted this? What actually triggered the decision to go all in?

JH: Well, I really think it's from what I experienced at Walnut Hill. The Walnut Hill community really changed my life. It opened me up to this idea of how important it is to have a community of people that support you and love you. And you have that, the things that you're capable of and the quality of your life is just so rich. And so that's always been a really important thing to me is finding community and building community and supporting community. And when I went to the guild meetings and you know, these ten people that were showing up, they were just as lovely as can be and it just felt like there was so much excitement and so much desire to soak up what this art form has to offer. And also, it was just important to the people to get out of the house and come together. And I just looked at that and thought yeah, there are a lot more people in this city that could benefit from coming together. And I think it would not be terribly difficult to do that. And so, that is really what drove me was the community. Really trying to think about an opportunity to really make a difference with this incredible group of people.

JB: Exactly. You've been very ambitious in getting programs together. What do you have planned for the next couple of years for PGOGNY?

JH: I want to flout the clout of PGOGNY. I want your membership to PGOGNY to be a really full membership in that we gain the respect from arts organizations around the city in a way that we can get discount tickets, we can get on lists for comp tickets so that PGOGNY is a club that is important and can effect change and is a respectable group of people that you could turn to in the city. We already have a handful of messages coming to us saying we're looking for puppeteers.

I would love for that to continue for really this to be the central hub of puppetry in the New York City area. That to me feels accomplishable and really exciting that I really want you to become you to become a member and I give you this big list and say these are the local businesses that will give you a discount, these are the theaters that will give you a discount. Here's a network of people that you now have access to and welcome to the family. So that's one goal. I would like to start fostering the creation of new work within PGOGNY. I'm not talking about a residency. I'm talking about just trying to create more programming that gets people up on their feet. And also have some opportunities for people to come in and throw something up against the wall and for it to land flat on the ground and feel okay in doing that and we all can help you pick it back up and look at that. And I don't know exactly how to do that, but we're in our early conversations about what does it mean to be a supportive community and what value do we have with having all these people coming together and how can we really take the most advantage of that in a positive way for people, while also keeping it simple. I mean, I have big dreams for it, but you've got to also keep it simple, because I'm managing a board of eleven people and as much as I'd like to just make decisions and go out the door with them, it's a slow process with that. It's not all up to me and certainly I represent the guild, but I'm really a facilitator for conversation. It's a slow moving, but I think it's great.

JB: Recently, you started an internship with the Henson Company which is just finishing up. What are you doing for them?

JH: It is amazing! Well, it changes every day. There are some days where they're a little over-worked. We just got like six giant, giant crates full of puppets out yesterday and that took like two days to pack up and it was a build that they had been working on for about four months. It's amazing how they build all this stuff and it's managed so beautifully by Melissa Creighton (senior production manager of Jim Henson's Creature Shop, NY).

I don't understand how she schedules this all out, but it gets done and there are days where it's like we don't have enough hands and I get to jump on and help. My main project right now that I'm working on is organizing the props, which is very exciting. They have a big prop-file there. So, I'm doing an inventory and taking some stock of the props that they're doing there. I've been photographing some puppets from time to time and it's very exciting. And they asked me to bring something over to Sesame Street, like, will you grab Ernie and bring him to Sesame Street? And I'm like, will I ever! So, I put him in a bag and we walked down the street together. Yeah, we're walking down the street and people are passing by and I'm like, you have no idea right now because inside my bag is Ernie! Sesame Street is the most magical place on Earth. Everyone is so happy to be there and it is beautiful. I love being there. But the thing that I'm most excited about is I feel like I'm building a vocabulary to be able to understand how to build quality puppets, more than I do now and also an understanding of how to properly talk to a builder. So, I feel like I'm building a vocabulary now that I didn't have before based on the things that I've seen in the shop. I mean I just wander around and see people just working with the most extraordinary, most interesting and mysterious materials and coming together to make something really fantastic.

So that is something that I'm really grateful for with this internship is it the opportunity to be amongst these incredible artisans. Any question that I have, they are happy to tell me where they get stuff, how they make it, why they make it and why they're supposed to make it like that. These people are just as giving and generous as we see at the festivals, as we see at the guild meetings, as we see when we go to see a show and someone turns their puppets inside out at the end to show you what they're doing. It's the same thing up there. It's so awesome. That is so awesome. In other industries, I feel like you get to that same level and there isn't necessarily that openness and kindness, but we still got it. We still have that at the very top and that is just awesome. I think anytime I see someone who is, you know, pulling a diva attitude, I think it's our duty to say, you know, we don't really do that here. It's just not done. So that behavior is not acceptable because there's no one doing it and anyone that is, you're robbing yourself, but we don't do that here.

JB: From what little I've seen, a lot of the folks at Henson seemed to be selected, not just for their skills, but for their kindness.

JH: Oh yes. Oh yeah, it's very much feels like a family for sure.

JB: When I visited there everyone was kind, everyone was friendly, so you must be having a really good time there.

JH: I am. This internship ends at the end of December and I'm looking forward to having a little more time in my schedule, because I'm balancing that with my job as a puppet wrangler and wardrobe supervisor Avenue Q on Broadway right now too.

JB: That was another thing I wanted to ask you about. You're the puppet wrangler for Avenue Q. You were in the national tour in 2010. So, it's eight years later and now you're wrangling for these guys on Broadway. What's that like?

JH: That's great. It's a lovely little job. I remember when I first started working there, how captivated I was by the puppets, now it's a little more part of my everyday norm, but Rick Lyon has built just incredible, incredible characters and it's an honor to be maintaining those every day. It's a lot of work because (originally) it was two separate departments. You had the puppetry department and the wardrobe department and that consisted of four people total and now the job is mixed down into one, which is just me. So, I'm doing puppets and I'm doing wardrobe. That's how the show has been able to maintain itself for the past fifteen years. But, you know, it's eight shows a week, every week and I'm not sick of the show. The show is just, it's awesome. The music is great. The message, I feel like it teaches me something every day, it connects to the different part of my life every day. And I really enjoy it. It's a well-oiled machine and I appreciate that and it's efficient. It's a nice little job. It's flexible. So really, that's what it's helping me while I'm pursuing the Joshua Show, which I hope to be moving into full time in the next year or two.

JB: So, what's the future look like? Will you be developing the Joshua Show? Will there be an episode three?

JH: I'm currently, right now, building my holiday, Christmas show that's going to be performing at two private events and then I'm going out to Sag Harbor at the end of the month. And it's called the Joyfully, Jolly Jamboree with Joshua and Jeb. Of course, Mr. Nicholas plays the Scroogiest, Scrooge. He has a beautiful little song that I wrote called Skipping Christmas, and oh goodness, it's so beautiful. I'm hoping to have that booked next year and it's really a goal of mine to have my father join the show with me. My father is a "real beard" Santa Claus.

JB: Oh really?

JH: Yeah. I mean he is Santa Claus. It's like, my father is Santa Claus, like 100 percent. He is just beautiful. His connection with children is unlike anything I've ever seen, and he is full of Christmas spirit, so I kind of want to bring them into what I'm doing and kind of tour around with him a bit. I think that would be really fun. So, I'm talking to my booking agents about what that possibility would be like, but I'll certainly hopefully have the Christmas show booked in a real way next year.

JB: And finally, it appears that we both have a scientist crush on the same person. And that would be Dr. Jane Goodall. Talk about it a little bit. Why? Why is she important to you?

JH: Oh, she's so compassionate and she's so gentle and she's pursuing something that she really believes in and it's good and just. I think through her efforts, she teaches us a lot about what it means to be a compassionate human being. And I also just love monkeys, so that I'm wildly jealous of her making friends with all these monkeys and I've always wanted to be friends with one!

JB: What else do you have on the horizon? What other

ambitions do you intend to realize?

JH: I want to have my own TV show. That's, that's, that's really what I'm working towards these days.

JB: I think we all want you to have your own TV show. Thanks for talking with us Joshua, it's been a delight.

ROLLIE KREWSON

JB: How did this all start? Were there childhood influences?

Rollie Krewson: I grew up watching Shari Lewis and Lambchop, which I adored. Lampchop, Charlie horse, the whole kit and kaboodle. And on Sunday nights, we had family dinners in the living room around the TV and we watched Ed Sullivan, so of course, I got Topo Gigio, and I got Jim and Frank. And then Jimmy Dean I would occasionally see, although I think it was a little late for me, but I think somehow I managed to see Rowlf a few times. I think it was mostly with my grandmother, she liked Jimmy Dean. Rowlf was great.

JB: Yeah, a talking, piano playing dog with a big spherical head and floppy ears! What could be wrong with that?

RK: And the ears would get stuck over on one side!

JB: Were there any cartoons that you liked?

RK: Beany and Cecil, the Jetsons. I was not a great Bugs Bunny fan. I don't know why. I loved the Road Runner. I liked Tweety Bird. Mickey Mouse. The first movie I remember seeing was Bambi. The fire and the mother dying! I was a little-bitty kid!

JB: Did you make puppets as a child?

RK: I did not. I had a Lambchop. I had a Charlie Horse. My cousins had puppets. They had those old Stieff ones and I remember playing with those. Every summer we put on a show in the backyard. We had record players and they were all based on records. It was a pantomime to a record. Everybody in the neighborhood would get together and we would all make our costumes or get our moms to make them, and we made antlers for everybody out of tinfoil, and get together in somebody's back yard, and somebody would sell tickets for five cents, and we'd stick the Bambi record on and we put on a show. We probably prepared for a week. We did Bambi, we did Snow White. Whatever was on a record. So (my experience) was more larger-scale, it wasn't exactly puppetry, but it was definitely going the direction that I ended up. I sang in choir and I always liked being in the theater, but I wasn't a great actor or anything. I was mostly backstage.

JB: You attended Denison University in Ohio. Did you start in theater studies?

RK: I was going to be a social worker, I wasn't going theater, at all. My roommate Barbara was a BFA major and I went to the theater with her one day and decided I was going to be an usher for a show that she was in and I got down there and that was IT. I fell madly in love with it. It was the greatest thing since sliced bread. I was watching them build a set and I thought, I can do that! I got terrible grades, except in theater. I got rid of the courses I had to take as soon as I could and all I did was take theater. We're still good friends, all of us that were in the theater department at the same time. We get together, whoever's in New York at the time, three, four times a year.

JB: Did you get into acting or did you gravitate more to backstage?

RK: It was mostly backstage. That's where I first started learning how to costume. My mother had a sewing machine and she would never teach me how to use it, because she couldn't use it. I had troll dolls and I would make them clothes. I was always making stuff for dolls. But the theater at Denison was great. We had a couple of really good theater professors. I took acting courses and I got to act, but I wasn't that great. There was a man whose name was Cal Morgan and in my junior year, he did a puppetry course and we learned about all different kinds of puppets, and at the end of the course, we had to do a show. I ended up doing an adaptation of The Sword in the Stone, and we designed and built marionettes. I designed the set, which was a big castle and the drawbridge came down and that was the marionette stage. I wrote the script and directed it, and it was great! We had a fabulous time. I don't think there had ever been a puppetry course at Denison before, and I don't think there was a puppetry course after that! But we had a blast! Eventually, I went to New York as an intern for a lady whose name was named Judy Licht. Her husband was Manny Azenberg at the time, and Manny and Jim were working on the Broadway Show. I was working with Judy on a show called Almanac, on the public broadcasting channel, and she eventually left there and became a newscaster, and couldn't take me with her. She knew I liked puppets and that's when she told me about her husband

and working with Jim. At that point I hadn't really seen Sesame. I was in college and never watched television, but I made a point of finding a TV in New York City, so I could watch Sesame Street before I had my interview.

JB: When did your internship at Henson Begin?

RK: It was September through December (1973). It was a whole semester. It was organized by the Great Lakes College Association. I don't know if they exist anymore, but they would send kids specifically to New York to work with Broadway producers and all sorts of people. That was how I got placed with Judy, because I was interested in television. I maybe did a month with her before she went to FOX (and she) couldn't take me with her. That was when she got me the interview with Diana Birkenfield, and that was when I met Bonnie, and Caroly, and John Lovelady, and Faz, and Dave Goelz, and Kermit (Love). Eric Jenkins was there then. Don Sahlin was there. I loved Don, Don was great. I interviewed with Diana and she said, "Let's go talk to Bonnie." I can't even remember what the interview was like. They said, "What have you done?" And I showed them my puppets. And they said, "Oh, go look around. Go Look in the drawers."

JB: Was that when you knew you had a job?

RK: Uh huh! And I said, "I guess I'm an intern, okay!"

JB: Was this paid?

RK: No, it was (for) credit. They actually did give me a stipend. I can't remember how much it was, I think when I came on board the stipend was $50. I know Diana was really good to me.

JB: Where were you living in New York City?

RK: I lived on the Upper West Side on 72nd Street between West End (Ave) and Broadway in a place called the Coliseum House [now the Parc Coliseum Apartments] which was awful, especially for somebody who came from Ohio! There were three of us in there and we all had various internships There was a living room, a kitchenet and a bedroom and a bathroom. We all had beds in the bedroom and you'd come in after a long day and you'd find a big piece of plaster on your bed! And the cockroaches were the size of waterbugs! Okay, welcome to New York. I never told my parents about that. They would have been horrified!

JB: When I interviewed Bonnie Erickson, she made a similar experience of her early days in the city sound like a grand adventure.

RK: It was! I can remember running around New York and I was never afraid, and I probably should have been, but everything was exciting. I was working for Jim, but one friend was working for Tony Walton and they were doing "Free To Be You And Me," and I got to put felt stars and moons and hearts on top of a carousel, in Central Park, that they had brought in and they needed somebody small to crawl up on the top of it. So, here I am, crawling around putting up suns and moons and stars on top of the carousel!

JB: And you went back to finish college right after your internship?

RK: I did. I went back to Ohio for my last semester. I kept in touch with Bonnie. You have to know about The Crumpet That Died. When I was working as an intern, they were doing the Valentine's Day special. They actually made me a Production Assistant for that. There's a little thing, it was a crumpet that appears in the Valentine's Day special and somehow it ended up in my bag and I found it when I was on the plane flying home, and I don't know who put it there. This is still a mystery. It was either Bonnie or Don, and I still have it and it's still fine. It's perfectly fine. It's been in the dark the whole time. I go and look at it. It's just soft foam, it's got little bead eyes. It's got a little bit of spray paint on it.

JB: Did you go right back to NYC after you graduated from Denison?

RK: I went back to New York to work for Jim the day after I graduated. I still have the letter. My friends that I graduated with went and we found an apartment on the Upper West Side, more toward the river. It was a Brownstone and we had the whole floor and there were three of us, sometimes four, depending.

JB: So, you're there. What was going on? What was the workshop like in those days?

RK: It was small. We all did everything, which is great. It was a lot more fun than being only a puppet builder. So, we all got a chance to do stuff.

JB: What productions were they working on and what was the first thing that you're given to do?

RK: It was Sex and Violence. I worked on Heaps and Stalks [for the sketch Aggression]. I love Jim's drawings. Jim's drawings are, you know, they're just five lines, and it's a world. But if you don't know how to interpret them, which I didn't at first, it was soooo hard! It was like, I don't know how to do this, so it took me a while to find that in myself, that I could interpret his lines. He seemed like he was very easy-going, but he knew exactly what he wanted to see and if you weren't doing what he wanted, it was like "Hmmm." We worked on Ice Follies, too and I get the timeline confused, whether (Sex and Violence) was first or Ice Follies. The Ice Follies story is funny. We built all the Sesame costumes, so it was Ernie and Bert and there was a Snuffleupagas. I was working on shoes that went over ice skates, that was my thing. At that point I wasn't ready to make heads. They do have a way of introducing you; you get to make bodies first, you work your way up to heads and we still kinda' do that, just to make sure everybody's got the right feel for everything and does the style right. But these things were huge, they were really big and they weren't going to ship them out there. You have a get a truck and pack them all up, so Eric Jenkins and I drove a U-Haul truck across the country to San Francisco with all these costumes in the back. Somewhere there's a picture of Kermit pushing the back end of Snuffy into this U-Haul truck. And Eric and I didn't have that long to get there, so it was pretty much straight through, so I'd drive, he'd sleep, he drove, I'd sleep. And he would pick up a really stinky hitchhiker and I was like, Eric, really? I only remember stopping overnight and showering a couple of times, so we must have just trucked through. I figured out that my favorite time of day to drive was early in the morning and there was one morning where we were going through the desert and the mists were kind of rising up and I went, "Eric! Eric! Wake up! We have to take Snuffy out and put him over there!" It would have been a great picture with the mists coming up! And the Snuffleupagus standing in the middle!

JB: Did you do it?

RK: No! No picture! That was also the trip where I picked up a tumbleweed for Caroly (Wilcox). They were beautiful! I'd never really seen one other than cowboy movies. And I picked up this tumbleweed and taped it to the inside of the truck and then found out you weren't supposed to take them across state lines. I managed to get it back home again. I don't know how I did that though because we flew back. It got back somehow. And she had it for the longest time. That trip was great, and I wasn't very far from having been an intern at that point. How many people can say that they've taken a bunch of Ice Follies characters across the country from New York to San Francisco?

JB: Back to Sex and Violence, outside of being sketch based, it seems so different that what it turned into, The Muppet Show.

RK: But the elements are there, and you can kinda' see...I mean Nigel didn't work. I love Nigel. If you ever talk to Dave Goelz, he was trying to make puppet that could whistle and that was his attempt: Nigel. He was bound and determined that Nigel was going to whistle, and I have a feeling that Dave still wants a puppet that really whistles well.

JB: Both the entire pilot and The Muppet Show have such a raucous, improvised feel. I just watched the John Cleese episode the other day...

RK: I made the parrot!

JB: And you went to England? You weren't shipping stuff over from the New York shop?

RK: I went to London for six weeks and ended up living there for six years. When we first got there, our workshop was right off the studio. As you walked through the door into the studio you had to pass where the lighting guys hung out and they had about ten calendars of "calendar girls" and Bonnie especially was just incensed that they should have those up there and we had to pass them all the time. So, we asked them nicely a couple of times to please take them down and then finally I think she had words with somebody, and they disappeared.

JB: What were some of your other responsibilities on The Muppet Show?

RK: I did stuff like Scooter's body. I got to do Wayne, of Wayne and Wanda. He was mine. I made a lot of Whatnot puppets. I didn't do any main characters at that point, but I did parts of main characters. At that point, I was still very much Bonnie's Assistant. She did the Newscaster and she clipped him all out of foam. I actually loved to get on the belt sander and I loved to sand the foam and she let me sand (the Newscaster) and normally you get into a Zen mode and you just do it and it's fine, but if you get distracted…if you look at that very first one, there's a little dip in his lip that's not in the center, it's off to the side. We had to use him because she didn't have time to do another one. It didn't show that much. I doubt anybody but me would notice, but I sat on the stairs and cried for half an hour because I was so afraid to go back and show her. She was fine about it! I was mortified!

JB: What was the turnaround on the show?

RK: Sunday was the read-through. Monday was vocal recording, so we were in the shop doing whatever we had to do to get ready for the show and then the actual show was taped Tuesday, Wednesday, Thursday, so our weekend was Friday, Saturday. But again, it was union. They did go late, but they didn't go late all the time. A lot of times you'd get something set up and (not have time to shoot it). Halfway Down the Stairs with little Robin the Frog, that got set up every week to have it done and I swear it took us an like entire season to finally shoot it, because it was like, "If we have a few minutes, we'll shoot it. There was never that few minutes. [editor's note: this beloved scene, performed by the late Jerry Nelson as Robin, appears in season one, episode ten]

JB: Would scripts be arriving well before the read-through so the puppets could be built and be ready in time?

RK: A couple days before. Although Jim would come by and say if he actually needed something, then he would tell us beforehand. We were usually working a week in advance. I did the scientist for Time in a Bottle [song by Jim Croce, performed by Jim Henson; season two, episode seven] and that I did that over a week off or something. I think I stayed and did it, because there were a lot of pieces to that one. I remember I did Foo Foo [fourth and fifth seasons], which had to match the real dog and that I built, it was like Easter break or something. And Foo Foo the puppet was actually built in Wales, because my friend and I went to Wales for the few days, so I was stitching away while I was in Wales.

JB: Not much mention is made of how English The Muppet Show really was and it wasn't just that you had English comedians like Chris Langham writing for it.

RK: We did all the Pearly Kings stuff, too. Which was great, the two -minute things. A lot of them never got seen here, because they stuck in an extra commercial, but we did all the British stuff and all the music. We did a whole musical thing, all of us, one night. We rehearsed it and we rented a hall, invited a whole bunch of people and we all got up and sang songs and did Pearly King stuff. It was weird and wonderful! It was great. I can't remember what I did, but I know that I was up there!

JB: Let's talk about Emmet Otter's Jug Band Christmas a bit. Did you have to make a new batch of puppets for the stage version almost thirty years later?

RK: Some of them were the same. Emmet and Ma were from the TV (version). They were the original Emmet and Ma. They were just basically seen in the rowboat and then they (the characters) were performers dressed in costume. A lot of what we did were larger versions. Dave did the original snake for the TV. I made the snake that was for the stage version and I copied his techniques and made it bigger.

JB: Enlarging the puppet changes things.

RK: It smiled, but not like his did.

RK: We always were trying to get people with the fake cookies. We got a lot of people with fake cookies! Because they looked pretty good. And Caroly, she would bring in various mice and stuff that were dead and put them in the freezer and then forget that they were in there! And you'd go in for something and go, "Oh…that's Caroly's." She bring it in and go, "Look! Look at what was in my garden! Isn't it cool?" And then she'd put it in the freezer, so it wouldn't be sitting out and it would remain in the freezer for quite some time. I think she brought in a mole once. She had lots of stuff that she brought in.

JB: Was this because they'd be used for puppet design purposes?

RK: She just thought they were interesting and "weren't they cool?" I mean, Caroly built fabulous animal puppets, she's the best animal puppet builder ever and that's why she would do that. She'd just find something that she thought we would find interesting. Caroly would bring basil in and make pesto and we'd all sit around and have pesto lunches. That was the fun thing about the shop and still is, although we don't do it as much.

JB: Let's talk more about puppet building. Talk about the first time you carved a puppet from foam.

RK: The first puppet that I carved out of foam was a Koozie pup. (Dave Goelz) did the male and John Lovelady did the female. Dave was carving the pups and we were using a hot-wire, which we found out later was really bad for you! But whatever!

JB: I remember Bonnie telling me about smoking over an open can of Barge cement!

RK: We had a shoemaker across the street, a Russian guy who was there for years and years and years, and you'd go in and get your shoes and he (was smoking cigarettes) one right after the other (with) the open Barge can! But Dave was the one that actually helped me do a Koozie pup, so under his eye, I got to do a Koozie pup. That was lots of fun.

JB: Let's talk about Sesame Street and Elmo. Caroly did the first Elmo, when he was called Little Red?

RK: Caroly did the first one. I wasn't around when he was built the first time. I came in (to Sesame Street) in '87, so I think there were two before I got to him. I don't even know how I came to have Elmo. I'm assuming that Caroly said, "She's doing it."

JB: Tell me about his arms.

RK: Elmo's arms, because they didn't want elbows in them, they have beads, so it's a cord with wooden beads with a knot in between each bead so you get a nice kind of loopy movement to it. The first ones, I'm sure it was Caroly found, had little faces on them and so I reuse a lot of those beads and if an Elmo becomes too grotty to use again, then I'll get a new chord and reuse the beads and I still have some of the beads with the faces on them and they're still in the Elmos.

JB: I've read that Cookie Monster is made from a basketball.

RK: It is. I just made a Cookie Monster at home and yes, it's a basketball. I cut it out of a basketball. The eyes go into the basketball, then there's a leather piece that holds them in. Your hands are on the other side of that leather piece. That is the top and the bottom is the opposite curve. It's sort of a clamshell shape. Your hand's in a glove. And your thumb goes on the bottom part. It's got a really loose hinge, with a little piece of gaffer's tape that holds the two pieces together. The actual mouth itself is just a piece of black velour with a swallow hole.

JB: How about Ernie. Is his neck really a coffee can?

RK: Ernie's neck is still a coffee can. A little more than half a metal coffee can and you sand it all off so you don't get cut and you put gaffer's tape around the bottom. It was hard to find a coffee can that was the same size as Ernie's first one. They vary in size slightly, so you have to be very careful about what coffee can you get. Why change it? It worked. There's no reason to change it. And maybe you can make Cookie Monster out of Plastizote, but it's not going to be the same.

JB: You also did Abby Cadabby, Murray, and Ovejita.

RK: I love Abby. LOVE Abby.

JB: Everyone that meets Leslie loves her, too.

RK: We are Abby's two moms, so we share Abby.

JB: You have 13 Emmy Awards for Sesame Street.

RK: The very first one meant the most and was the most surprising because I actually got it. It was the very first year for Muppets, so I was helping Caroly do Sesame and they were nice enough to put my name on. So that's the generosity of that group. I worked on it, I helped her, so she thought I needed credit, so that's the best one. That one means the most to me.

JB: They are really pointy statues.

RK: They are really pointy statues. And they changed every year. They're all different colors. One of them, the gold has flaked off in places. I've been trying to figure out who to give my Emmys to. My daughter has one already. I figured I would give them all to my nieces and nephews.

JB: Let's talk Fraggles, because they're coming back.

RK: They're coming back! I was just on a phone call yesterday. There's a lot of discussion on what themes we should continue, you know, compassion and everything that's happening in the world now is a good thing for the Fraggle to deal with, because that's what they were dealing with back then and trying to make the world a better place. Everybody figures this is a good time for Fraggle to come back.

JB: In the original you built…

RK: Wembley and Red. I love building Wembley. Sometimes puppets just sort of happen and they feel right and Wembley was one of those. He just sort of came out and there he was fully formed. I kind of feel that I've got a lot of Wembley issues: he can't always make up his mind, he's a little fearful of things. That's one side of me. And then I made Red and that's the other side, that's the side I want to be. I want to be the cheerleader, I want to be the rah, rah girl, but I'm somewhere in the middle. Jan (Rosenthal) and I made almost all the background Fraggles. Jane Gootnick and Tim Miller did the Gaggles which were the RC [radio controlled] background Fraggles. It's so funny now, when they're taking about them, they call all the background characters Gaggles. No they were Fraggles, the RCs were the Gaggles. The thing about Fraggle that was different that the Muppet Show was that you went over for the entire time of the Muppet Show. There were a few people who came over for a few weeks at a time, but I was at The Muppet Show the entire time. I got taken off of it to work on Dark Crystal and wasn't in the final picture. I was so upset. They had everybody in the shop that worked on the show and I was building Fizzgig, but they didn't call me and let me know! So, I was not in that picture, I want to photoshop myself in there.

JB: If it's any consolation, one of the only two Henson character puppets I own is the Fizzgig that came out recently.

RK: It's a really nice puppet. They did a really nice job.

JB: How many Fizzgigs did you make?

RK: I made three good ones that were "camera perfect." Then a couple that were "stunt" ones that you could pull them along. I made a furry, rolling ball one. There was one that had a big, wide, open mouth. There was one that had a smaller mouth. I ended up cutting one down. They were dreamfasting and they showed a little Fizzgig. I could have used a big Fizzgig and it wouldn't have made any difference, but I cut one down and made it smaller, which I gave to the Museum of the Moving Image. There were probably six or seven of them.

JB: Were there prototypes?

RK: I seemed to have worked on it forever. I don't remember going through a whole lot of prototypes. Building that way was a totally different thing for me at that point. That was the first time I had (worked from) a mold of Dave's hands, so that puppet fit him like a glove. It fit his hand exactly. Somebody else made the mold. I sculpted what he was going to look like under all that fur, and somebody made the mold of that. It was a lot of stuff I hadn't done before, which was a real growth experience. Jim had insisted that I do him, because I was getting the reputation of being the "queen of cute."

JB: And Fizzgig's body was cast in latex?

RK: Yes.

JB: What was Fizzgig covered with

RK: From the drawings, he looked to me like he was made out of fur, but it wasn't going to be a fake fur, it was going to be real fur. I felt really badly about using real fur, it didn't seem like the thing to do. What I found, in looking around, were some old collars and stuff off of coats and I thought well, at least I'm recycling.

JB: And this was in London, Right?

RK: This was all in London, yeah. I had gone to the "fur district" and found old pieces that had been taken off of things and that's what Fizzgig was made of. I took some collars for the curly bits, then there were some other pieces that were maybe fox or something, and I intermixed everything. You had to take the skin off the back, so I put it in gelatin and got it hard and then sliced the actual skin off the back of it and then put it on fabric and then melted the gel off. It was a very interesting process, which worked in some ways and not in others. It finally ended up that I cut individual little pieces out and mounted it on net, so it had a "stretch" to it. But we had all the time in the world. Now it's how much can you get done in this amount of time and this amount of money. Jim just let us go and just do stuff and if it didn't work, it didn't work, he moved on to something else.

JB: Using all these different collars and furs, it must have been very hard to match stuff.

RK: It was! I was going to run into big trouble if he ended up asking me to build yet another one. Which luckily didn't happen. That's why there were some that were "camera" and some that were "background." The background ones got to the point where I was using dribs and drabs of what I had to try and match the camera ones, because I only had so much.

JB: Did Fizzgig have cable control for the eyes?

RK: Yes, it was cable.

JB: I remember when it was released, Dark Crystal didn't do all that well, but now it's a classic.

RK: What was so cool about Dark Crystal is that it was before CG. It was before any of that. It was all built. We built all of it. It was hard work. The hard part was the actual doing it, crawling around underneath! I worked on Dave Goelz's cables for the Garthim Master and so I was always being dragged around underneath and behind him, so that was hard.

JB: I can see how that must have been difficult. Those Skeksis were much smaller than they are in Age of Resistance.

RK: Just the cables themselves were archaic compared to what they have now. That was when Faz first did the RC controls for Jen and Kira. And Jen was extraordinarily uncomfortable. Jim never complained. Bobby Payne was one of the Skeksis, too, and for some reason he had to get into Jim's Skeksis and he said, "Oh my God this is so uncomfortable! How does he do this?" Jim never complained.

JB: What other memories do you have of this remarkable film?

RK: On our downtime, we would hang out in peoples dressing rooms and make stop-motion animation films. Steve (Whitmire) was always doing stuff like that. We had a lot of fun doing that. I loved working on that movie. That was fabulous!

JB: Did you have anything to do with Age of Resistance?

RK: They asked me to do the Fizzgigs for that, but I would have been building them in the New York workshop and everybody else was going to be in LA and I said I didn't want to do that. I wanted to be with the group that was doing it. They took Jason Weber, who's the creative supervisor of the New York workshop out there and he was doing a lot of the dyeing of the costumes, but there didn't have enough money to send two people out. I would have done stuff here, had to send it to LA, and they would have had to send it back to me. It just wasn't going to work. Robert (Bennett) ended up making Fizzgig.

JB: Rollie, this has been wonderful. Thank you so much for your time, stories and wisdom.

ALLAN STEVENS

JB: Tell us about your early years.

Allan Stevens: I was born in Alexandria [Virginia]. I grew up in four "environments." The first was my grandmother's house, which was in Alexandria, on South Pitt Street. I lived there with my mother because in the very beginning daddy and momma couldn't afford to live together. Daddy came visiting on weekends and that was about all. But Grandma's house during those early days on Pitt Street, were really kind of wonderful. Grandpap was totally illiterate, couldn't read or write a thing. Grandma had mastered some writing, so she could communicate and sign things that they needed to have signed. The house had electricity, but the electricity was run "on" the walls, as opposed to "in" the walls and it was not a pretty sight, I can tell you that. The only running water in the house was cold water in the kitchen sink and there was an outhouse out back. On a street, in Alexandria, in the nineteen-forties. The house did not have indoor plumbing until the nineteen-fifties, when it became a law, so this was a very primitive kind of existence, with people who were…poor. But I can tell you there was never a harsh word, never a raised voice in that house and people came and went and I hardly even knew who they were. Some were relatives, some were friends. That was that part of my city living. My dad worked at a place called Hollin Hall Farms. It was a private estate owned by Merle and Lillian Thorpe, whose money was in oil. It was 56 acres off of Fort Hunt Road, in what is now the Mount Vernon area of Fairfax County. We lived in a house in the forest. Right up the road, so to speak, we came to the poultry farm, in which my daddy was a partner with Merle Thorpe. And it WAS a poultry farm! And all the chickens were free range, I have to tell you. Then you got further uphill into the gardens and there was a huge formal garden that was walled, and it was surrounded by informal gardens of all sorts. There was a maze that spelled out "Hollin Hall" that you could only possibly see from the air. There was a windmill. There was a kind of magical architecture that surrounded the mansion house itself. But there was nobody but me. There were people at Grandma's house, but when we moved to Hollin Hall, we first had an apartment over the garage (Which was an apartment I loved. I lived in it as an adult, as a matter of fact.), before we moved down the hill into a better house. Until I was probably twelve years old, I had no friends, and summers were spent just wandering the grounds at Hollin Hall, in the woods, in the poultry farm, and in the informal gardens. So that was kind of a strange atmosphere, so to speak.

I loved every minute of it. I had a dog. What else did I need? But I did a lot of imagination. That's what it comes down to.

JB: How old were you?

AS: This was my very early life. I couldn't read. Daddy would read to me. This was from the time I was five until I was seven, when we moved down to the bigger house in the wood. By that time, I had school friends, so I was not quite so much in isolation as I had been.

JB: You made your theatrical debut in the first grade.

AS: "I am Brownie Early To Bed. Early to bed, early to rise, makes a man healthy, wealthy, and wise." That was my entire role as Brownie Early To Bed.

JB: It's around this time that the suburban areas of Washington are starting to grow. How were you navigating this period?

AS: Around us, the Hollin Hills subdivision grew up and I commandeered everybody and put on little plays and little puppet shows, in the woods, in the back yard, on the patio, anywhere! We did big shows, little shows, but it was never ending.

JB: This is the mid-fifties and television is just starting to happen. Was this also influential?

AS: Yes, but in the funniest way. On Pitt Street in Alexandria where Grandma lived, down the block was the first person who had a television set and they positioned it so the kids could look through the window and see what's on. And what was on was Kukla, Fran, and Ollie.

JB: Was this the "Aha! I'm going to be a puppeteer!" moment?

AS: Nope. But there was a pivotal moment. I couldn't have been more than five. Alexandria was a tiny, little, sleepy southern town. At the corner of King and Washington in Alexandria, on King Street there was a hardware store. It was Knight's Hardware. I remember it dearly because it was still like an old-fashioned hardware store, with kegs of nails and tools that you had no idea what they're meant to do. Cast-iron skillets hanging on one side of the room and axes on the other. It was really terrific! On this particular occasion, I seem to recall snow or cold and we were walking up the street and as we passed Knight's Hardware, in the window, there was a puppet stage and some puppets, marionettes that had been built by Cub Scouts and apparently the store put it on for display. I said, "That's it." There was a king and queen and there were kids, they were wooden ball heads, I do remember that. They were real simple. But they were dressed and had headpieces and all that kind of stuff, but very simple puppet forms, and I think the stage was blue. So as soon as we got home, I went, "I must make one of these puppets, now how shall I do this?" I got out a piece of manila drawing paper and I draw a little circle and I put a little face on it. And then I go, "The paper's too thin. I have to glue this on cardboard and cut it out again." I knew that paste came in small jars. So, I got out a small jar and stuck my little puppet head on the cardboard…and it was Vaseline! So, my first puppet was a bit of a disaster, when you come right down to it. But even in the early days, I learned important lessons. I had a little Snap, Crackle, and Pop [Rice Krispies cereal characters], Snap puppet and a Howdy Doody hand puppet, that had a really soft head that I didn't like, and I made a couple of little rag-muffin things, a frog bean-bag which I used extensively. I remember sitting down in our basement with a little stage of piled-up books that I'd made, with Pinocchio, the book, open in my lap and I'd decided I was going to perform the whole book. So, I'm reading along and going, "This is ridiculous! You can't do this! You got to cut a lot of this stuff out!" And I went, "Aha!" I learned adaptation the hard way.

JB: And this continued as you got older?

AS: The puppets were always there. The first show that I got paid for, I was twelve and it was a birthday party. The mom asked if I would be interested in doing it and I said, "Yes, of course." So, I did a little Hansel and Gretel, mostly with patterns from Edith Flack Ackley. There may have been a papier-mâché head on the witch. But that earned me five dollars.

JB: Which was good money in those days!

AS: Indeed! It was the beginning of my career. Now mind you, I'd never seen a live puppet show! I'd seen Paul's Puppets [editor's note: Bernard Paul had a televised puppet show broadcast from Baltimore in the late 1940s and into the 1950s) on WBAL. It was grainy, but I could see them. So, I was making it up as I went along. I had the same books that everybody had. Edith Flack Ackley and Marjorie Bachelor, mostly from the library. But I started developing a visual style, even though I wasn't sure how to make the mechanics.

JB: Let's talk about college. Where did you go?

AS: A year at the University of Virginia, which was great for the art and the drama. My wonderful high school, Groveton High School, prepared me in no way for academic life. In no way whatsoever. One of the things I was signed up for was biology. The first term was botany, the second term, zoology. I'm looking forward to this. So, I go into the class and it's taught by Doctor Riopel. Doctor Riopel looked like he was about fifteen years old (editor's note: Dr. James L. Riopel was about a decade older than Allan) and the first thing he did was write on this chalkboard the formula for photosynthesis. And I went like, "The whhaaatttt????" I'd never had any biochemistry or any of those things and that's all the class was. There was a lab and I got to see one of the true miracles of life. There was a microscope with two eyepieces so that you could see in 3D. It was the prothallus of a fern. It's the thing that the fern germinates from and it was one of the most breathtaking things I've ever seen. It was worth it for that moment and it was very momentary, because everybody was standing in line to look at this thing. That's the one thing I remember from the year at the University of Virginia. I did lots of stuff in the theater department, almost always relegated to paint. I hadn't been there a month before I got (to be) in charge of the paint department, which in that time was ground pigment, you just got pigments in big bags and boxes. Hot glue, but not (with) glue guns, rabbit skin glue, hide-glue, and you mix that up and put in the white and you put in the color and it's a mess, but that's what I did, basically. Did a lot of background painting and stuff like that and enjoyed it all. But Bennington was a whole different thing. I was a Fellow. My four years at Bennington cost me not one penny for anything, except getting there and getting home. I did have to work. The work consisted of probably a half-hour of work in the workshop and it was usually dusting props or sweeping the studio floor, or something completely innocuous, that you would do anyway. This is what's earning me this education. But Bill Sherman was the person who really turned me around to everything. He was, at the time, the chairman of the drama department. I went up for an interview and I was the only person who interviewed that year. They were supposed to have five boys for the dance department and five boys for the drama department, because Bennington at that time was a girl's school. It was actually founded as coeducational, but during the wars it became, more and more, a girl's school and had remained that way. They just brought in men to work with the girl's in dance and in theater, so they wouldn't have to be playing "pants parts" all the time. I think he saw the puppeteer in me. When I worked on design with Bill, it was always finding "concept" and how to develop the concept, what sources we were using, and how we were using them, and what part does imagination play in this. Can you take this concept that really happened and broaden it into something more abstract? And that was four years-worth doing extraordinary things. Hippolytus, which I designed the set for, Tidings Brought to Mary – I did the costumes. Tons and tons of stuff

JB: And this is what launched you after college?

AS: It was actually when I was in college. Bennington has a non-resident term in the middle of the winter, because everything gets snowed in and they don't want you snowed in up there, as well as a summer break. In my non-resident terms, I went back to my old high school. Dorthie Kogelman was a teacher there and we were very good friends and that time of year was when she was preparing her festival play, because they had one-act play festivals in high school. And we talked about it and ultimately, I ended up one year working with her on Prometheus Bound. The next year was Everyman. The Seven Princesses, an obscure Maurice Maeterlinck play. Abraham and Isaac from the medieval pageants and Aria Da Capo, an Edna St.

Vincent Millay play. All of that was wonderful stuff. In the summer, I started doing summer stock. The first year was in Bar Harbor, Maine and I took the puppets with me, so I would do puppet shows on the weekend and scenery and costumes the rest of the week. That was not a bad year. I think it kind of went bust. Obviously, Bar Harbor is a tourist town and the theater just didn't attract as it should have. We had some good audiences, but it was not a blockbuster season, by any stretch of the imagination. I think it was eight shows, eight shows in eight weeks and that was kind-of doable. My next year, one of the directors from Bennington hired a couple of us; myself as designer, another Bennington student as technical director, and a couple of other people as well, for twelve weeks in White Lake, Michigan and they were all huge shows. Tea House of the August Moon; Bye, Bye Birdie; The Pajama Game; Roberta. One a week. Costumes and scenery. That was a hell of a summer, I can tell you. There was a lot of in-fighting and fuss that went throughout the whole season. The last show was The Fantasticks and I designed it as a commedia [dell'arte] show with kind of unusual costumes. I had discovered in this loft, from God knows when, a set of drapes that were kind-of a medium-dusty teal that had a really wonderful quality to it. So, we used those and we painted the floor the same color and there was a rakish platform and the usual swag sign. It went very well, after this year of horror. At the end of the opening night, everyone in the company came up and kissed me! One of them sat up with me all night long listening to me babble about absolutely nothing!

It was actually during this same period that I moved on. While I was at Bennington, there was a year that Bill Sherman spent in Greece, because we were getting ready to do Hippolyta. During that time, I was the costumer at Bennington College. I also, with my advisor, did a puppet production of Doctor Fautus, which was flawed, but beginning to point the right direction. One of the last shows we did at Bennington was The King's Stag. This is a Carlo Gozzi, seventeenth century, Italian comedy in commedia style. Bill had this wonderful concept: all the costumes were made out of white duvetyne, which pretty much looks like white velvet at a quarter of the price, with brilliantly colored linings and facings and collars. I did masks and props and I played Truffaldino as well. I felt that it looked gorgeous, but there was something I didn't feel was right in the direction and I'm sitting around home one day and I hear that the Smithsonian is going to have a children's theater and I said, "They ARE?" Now oddly enough, I knew the director of the division of performing arts, so I was able to call him up and say, "Hey, I want to do this." I did some drawings and he said, "Okay, we're going to do this." I chose two shows. One of them was The King Stag, which I hoped to get right this time and it incorporated puppets. The theater was in a tent on the Mall, that had been specially designed. It was a circular tent with kind-of a scooped roof, in blue and white. The roof was supposed to be white on the outside and black on the inside to reflect heat and we were guaranteed it would be ten degrees cooler in the tent. Unfortunately, it was manufactured incorrectly, and it was installed with the black, outside and the white, inside. Which meant that it was ten degrees hotter inside than it was out. And there we were, in these amazing, huge costumes that were all lined and velvet and headpieces… melting! We stopped using makeup. It was ridiculous! It wouldn't stay on your face. You had to go by the water fountain and literally stick your face in it to keep from passing out, it was that awful. The tent was supposed to accomplish two things: the children's theater in the daytime and an American musical theater at night. The first production that they did was Annie Get Your Gun. It was a great choice. Ethel Merman had just done a revival on Broadway. They got the Broadway costumes, which were wonderful. The Indian things in particular were just incredible. Ball gowns with all the hoohah and gimcrack you'd ever want to see. The got real firearms. The furniture was all antique stuff. It was all like the real live thing. So, the costumes were hanging back in this backstage area and it being a tent, it had a dirt floor. And it rained. And there were these Indian blankets and the trains on these incredible dresses in the mud! So, we're running around in ridiculously elaborate outfits trying to rescue the costumes from Annie Get Your Gun. We succeeded only partially. They did get on the second show, which was Of Thee I Sing. Congress stepped in and just closed it. The third show was supposed to be Guys and Dolls, which is one of my two or three favorite shows ever and I was looking forward to that. But for Annie Get Your Gun, the costumes were all destroyed, the guns, the antique furniture, were all destroyed. The losses I can't begin to calculate. Toward the middle of that, I was in a magazine store on 14th Street and who should walk in the door but Jim Morris, the Director of the Division of Performing Arts and we said hello and he said to me, "By the way, do you want to do this puppet tour that we have going out this fall." And I said, "Yes, I'd like to." That was it. That was the entire contract made in twenty seconds or more and it was the end of my life doing anything except puppets.

JB: Who was doing this before you?

AS: Fred Thompson. Fred Thompson had rotten breaks, one after the other and Fred is a wonderful person, he's a wonderful puppet maker, he's a wonderful performer. Besides thinking of what he wanted to do himself, he had the Rufus Rose shows that he could borrow at any time and that was wonderful.

But it all started off with the great Smithsonian fire. My good friend at the time, Vera Hughes, and I were going to go to the opening of Fred's show together. And I'm getting ready to go and the phone rings and it's Vera and she says, "Allan, have you heard the news?" And I went, "What news?" And she said, "Well, there's been a fire at the Smithsonian." And I said, "Oh gee, which building?" And she said, "History and Technology." I said, "Oh, that's awful. Whereabouts?" And she said, "On the third floor." And I said, "What?!?" And she said, "Allan, the fire was in the puppet theater." We went, "What are we going to do now?" I had been instrumental in bringing Fred to town. He came with his friend Russell Metheny. Vera and I went down to the Mall and we found Russell and Fred. Russell was green and they said, "We haven't been back in." And just about that time a guy came up and said, "You may go in now." So, we crept slowly in. We went up to the third floor. Obviously, the escalators and elevators weren't running. We had to walk up. Everything that had looked like marble, glass, and metal had melted and was hanging off the wall. We apprehensively moved forward. Basically, the puppet theater was gone and on what had been the stage, were Rufus Rose's Puppets…hanging untouched. It was absolutely amazing.

foot on which Fred started, and it got worse. You'll hear different stories about what life at the Smithsonian was like. I got along. There were only a couple of moments in which I wanted to smack somebody or take them by the shoulders and shake them, but generally, within a perimeter of sorts, I got to do what I wanted to do. The things that was interesting, out of it all, was that I was being protected, so that I was never at the "upper end" meetings, so I never really knew what was going on, on top. What I did finally realize at one point was, apparently, we weren't making as much money as everybody hoped we would, and apparently, there was some talk about what were we doing that didn't bring in more money. First of all, after the upstairs theater burned, the new theater opened up in the Carmichael Auditorium, which is on the ground floor of what was History and Technology and is now American History.

To be in the museum, we had to do museum related shows and how on Earth were we gonna' do that? We developed a good friend by the name of Judy Morris, who wrote some shows for us. Judy is a wonderful writer and always was, but she inherited it fairly. Her father was Elia Kazan. She was good and it was fun. The first show we did with Judy was The Waywardly Wandering Wagon Full of Banjo and Jack, which was Southern folklore and we did a scavenger hunt related to exhibits in the theater, you know, the wagon that they were performing on, things that they talked about, so there was definitely a link to the museum. In 1972, we did a show which was called The Hullaballoo Election of Osbert or Jess. I was working with Ingrid Crepeau from very early on and she was developing her own puppetry style, so we said hey, we'll do these puppets together. She did the principal characters and they were Muppet-like, fabric puppets. The whole idea of the show was these two characters, Osbert and Jess, were running for president of the puppet theater and through this we went through the whole process of campaigning, of doing door-to-door, making flyers. And at the end of the show, everybody goes into a voting machine and votes, and so the kids got to vote, too. Now Osbert was orange, Jess was green, and we learned an important lesson. The white audiences voted for Osbert. The black audiences all voted for Jess. So, the difference between the warm and cool colors actually split on a racial divide. I have borne that piece of information with me ever since that even if you're avoiding the subject of race, by just using colors, you're not avoiding it. But those years at the Smithsonian, all the pieces came together. Slowly but surely, I learned how to do all the things I didn't know how to do before. I knew how to make a wrist joint, the head joint was really kind-of transformational. It's a very simple thing in which the head is balanced on elastic. Fifty percent rubber, fifty percent cotton elastic, so that the head can be nodded by triggers on the handle of the rod puppet. The first time we did it, we were working on Tom Sawyer. Russell Metheny was working with us at that time. We put the first one together and tried it, and we all went, "Look at that!" We scrambled getting puppets together, left and right! And going, "Hey! It worked again!" It was really a wonderful moment.

JB: During this time, you also worked with some other interesting people. Grammy winner Ken Bloom worked as a puppeteer for you.

AS: Ken was in the touring shows and I know he did the Marvelous Land of Oz. He may have done Tom Sawyer as well. The only time he performed at the Smithsonian was when we were doing Alice in Wonderland. We did a new show every three months and none of them were little, so everybody was really worn out and they wanted to take a break at the same time that the touring company came back from the tour. So, we let the resident company off on a holiday and the touring company, to earn a few more bucks, got to do the resident show, which was Alice in Wonderland. At that time, Ken started doing shows that were called things like The Unsung Jerome Kern or The Unsung Cole Porter, in which he would put together programs of the lesser known music of these greats of the American musical theater. After the success of the election year show, we developed a show called Patchwork, which was not only a patchwork in terms of little bits of Americana, and shorts stories and things you've heard, but never saw happen and the patchwork being the fabric that Ingrid used to create the puppets. It was hysterical! Absolutely wonderful! It ran for quite a while. One of the characters was this little girl who liked to put on plays, and so she would get all the other characters out and get them dressed up in outrageous things and put on a little pageant.

So, they did a Thanksgiving pageant, they did a holiday pageant. It was wonderful. All I had to do was sit back and watch. But that really launched Ingrid. She went from that into Kids on the Block, the series of puppets that have physical handicaps. She developed puppet for all these disabilities. She and another puppeteer working with us, Sarah Toth worked out Patchwork Productions which was carrying this whole thing forward into a new generation. Something happened. I think it was as simple as they wanted to do a national tour, and they did a brochure and a huge mailing, and I think they got absolutely no bites and they just went, "This isn't going to work." And it was at that time Ingrid happened to bump into Michele (Valeri) and Dino-rock was born.

JB: And Vera Hughes played a big part, too.

AS: Vera did a lot of the adaptation. She was good. She did Tom Sawyer, Aladdin, a couple of others. We closed the Smithsonian Puppet Theater, as I knew it, in 1975. The idea was the place was going to be renovated for the bicentennial exhibit, which was the next year. Before we closed they were already working on the building, because it was a huge piece of work that they did in a very short time. The idea was that for the 1976 show, that we'd submit a new application. There were those that thought I could just walk back in the door. Working with one of the guys at the Smithsonian, we were going to do The Wizard of Oz, but base it on the stage play that Frank Baum wrote, after the popularity of his book and the popularity of Babes in Toyland. At the same time, Nic Coppola submitted a proposal to actually recreate the 1876 centennial show. The Smithsonian came to both of us. They wanted me to choose something better or him to charge less. (Nic's show was) exactly what it ought to be. So, I withdrew my proposal. And actually, happily. That show ended up being very good. The stage was absolutely gorgeous, stunning. But that put me on the street, so to speak. I had a number of small jobs. A job with Voice of America. A job with the Pentagon, believe it or not, a series of Army training films. We did a puppet for them and operated it. It took, I think, about four years to get the whole thing done. I had a near-death experience!

JB: Let's hear more about that!

AS: The first series was training bartenders, actually.

JB: An essential occupation.

AS: They set up a whole bar in the Pentagon studio and I'm sitting there doing my puppet stuff and the lighting grid fell. It was just one bar, but all the lights slid straight off of it. Missed me by a foot. We took a deep breath I can tell you. They were great people to work with, they really were. I enjoyed being with the Pentagon. I thought it was sort of ironic, as a matter of fact. At any rate, I've got all these shows that I've built, I ought to be doing something with them and I'm back in Alexandria and thinking it would be nice to have a little theater in Alexandria, so I was walking around looking for a storefront and wondering what you had to do to it to get it open, as a theater. And I had a little bit of money from the Smithsonian days and I was in downtown D.C. one day and I bumped into a friend who had worked with us at the Smithsonian. And we went and had a drink at a place called the Bavarian, a little downstairs bar and grill. And this person suggested that maybe we should go on from the idea of just my little theater, that would be a storefront and into maybe a national center. And I said, "Well, you know in Alexandria there's the old Richmond Theater that's been sitting there vacant all these years. Let's go and see if we can go inside. Well, we did. The roof was gone, which meant that the decorative tin ceiling and the cornices and all that stuff were hanging by a thread. But we talked to the owner and the owner said, "Well, we can do this. We'll replace the roof if you'll do everything else," and then we'll charge you this much rent and so forth and so on. So, this person started a limited partnership in which she was the principle partner and she started getting investors for a thousand dollars a pop and she basically hired me to be artistic director. Well, we opened, and it was a great opening, it really was. The place looked incredible. And then business wasn't doing so good and we're wondering why, and we are trying to make connections and going, "Well this is strange, because this show did awfully well at the Smithsonian, and nobody comes to it six miles away?" That's what it was; Alexandria, except for a few dedicated citizens, wasn't ready for a puppet theater. We couldn't get schools to come, although there was bus parking, they kind'a didn't want to deal with it and this person, who was the producer, vanished! We were left alone holding the bag. Around Christmas time, she reappeared, and we talked about converting what had been this limited partnership, into a non-profit. During that time, Donna and David Wisniewski were working for Prince Georges County and I had done Peter and the Wolf with them the year before, and they wanted to do Hansel and Gretel with live singers. The opera, but of course edited way down to forty-five minutes and I thought, "Neat," and so I went and did that and traveled back and forth, with the theater in Alexandria on Sundays, and Hansel and Gretel on others, to earn a little money to pay people back at the Alexandria theater

We were at a meeting with our attorney and she and her associate producer accused me of dereliction of duty for having gone and done the Hansel and Gretel show and I said, "That's it." But it didn't matter, because there just was not the right attitude in Alexandria. We had some wonderful people come onto the board, but they didn't quite grasp what being a non-profit means, what you have to do with the money, if you get a project grant or you get a regular grant, and what you can repay with what, and all of that stuff. And I had a breakdown. I just went flop! We closed it. We went down, for a short period of time, and worked at the Torpedo Factory and that finally just literally petered out. I was at loose ends and my health had gone to hell-in-a-handbasket. I had to sell my house to pay off construction bills on the theater in Alexandria. I was penniless, as a matter of fact, not well and drinking an awful lot of alcohol and eating very little food, at which time there was an offer to come out to Glen Echo Park and direct a piece for Adventure Theater. They had what they called their puppetry division. A guy by the name of Ed Tamulevich was in the puppetry division and he wanted me to do the puppets for a piece called Jack and the Beanstalk and Other English Folk Tales, which he produced. And at the auditions, who should be there but Christopher Piper and by the time we got Jack and the Beanstalk open, we were fast friends. Chris was coming from Hawaii, he'd been across the country and to France and back again, so he was really interested in settling here and he had decided he wanted to apply for a yurt studio (at Glen Echo Park), because those applications were coming up. He wanted one of the big ones and he didn't think he could get it by himself. But would I join in with him? And we did. Once together we were contacted by the Smithsonian to do a show. They were doing a season of traditional fairy tales and wanted to know what we could do. I suggested we do a composite fairy tale which we called The Magic Mirror. Chris wrote it. Chris made the creatures. I made the human characters. We were off and here we are.

JB: The creation of the Puppet Co was a major undertaking, from its early days in the park, through the construction of this beautiful theater that you and the Pipers are about to hand over to a new artistic director and team. Just how hard was it to make this all possible?

AS: We had actually submitted proposals before. One time it was for what was then the rehearsal hall at Adventure Theater, which was big enough to be a small theater. I believe there was another space we applied for as well, but we kept getting turned down. But our program had become so popular, that we were having up to a hundred thousand people a year. We had managed to get the schedule of the carousel changed. It used to be just Wednesdays, Saturdays, and Sundays. We first got Thursdays and then later, Fridays, because we could bring in the visitation. The director from the George Washington Memorial Parkway for the National Park Service said, "We have to find you a space. We have to do this. Obviously, the public wants it." When we were settled over there, it was with good reason, and our relationship with the National Park Service was very good. The whole process of the restoration and the rescue of the park took over seven years from the time Audrey Calhoun said, "We're going to do this," to the time we that actually walked in the door. And there were promises that couldn't be helped. Originally, we were supposed to be able to walk from the old playhouse into the new one with no interruption in between and it couldn't possibly work. And we really knew that. So, we went into exile, so to speak, in the back room of the ballroom for at least two years. Longer than we wanted to, but through the design of this facility, a lot of which Christopher did… the ground plan of the theater and the stage was really what Christopher offered to the National Park Service and the architect worked those things in, so we had a good deal to say about what was going to happen in this space. It totaled out at $500,000. More than $350,000 was to the contractor. Christopher installed all the sound equipment, on the stage and in the house and everyplace else. Dan Brooks, who was our lighting designer for thirty years, did all the installation of the lighting. That we saved money on. There were lots of ways we cut corners, because believe me, we got a lot for our half-million dollars.

JB: What was the most difficult thing to deal with?

AS: General aggravation. There were people on these various committees that were with Montgomery County who really wanted to slow the process down and there were people like me who wanted to speed the process up. We could have been a year earlier getting into the process, except there was this group of people, for reasons I don't really understand, thought a slower and more meticulous way would be more beneficial, to whom I don't know. It wasn't beneficial to us, I can tell you. So that was disturbing.

Now Audrey Calhoun was the Superintendent at that time. She had been the site manager at Glen Echo Park when we first came on. She actually accomplished miracles in those early days, in the early 1980s. She had said that one of the things she wanted to do was get the infrastructure, the wiring and plumbing and so forth installed in the park so that when we got to actually renovating the buildings, that would be done. So then twenty, thirty years later she comes back as Superintendent, and guess what. She gets her wish, so before the buildings went up, all the utilities had already been installed and that saved a huge amount of money on that, There were those who said, "She's just fixing the place up so she can sell it." This was never true. Audrey really loved Glen Echo Park, she was eager to see it get back together and blossom. And when the process was over, we had a conversation and she said, "Well Allan, we did it." And I said, "Yes Audrey, we did. But I wish it hadn't been so divisive and cantankerous. " And she shocked me when she said, "Oh no, Allan. That's part of the process." Going through that you really find out what people want and you're able to do a better job of reaching the greater public and that input works to your advantage.

JB: Let's change the subject for a minute. I understand that you love musicals.

AS: Actually, I'm into opera right now. I'm on Tannhäuser right now. I love Wagner. He wrote some of the most boring scenes I've ever read in my life, but with some of the most glorious music. I do like musicals, but I'm not crazy about Rogers and Hammerstein. Richard Rogers, I love. I'm not sure what I think about Hammerstein, at all. You know, he never could write a second act.

JB: Second acts are where all the problems are anyway.

AS: I'll give you two examples, one being The King and I, the other being South Pacific. In the second act of each of those, we lose a major character off-stage. Lun Tha gets killed in a revolution, we just hear about it and Cable, who's extremely important member in South Pacific, does the same thing! He goes off and gets killed somewhere and this is the great dramatic moment and oh yeah, he's dead! He got killed over there. Which I can't much tolerate. I've got two favorite shows and it's real simple and real easy. One is Guys and Dolls and the other is She Loves Me. And they're very similar shows, in which an improbable romance actually works out.

JB: Let's talk more about the partnership with you, and Christopher and MayField Piper.

AS: MayField coming into the company was pivotal, absolutely pivotal. She had known Chris's family for a long time and worked for them as a costumer. Chris's dad [Len Piper] did a renaissance heritage fair in Honolulu and he invited us to come out and do The Magic Mirror and Chris was also going to perform Peter and the Wolf, which we did. Then Chris met MayField and even though she had known the other brothers, he was The One. And within a couple of years they were married and, of course, she married the Puppet Company as well. But the minute she walked in the door, we started making money. I think we were easier to perceive as these two guys doing this very peculiar work when MayField came in. It was more like a family. MayField has succeeded at anything she ever tried. She does needlepoint that is incredible. She did pottery for a while and it's incredible. She's made an incredible business manager. She's done such a fabulous job. As well as being (Cinderella), she never imagined she was going to play Cinderella. Somebody stuck the puppet in her hand and said, "No! Say it like this!" Her roles in Cinderella and Pinocchio, in particular, are exemplary. Working on costumes with her has been a joy.

JB: The three of you have made a great team.

AS: I've often thought, how have we managed to do this without killing each other? Living together and working together. We all three think on both sides of our brains. We have a creative end, as well as a cognitive end and it's through that, that we've been able to do this three-person show here, thirty-seven years later.

JB: Let's talk a bit about the current state of puppetry.

AS: I think there's a pivotal moment. Jim Henson produced an extraordinary experience for children and for families through his television shows, but he always espoused a more sophisticated theater for adults, with puppets. But it really didn't happen. What's odd is just after his death, all of a sudden, little theaters started springing up here and there. When we started here, the nearest was Boston, to the north and Atlanta, to the south. Well, that's not true anymore. I find that interesting. A lot of it is through people like Heather (Henson).

JB: Her own beautiful work and the series of short puppet films, Handmade Puppet Dreams, come to mind.

AS: That and sponsoring slams and all of those things. Julie Taymor has to get some credit. I'm sorry she doesn't like to hire puppeteers and hires dancers instead, but certainly her design and the way she's integrated into stage-play has resulted in things like the boy in Madame Butterfly being (a puppet). Olney, in the past couple of years, did Our Town with puppets. It's almost difficult to see a show that doesn't have a puppet hanging around somewhere or other. Which is a good thing, because people like Matt McGee. He gets all kinds of work making puppets that are being incorporated into other things. Dre Moore, at Adventure Theater, is turning out some wonderful stuff as well. She's a prop person who's moved into puppetry and very successfully. I don't think that the puppetry disciplines are always applied to what goes on onstage. There is a Philip Glass opera about Gandhi [Satyagraha]. It has fantastic puppets in it. Huge! They're made out of newspaper. They're absolutely gorgeous. Warhorse. Shows like that.

JB: There's also The Oldest Boy by Sarah Ruhl, about a young boy who is recognized as a reborn Tibetan Buddhist teacher. The entire cast alternated as puppeteers to invisibly integrate the manipulation into the show. A couple of year's ago, I saw The Woodsman, James Ortiz's adaptation of the back story of the Tin Woodsman from the Oz stories. Brilliant. It's a joy to see puppetry affect an adult audience as if they were children, to see the suspension of disbelief.

AS: You know seeing is believing and we have experiences here (where) the adults don't know what's going to happen when they walk in the door. Particularly in the first decade or two of The Nutcracker, dads would come and say, "All these times I've been dragged to The Nutcracker and at last I know what the story is about." That conversation happened timed after time. It's kind of a magical thing and this reflects on the adult response to what's happening on the stage. When we first did Cinderella, one of the early difficulties was how we were going to do the transformations. We bought our first really expensive piece of fabric, which was called Cracked Ice, for Cinderella's ball dress. It was a hundred dollars a yard and I think we got three-quarters of a yard. Then how are we going to reveal it? Well, we'll just over-dress it and she'll spin around, and it'll come off. So, we started doing the show and people were having their minds blown, because we're tearing a rag off this shiny thing. And the device shows! I've watched in on tape and it's right there, but the audience (doesn't want) to see it and so they erase the rough edges and it just goes from wham to sparkle. The same is true for the transformation in Snow White, when the queen turns into the hag and it's a turnaround and there's nothing complicated in what actually happens except the audience is ready for it and so they make the magic!

JB: Let's talk a little about the Rapunzel gallery show.

AS: Boy, that was a funny thing. First of all, it was for the Museum of Women and the Arts and it was (in) their library. I got a phone call from the curator who wondered if we happened to have puppets of Rapunzel because they were doing a Rapunzel exhibit. Rapunzel from every possible point of view. She came over and looked and said, “That’s exactly what I want.” I had no idea how they were going to be displayed and they ended up in flat library cases that weren’t that deep, with glass tops. We had to tuck their costumes under them. They all fit, and they all stood up, but was not the way I would have preferred they be displayed. But, you know, that was fun. The big gallery thing came out of the 1980 puppetry exhibit. That exhibit toured practically every major gallery in the United States and it had my caterpillar from Alice in Wonderland was in that exhibit, so I got included a lot of other places.

JB: You also were the Director of Capital Fireworks, the 2008 regional Puppeteers of America Festival.

AS: What I was pleased with was in that festival all of the shows were first time, none of the shows had been performed at a festival before. My pet project, a day of solo performances, was great because people don’t really realize the range of things that a solo performer can do, so I loved that. We had a great exhibit, we had an extraordinary store. But the thing lost money and part of the reason it lost money was because we were trying so hard to not interfere with anything else going on, but Peter Allen and his wife had PuppetFest MidWest, which ended up being exactly the same time as our festival and we lost what would have been the difference in breaking even.

JB: You, along with Christopher and MayField are poised to retire in two months and we plan to feature the three of you along with your new artistic director Liz Dapo, in our next newsletter. How do you feel about retiring?

AS: It was a surprise. This is important to know. We had talked about retiring when Chris reached his seventieth birthday, but as we’ve gone into this period in which we have had audiences diminishing and finding it really difficult to make ends meet, we’re all played out. I’ll give this example which I gave to the County Arts Council and they got a big laugh out of it. Here am I, I'm sitting at my computer in a dimly lit room and I'm writing the Great American Novel or the Great American Puppet Play or whatever it is. And I know I've just got a couple more lines to write. And I think like, oh God, do I need a cup of coffee or what? But I don't have the wherewithal to get up. And I go, oh my God, this chair is breaking my back! But I don't have the wherewithal to get up and change chairs. And all of a sudden, here comes the Glen Echo Partnership in the door and they go, "Look at you! You look terrible! Let me get you a cushion. Then Liz comes in the other door and says, "Ah, you look awful. Let me get you a cup of coffee I'll put the kettle on!" And all of a sudden, the lights come on and I write, "And they all lived happily ever after."

JB: You've had such an amazing career, what amazing things do you plan to do after June 30th?

AS: Probably a couple of days a week, at least through the end of the year, I'm going to be doing archives. The pictures that I sent you [included in this interview] are the tip of an iceberg. I can't do more than four or five hours a day. It doesn't work, that's all. I have emphysema, and that's puppetry related. Acetone. Back when we were building the Smithsonian puppets, the only instruction you got was "use in a ventilated space" and my studio was in a basement. So, for five or six years, every day, I had my nose over an acetone bucket.

JB: But now that it's here, how do you feel about retirement?

AS: You know, I was ready to plod through for another two years. I would have and it would have been a diminishing return, but I still would have done it, but I am actually much relieved. And it's not that there aren't shows that I wouldn't like to do. As a matter of fact, I've been giving Liz a challenge of real theater pieces. I'm going to challenge her to do things like Archy and Mehitabel to Prometheus Bound, other complicated shows, all of which can lend themselves to puppetry very well. It's the sort of thing she'd want to do. She's done a lot of adult theater using puppets.

JB: I can tell you that you will be missed in retirement. Allan, it's been an honor to speak with you. What other thoughts would you like to leave us with?

AS: I like to define terms. I like to know where I am. Now mind you, things which I have developed for myself, may have never even been spoken of, to Christopher and MayField, even though they were playing it out on the stage, they may not have known why. Recently Chris made me tell him why a certain gesture had to be made at such a time, and I said alright, here it goes. First thing, I divide puppeteers into two categories, professionals and hobbyists. Professionals make all, or the greater part of their income from puppetry, the hobbyists do not. There's no such thing as an amateur puppeteer. It doesn't exist. Anybody, for me, giving a first read to a new script to some twelve year old sitting at the kitchen table, with two library books and a shoebox full of dreams, there's no difference, because the path toward the production itself is going to be the same. I will say this, from time to time you will have amateurish behaviors, but that can happen to the professionals or the hobbyist. Part of my reason for doing this is I used to be so amused (by) Mabel Beaton's book, Marionettes: A Hobby for Everyone. And you go like, a hobby for everyone?!? Who's got these talents and that workshop and knows how to use these materials and everything else! But the fact is, her husband never quit his job. They never lived off puppetry. They did the puppetry mostly for fun. They did the parables, I think it was called Lamp Unto My Feet (editor's note: apparently this show was called Bible Puppets), a religious television show. I always gathered that they were probably being paid for it, but I don't know that. Even if they were paid for it, it probably wasn't very much. Have you seen the parables?

JB: Most of them. That sort of thing was big where I grew up.

AS: They're really quite wonderful. The original piece, The Nativity, is a little bit creaky, quite frankly. They are beautiful things to look at, but some of the manipulation…the Three Kings looks like they've got loads in their britches. But they got past that when they got to the parables and they're very well done. Also, the story of Moses and the story of Joseph, those are also very well done. I think both of those are in color. The parables are in black and white. But it's all very worth seeing. At a workshop recently, I did my definition of puppetry. Now I have to tell you, all these definitions are fluid. They're fluid because I think puppetry is a moving target and you know you can't say puppetry is only this or only this, because you're only going to get caught in your own trap sooner or later.

JB: The word puppet seems to mean many different things to different people.

AS: I needed to find, for myself, a definition of "puppet" that went beyond inanimate objects being brought to life. This is a work in progress. I keep looking for ways to clarify my thoughts - and my definition.

To me, puppet is any inanimate object, shadow image, or disassociated body part made to move and given the illusion of life and personality, directly or indirectly, by a puppeteer - an individual trained in puppetry. I add the personality along with it because if the personality ain't there, you're just moving a chair around. You're moving the furniture and that's all. When you think of Kermit, you don't look at him and think, oh yeah, isn't that a piece of old coat? Which he is. You think about this wonderful character, not what he's made out of or the fact that he has a hand in his face. It's the personality of the character that comes through and it's what has made the Muppets and The Muppet Show overwhelmingly successful. Puppetry is a process of distillation and purification. In a way, it is the same for the puppeteer as it is for the show, that it is a process that has a catharsis whether you realize it or not. The you will be changed by your experience. You start with a story and you say, "Alright, do I need a script?" And then you look at the script. Do I need all these words? Do I think that I can just do silence there? Or how about do a little dance there or maybe sing a little song there? What color is going to suit this moment the best? What about the lighting? If I want this to be translated in some way, how do I do that? Just to keep tearing stuff away. I saw a show recently, this was a show that included puppets and it was a popular, but very complicated children's piece, that you wonder whether it's really for children at all. (It was) done by an extremely reputable company and they were in concert with the Washington Ballet and it was a show that was a long time coming together. I go to see it and I expect to see the dance incorporated into the story. What happened was the actors would play out a scene, and then the dancers would come out a dance the same scene! And what's more, the actors when they spoke, intoned the lines. There was no inflection whatsoever. I can tell you that no child that went into that theater, not knowing the story, came out knowing it any better! Which is too bad. Don't do that. Don't complicate matters! You get rid of (things) until you've got…Snow White has a blue dress and she has a medallion that's a snowflake. That's what it must be. Generally, I think there is a difference between looking at art and looking at illustration. If you go into a gallery and you turn a corner and you see Renoir's Luncheon of the Boating Party, chances are the first thing you're going to do is step back because there's a shield between you and the extraordinary experience going on in the painting. With an Illustration, it's the opposite. You see the image and you're drawn to it. That accounts for most of our repertory. We want to embrace the audience; we want to give them this treat. I have very different feelings about Snow White, I don't know why. Snow White has that particular power. From the first time I started reading the script and the fact that the name takes on major proportions; your name means something, and the idea is that the queen knows your name. She can use it as a weapon, so everybody is just brother and sister, until unfortunately, Snow White slips and tells the prince her name and then two-hundred kids in the audience go, "!!!!" That's very rewarding.

JB: What are your criteria for judging a performance?

AS: At some point, I realized that I needed to be able to discuss puppet productions, often with their makers… even if I did not personally like the show. I wanted to keep it simple. I put together four simple criteria: could I see everything? This applies to all of the visual aspects of the show such as the design of the puppets, the scenery, the lighting, the staging, the sight-lines, the color - anything visual. Could I hear everything? This applies to all things auditory, such as voices, music, or sound effects. Did I become confused at any time? Confusion could be the result a problematic script, or problematic staging or the blocking of the show. Did I become bored during the performance? This is the kiss of death for any show, especially a show for children or family audiences. It is also the most difficult one to put your finger on. You may become bored because a scene is too static or too long. It could also be the product poor visuals, or sound - individually or together. When you approach this criterion, choose your words carefully.

I have had good luck using this critique system in difficult situations. Do I ever stray from this format? Yes… and I always wish that I hadn't.

Editor's note: If anyone is interested, Renoir's Luncheon of the Boating Party hangs in the Phillips Gallery in Washington, DC.

CAROLY WILCOX

JB: Let's start with your childhood. You grew up in Swarthmore, Pennsylvania.

Caroly Wilcox: Yup. My father was a college professor. I went to a private progressive, sort-of John Dewey (an American philosopher, psychologist, and educational reformer whose ideas have been influential in education and social reform] school, which was great fun. It was on the edge of some woods. We'd get tadpoles and watch them change into frogs. We had guinea pigs and bantam chickens and goats. At the end of each year the kids would go on a camping trip: the youngest (3-4) for one night, the oldest for a five-day trip. In eighth grade there was a biking or hiking trip on the Horseshoe Trail in the Pennsylvania Dutch area. Great learning experiences.

JB: And you went to Swarthmore College? The school's philosophy is based on Quaker values. What was that like?

CW: Although I was raised as a member of the Society of Friends and I respect it a great deal, I am not active with it. I did go to some work-camps in Mexico that were affiliated with the Society. My first experience of a different life.

JB: You are known for your puppet building skills. Did you acquire your skills early in life?

CW: I guess I took after my mom. I made dolls. I sewed. She taught art at the school I went to - we did all different sorts of crafts: plaster casting, etching. We didn't have a television when I was young. My dad got one of those big boxes with an 8-inch screen to watch the news: Edward Murrow, David Brinkley, Chet Huntley. But that was it. We would watch the news and then it was off. We would read, play games, sing. It never occurred to us to watch it for shows or anything else. Eight -inch B&W was not a very exciting format.

JB: What brought you from Pennsylvania to New York City?

CW: I had a college friend there. I was at a loss as to what to do. I had studied some education, but it was not a good fit.

JB: When was this?

CW: 1954. My mother had died and my father was working in Pakistan (with his new wife, a good lady) and my sister was up at Cornell and later in Indonesia. I tried this and that: waited table, worked in leathercraft making belts and bags.

JB: I found out that you were in a musical, The Next President, with the political satirist, Mort Sahl. This was in 1958. How did that come about?

CW: I had dated a man who knew they were looking for folksingers. It was the weirdest show. The folk singing group with Mary Travers [Later of Peter, Paul, and Mary fame] and Erik Darling -- six in all. Mort would do a set, then he would be supported by the singers or by the Jimmy Giuffre jazz trio, with a modern dancer (!!!). This bizarre combination only lasted a week and a half.

JB: Were you living in the Village at that time?

CW: Yeah. On Barrow Street.

JB: That was an incredibly exciting time to be in New York City in the Village with the folk music explosion happening.

CW: People would be singing in Washington Square. I sang on two folk music records, too. The first was with Erik Darling, "Run Come Hear the Folk Singers" and the second with Tom Glazer and Sandy Bull [aka. Benjy Bull]. Sandy was the son of a jazz harpist [Daphne Hellman]. Tom did a lot of folksongs for children, had a nice baritone voice and played the guitar. Benjy played banjo. The record was titled "The Samplers in Person". We did about four concerts and that was it!

JB: What were you doing before for work and then how did you become involved in puppetry?

CW: Odds and ends of jobs, waitressing in coffee shops. A friend said, "Well, you've tried all these different things, why don't you try puppetry?" She had a friend working at the Park Department's Marionette Theater. So I interviewed and got in. I worked there for two years. There was a show called "Happy the Humbug" in which the hero was part turtle, part monkey, part giraffe. I made and performed Miss Pink Elephant for that show. The Marionette Theater had been set up during WPA days. The director, Ascanio Spolidoro had a good ear for music for the production--wonderful themes by classical composers. In summer we would perform in the parks from a stage built into a van that would be driven to various parks in the city. The Circus show was quite spectacular, with weightlifters, animals, and as finale, a giant. Huge Legs walked onto the stage, the top of the van opened up and the head and arms of the giant emerged! Good shtick! The kids would sit on the asphalt and sometimes it was too hot! We'd build a production in spring and fall, perform in schools in the winter. The "parkies" would assemble the stage and then the puppeteers would hang the marionettes and do the show. We'd eat the school lunches [laughs]. Brown bread, with cream cheese and marmalade.

JB: I think I would have left off the marmalade myself.

CW: It was on it! You didn't have a choice! While I was with this someone from Swarthmore College called to ask if I would like to do the puppets for their production of Ben Jonson's satirical play "Bartholomew Fair". In one scene the Puritan (and hypocrite) came up and scolded the puppets for being licentious, and he is answered by a puppet pulling up his robes and saying, "Here we are! We're just made of wood and cloth! How can we be licentious?!" These puppets are at the Puppetry Center in Atlanta.

And then I got a job with Larry Berthelson's Pickwick Puppets. We did shows at Lincoln Center with Thomas Scherman's Little Symphony Orchestra. We performed De Falla's "Master Peter's Puppet Show", Mozart's "The Magic Flute" (in an abridged version by Oscar Hammerstein's daughter), and also Ravel's "L'Enfant et les Sortileges". I built and performed the Armchair in this last one. I also toured with Larry puppeteering on his smaller shows. I built small fold-up sets for "Rumpelstiltskin" and other shows. For "Scheherazade" I built the sets and Penny Jones did the puppets.

Later on I worked on "All Join Hands", a local CBS-TV children's show (it fulfilled the public affairs requirement). Beryl Bernay created the show. Each week we would focus on a different country. I would research folk tales and customs to find what would be interesting to present. I would phone the consulates to see about props.

(For Switzerland I got to blow an alphorn). There were big drawings of village life and small magnetized figures would walk down the streets. I also made many quick hand puppets with rubber ball heads for this show.

Larry passed on to me a job with Project Arise - educational experiences for high school kids. So I went to Berlin, New Hampshire, and in two weeks we built and performed "Peter and the Wolf". They did a great job. In 1965 I worked in the World's Fair: The Chrysler pavilion: Bil Baird's marionettes with a crank-case torso and sexy legs - a Rockette kick chorus.

JB: So, you kind of learned on the job. How did you get to Sesame Street?

CW: I read that Joan Cooney was starting show, so I wrote to them about my TV and puppet experience. And they said, well. eh. Then I read that Jim Henson was going to do it, so I went to Jim. He was looking for puppeteers and I am not a great puppeteer--or rather, I am good at mime, but absolutely cannot ad-lib. Jim really is happy with free ad lib creating characters. Fortunately, he also needed to expand his puppet-building staff, which consisted of only Don Sahlin at the time. So, I joined at the very beginning of Sesame Street production.

JB: You were involved in a lot of the early commercial work, too.

CW: I remember going on a shoot to Staten Island. I guess it was an ad for nutrition, with Cookie Monster. I was there to take care of the puppet and to do the right hand. Frank Oz would perform the left hand and the mouth of Cookie. The bit was fun. First it was eat peas, eat carrots, eat meat. Then finally it was eat cookies--and a whole payload of cookies dumped down on Cookie!

JB: Weren't you Ernie's right hand for a little while, off and on?

CW: Only occasionally the first year. The other Muppeteers were Frank Oz and Jerry Nelson. With many characters, even the director, Jon Stone was drafted. No one really knew that it would be such a hit in the 69th street building.

JB: How would a construction assignment go?

CW: Sesame Street was great because so many new things were needed. The writers would, say, give you a germ. What does a germ look like? So, I would invent a germ. A nasty, sort of hairy thing that was lots of fingers and angry eyes. It was great to be able to invent things. The educators would ask for something, the writers would write, and we would create a visual puppet of it. I had great fun making Bert's bottle cap collection. Talking French toast and peanut butter sandwiches. I made a whole set of teeth, too. I loved making the animals. That's one of the things I miss most on retiring was not inventing. I do not miss making budgets for movie. That was a nightmare. We'd get a movie to build. We always knew that the main characters were needed, so we could start with those. There were about eight or nine versions of Kermit the Frog.

JB: You also used to clean up Jim's sketches and sort of translate and annotate them.

CW: When Jim was around, he would give us a quick thumbnail sketch of a creature. if he was there, he would come by and critique how it was developing. Whatever we produced, even if it was not what he had dreamed or fantasized in his head, it was as close as we could get to what he had verbalized his dream was, he would work with it and make it work.

JB: Was this when you had space up on 67th.

CW: 67th and 3rd Avenue. At first we rented the fourth floor, and then added the fifth floor, then the third floor. We had the whole building, except for the storefront.

JB: It's interesting to see how the different puppet's look evolved over time.

CW: Yes. The first Big Bird was sort of ugly compared to later developments. The had quite long toes and they would trip up Caroll Spinney, so we shortened the toes. The first feathers were what they called hackle pads, made from chicken neck hackles glued onto a pad Kermit Love had started with those, but he had the aha to switch to the long body feathers from a Tom Turkey. The feathers took a lot of work. First the feather merchant bleached them white, scraped the spine halfway down the feather to make them supple, and then dyed them, two-tone. When the Muppets got them, we had a labor-intensive job of steaming them fluffy, and ironing a little sort of cup in the tip. The finish was hot gluing them onto a large hollow sort of bell-shaped basic body shape.

The first Ernie and Bert were both only slightly different. Their noses were larger and darker in tone. There was an article, I think, in Natural History magazine on the neotenization of Mickey Mouse [Mickey Mouse Meets Konrad Lorenz, Stephen Jay Gould, Natural History May 1979 - https://archive.org/details/naturalhistory88newy/page/n487]. Mickey's Nose got shorter, his pupils larger. Jim's first pass at Snuffy. It makes them more childlike. Jim's first pass at Snuffy had eyes that were green and yellow – even serpent like.

JB: He looked pretty creepy.

CW: Creepy, yeah. But those eyes were never used on the show Kermit Love also suggested the long, soft feathery ostrich feathers for the eyelashes.

JB: In the early days everybody pretty much did everything, right?

CW: Not really. The puppeteers only performed. Marty Robinson is a terribly talented puppet builder, as well as performer, but he only builds for his own projects, not Sesame Street.

JB: You have quite a list of builds.

CW: We all worked on everything. God knows how many Kermits I've built. As for a movie there was a radio-controlled version, versions with and without legs, and an old one from last year as a "throw": one to be thrown and hit a wall, etc.

JB: There were so many great scenes in those movies. The Great Muppet Caper, what memories stand out?

CW: The bike scene in London was something else again. One problem was the changing light on the background, and the fishlines would show one way against dark tree trunks and another against sunlit grass. The solution was to mottle them like camouflage-- sort of blotchy. It worked pretty well. Besides, if the puppets are fun to watch, the fishlines are not very visible. The bicycling was well done: two cherry-pickers with suspended platforms beneath them. This enabled Piggy and Kermit to circle around towards each other. The motion of the bicycles' pedals was what made the legs move.

JB: How about from The Muppets Take Manhattan.

CW: That was interesting for the swim scent a la Esther Williams. We had two kids in small Piggy costumes--two, because children cannot work too long. The costume could not be used too long, because it would get wet and sag. We took the Piggy legs to a pool to test if the flock would come off with the chlorine, etc. It worked pretty well, but we probably left a slight film of the hairs on the pool.

For the John Denver show in Colorado, Faz [Fazakas] and I had two things to check out ahead of time. First was the effect of Piggy's electronics on a horse-- would it bother the horse, would the gait bother the electronics. Yes to both-- the horse started trotting off and Piggy's head fell off (Not ruined, but educational.). The second was Gonzo swimming and coming along like a periscope.

JB: With his nose.

CW: Yeah. We weighted a plank of wood, put an extra Gonzo head on it and tested that rig by towing it in the river upstate near us.

JB: What is your favorite Bert and Ernie Sketch?

CW: My favorite is the one when Bert is asleep and Ernie goes "poke, poke, poke, poke" to wake Bert to ask him a question. Steve Whitmire does a very good Kermit - good manipulation and accent. But I always felt that Jim was a baritone, so the timbre of Kermit's voice was different. What was so horrible when everyone read of Jim's death, there were many calls the next day, jamming the lines, with people calling to say, "I can do Kermit". Horrible.

JB: You were workshop supervisor for a number of years. That must have been a big job. What were some of the responsibilities?

CW: Going to production meetings, designing characters, assigning jobs, hiring new crafts people. Some came from art schools. Tim

Miller had done costuming before-- he was just all-around talented. He ran the Fraggle Rock workshop while they were taping in Toronto. Bonnie Erickson came back for the initial supervision of Fraggle Rock. Ed Christie came as an intern from U Mass., and stayed on. Rollie Krewson came as an intern. She is still plugging away, keeping the faith. The Muppet Show was taped in London. While all this was going on, I just kept churning away with Sesame Street. I finally said to Jim, “Look, I don’t want to run the workshop anymore. I would like to be in charge of Sesame Street, but I would like some time off.” Bless him, he said okay. I went on a three week Sierra Club trip to Greece and Crete and then about three weeks in India, visiting a friend, and then to China and Szechuan province and the panda area. I worked six months of the year and then had the rest of the time off. If Sesame had a taping, I’d be there.

JB: You also trained a lot of the builders.

CW: Yes. We did a lot of workshops to try to find new builders. We would have a session with the builders given a chunk of soft urethane foam, and they would be challenged to carve a head and make it manipulable for talking. I also gave lectures on the way I would build animals out of sheets of foam.

JB: Let’s talk Elmo.

CW: Okay. Sesame Street had a song that needed a variety of monsters: little red, fat blue, tall orange. They could be grouped in different ways with the song, ”One of These Things is Not Like the Other.” And little red was cute, so various puppeteers began to play with him. The first was Brian Muehl, then Richard Hunt. Kevin Clash was the one who started Elmo talking about “Elmo do this” in the third person. He really created the character, and then the writers would start writing for it. One would write a bit with Elmo sitting on a table. So, I would have to make legs and a little bum for Elmo.

JB: You built the first Elmo, correct?

CW: Yes.

JB: What was the mouth plate built from birch plywood and gaffer’s tape?

CW: Yes.

JB: What about the flexible mouth plates?

CW: Red gasket rubber. It is stiff but flexible. Watch Kermit in particular. His head is only fabric, and Jim got wonderful expressions out of Kermit.

JB: What advice do you have for people wanting to learn how to pattern?

CW: I recommend that people look at toys and toy patterns, because they have some good ideas. I wound up having a great time making horses, cows, pigs. My animals are actually pretty simple in shape.

JB: So many of the folks at work became close friends. You and Bonnie Erickson have been friends for a long time.

CW: Yes.

JB: How long have you lived here?

CW: We've been in this loft since '77. This particular floor manufactured handbags. It was pretty dirty. Frank Misurski and I did the conversion. We've been together since '69.

JB: Bonnie told me this wonderful story about Don Sahlin keeping mice at the studio. Let's finish with a memory about him.

CW: Don built all these structures all over the studio. There were tubes like ventilation tubes, and they were all around, over the walls. The mice sometimes got out the other end. One day they were lost and were found in the pockets of a sweater hung on the wall. Don was a dear man, but he would buy things and not read the instructions so he never really could use them. Something Don did that was wonderful was play, which was great in inventing puppets. There was a sort of hunchback puppet. He would put it on a dressmaker's dummy, in the closet. When you opened the door, it would trundle out at you and scare the living daylights out of you!

I think what was so good about the Muppets or puppetry in general is the chance to create something---especially if you are working with other people-- all working together to make it happen. And it DOES happen, one way or another, and that is good. Not all are successes, some are flops, but most work out pretty well. And then, you get to work on the next one. That was what was great!

Jeff Bragg is a producer/director, musician, filmmaker, writer, and puppeteer. He formerly served as President of the National Capital Puppetry Guild and publisher/ editor of its newsletter, Puppetimes, in which these interviews were originally published.

He is a contributor to Puppetry Journal and currently resides in Virginia.

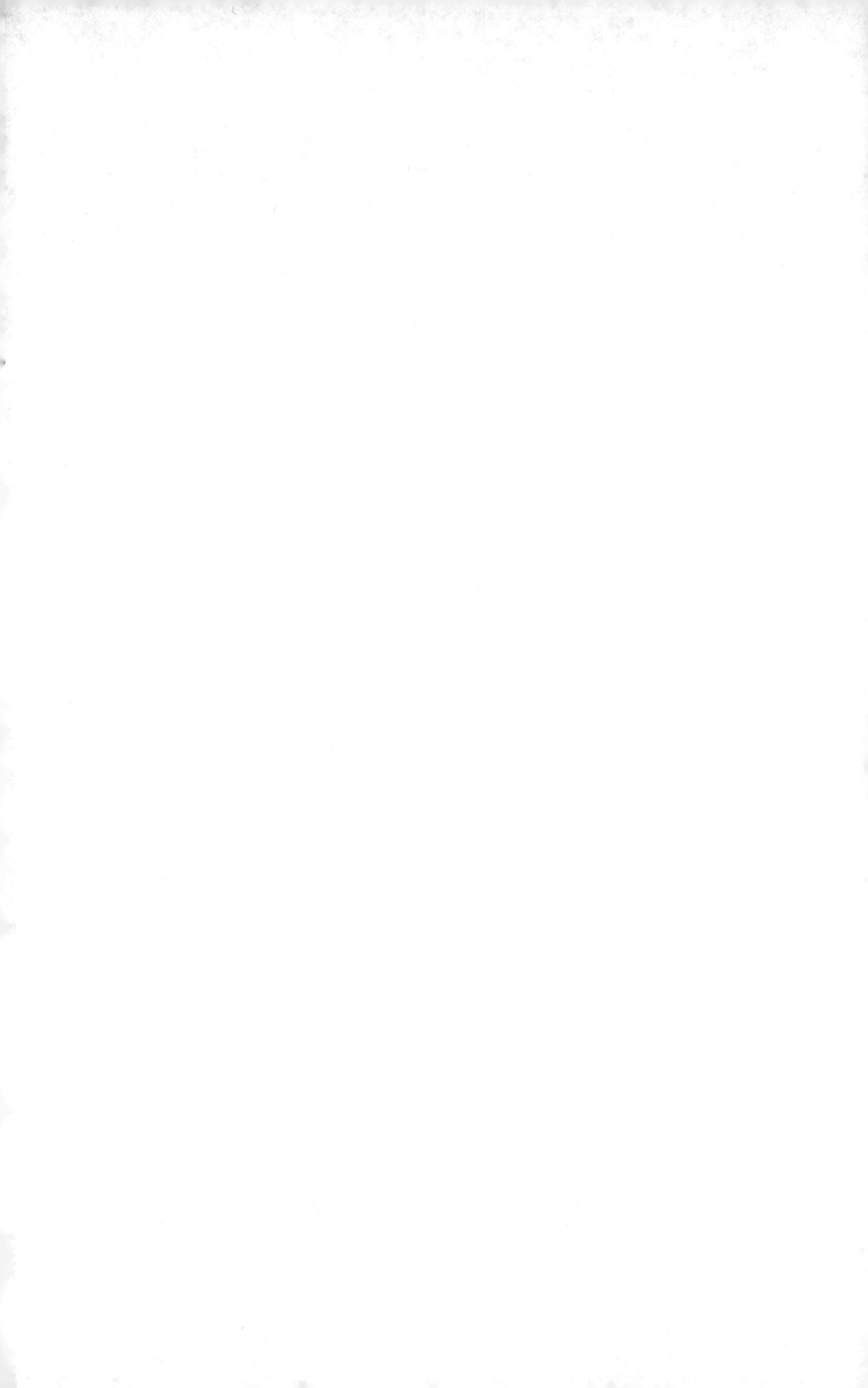